TONGUE-TIE

MORPHOGENESIS, IMPACT, ASSESSMENT, AND TREATMENT

ALISON K. HAZELBAKER
PhD, IBCLC, CST, RCST

AIDAN AND ÉVA PRESS

TONGUE-TIE: MORPHOGENESIS, IMPACT, ASSESSMENT AND TREATMENT

Published by:
AIDAN AND ÉVA PRESS, A DIVISION OF AIDAN & ÉVA, LLC
5115 Olentangy River Rd.
Columbus, Ohio 43235, USA
www.AidanandEvaPress.com

To order:
AIDAN AND ÉVA PRESS
Tel: (614) 451-1154
Fax: (614) 326-3509
Online: www.AidanandEvaPress.com

Permissions:
AIDAN AND ÉVA PRESS PERMISSIONS
5115 Olentangy River Rd.
Columbus, Ohio 43235, USA
www.AidanandEvaPress.com

Interior Illustration design: Paul Hughes
Cover design: Threepenny and Paul Hughes
Interior design: Threepenny and Anton Khodakovsky
Technical/Production editor: Jessica Hazelbaker-Buell
Copyeditor: Gretchen Hirsch
Indexer: Gina Pueblo
Author's photo: Cassie Lewis

Application submitted for The Library of Congress catalogue number.

ISBN 978-0-9845445-0-9

I DEDICATE THIS BOOK

to my formerly tongue-tied sons and grandson:
David, Bryan and Aidan. There's nothing like
personal experience to galvanize action.

ACKNOWLEDGEMENTS

A SIMPLE THANK YOU DOES NOT COMMUNICATE the depth of my feeling for those who have made such a significant contribution to both me, and to others, with their dedication to making sure that families receive the information they need to cultivate optimal health and well-being. It is the best I can do in this format. Know, however, that my heart is full.

Thank you to Kathleen Kendall Tackett for her unwavering kindness and support.

Thank you to Gretchen Hirsch and team who worked hard and fast to make me look good in black and white.

Thank you to Paul Hughes whose artistry created such an appealing aesthetic. Thank you to Anton for his amazing layout and cover design.

Thank you to Barbara Wilson Clay, Kay Hoover, Cathy Watson Genna, Brain Palmer, Greg Notestine, Larry Kotlow and especially Lisa Marasco for contributing photos, without which this book would remain relatively lifeless.

Thank you to the pioneers in the lactation field who chose to write about what they saw, knocking over the first tongue-tie domino. Most notably in my direct experience, Chele Marmet and Ellen Shell, whose mentoring I value supremely.

Thank you to those professionals who have come after, knocking over one domino after another with their vision, dedication and just plain hard work. It takes us all to make such immense change.

Thank you to the members of the International Affiliation of Tongue-Tie Professionals for the validation and the inspiration.

Thank you to my husband, children and grandchildren who sacrificed their wife, mother, and "Nanni-ma" for many, many, many hours as this book took shape and became real.

And, thank you to the many tongue-tied individuals whose stories inspire us all to determined action!

TABLE OF CONTENTS

FOREWORD

TONGUE-TIE TREATMENT HAS BEEN controversial since the 1700's. Until the 1940's, most English-language medical and surgical texts advocated treatment in infants who were unable to breastfeed well. Timothy Holmes in A treatise on surgery, its principles and practice (4th edition, 1884) admitted to sometimes performing frenotomy to satisfy parents, but states, "I have, however, seen cases in which the child undoubtedly could not take the breast till the tongue was released" (p. 613). Holmes cites treating the tongue-tied infant of a physician friend. The infant, whose mother died in childbirth, could not suck. Holmes writes of seeing the child and his wet-nurse a few days after the treatment, and "he then took the breast like other children" (p. 132).

Verrier, in his Practical Manual of Obstetrics (1884), classifies tongue-tie as one of the congenital deformities that must be corrected immediately, along with imperforate anus and umbilical hernia, as it may prevent the child from nursing. In general, the earlier the text was written, the more likely the author advocated treating tongue-tie for children with breastfeeding problems. Duncan, in Diseases of Infants and Children, with their Homeopathic Treatment (1878), used breastfeeding ability as the acid test to determine if frenotomy was warranted. He recommended snipping the frenulum if the doctor's finger could not pass under the tongue, the tongue could not lift to the palate, and the suck was obstructed. He also recommended placing a drop of calendula on the frenotomy site to aid healing. Holmes and Hulke (1883) likewise recommend frenotomy if the infant cannot use the tongue to "apply the nipple to the palate." They are among several authors who write that babies' frenula stretch with use or growth, a contention for which there is no evidence, but which has been repeated for well over one hundred years.

Charles Sumner Bacon (1915) writes in Obstetrical Nursing that in tongue-tie, the frenulum may interfere with free tongue motion and "very rarely ... interfere with nursing, and later in life with good articulation" (p. 314). In The Diseases of Infancy and Childhood (1918) p. 471, Henry Koplik recommends frenotomy for the tongue that appears bifid when protruded, which is now known as a "heart shaped" tongue. He states that though mothers ascribe inefficient nursing to tongue-tie, the condition should not prevent nursing if the breast secretes sufficient milk. This statement exposes a common misunderstanding of lactation physiology: blaming lack of the infant's ability to remove milk—the primary driver of milk production – on a deficiency in the function of the mother's breast. Koplik also states that half of women normally experience fissured nipples, which is unsurprising given that the latch technique he teaches deliberately prevents the infant from "drawing the nipple too far into the mouth" (p. 127). The attitude that women are untrustworthy to judge or manage their family's health was a common one. In his Clinical Manual for Practitioners and Students of Medicine (1885), Henry T. Butlin attacks the "evil custom" of lifting the tongue to cause the frenulum to tear back after it is snipped, blaming it specifically on midwives, though he admits many doctors of the day did the same, mostly under pressure from mothers.

As birth moved into the hospital in the 1930's, mother-infant separation and rigidly scheduled feeding interfered with milk production. Breastfeeding began to be seen as unreliable, and artificial feeding (bottle-feeding with modified cow's milk) rapidly became the cultural norm in the United States. Almost simultaneously, pediatric text books stopped recommending treatment of tongue-tie. By 1950, Textbook of Pediatrics by Waldo Emerson Nelson stated that a tight frenulum rarely interfered with feeding or speech, an unreferenced statement that was carried through to the 15th edition of the text in 1995. The 1950 edition also stated that "the action of the tongue itself is not important in nursing." Nelson certainly was not the first physician author to disparage the tongue's importance in sucking. Sir Charles Bell's 1929 anatomy text states, "The tongue, as I conceive, would sufficiently perform the necessary action on the mother's nipple, although its lower surface were universally adhering to the bottom of the mouth." This statement seems absurd to those of us with a basic understanding of sucking mechanics, but it still is occasionally heard from physicians.

McEnery and Gaines wrote several similar papers in the Journal of Pediatrics and American Journal of the Diseases of Childhood in 1941 and 1940, respectively, attesting that they had never seen a newborn with a tongue tie that required treatment. Any breastfeeding difficulties were blamed on a defect of the mother's nipples, and nipple massage during late pregnancy was prescribed as the answer (a technique that has failed to show any efficacy in modern clinical trials). They state that it is due to "a misunderstanding of the techniq (sic) of nursing that the frenum of the tongue is cut." The latter article includes a drawing of the position of a bottle teat in the infant's mouth, meant to illustrate that tongue movements past the gum or to the palate are not needed in sucking. What is purportedly infant anatomy is incorrect; the tongue is small and the palate high, the mouth is mostly empty space, whereas we now know that the tongue fills the mouth in infancy to aid in stabilizing the teat during sucking, and that babies feed poorly when a nipple rests only on the front of the tongue.

Antipathy toward tongue-tie as a cause of feeding problems continued in medical textbooks through the end of the 20th century. R. S. Illingsworth (The Normal Child, 1972) writes that mothers who ascribe feeding problems to tongue-tie are "almost invariably wrong." In 1987, he followed this up with a statement that he had "never seen feeding difficulties in the first year resulting from tongue-tie."

Interest in correctly identifying tongue-ties that require treatment has increased as more mothers are breastfeeding and looking for solutions to their baby's sucking difficulties. Though some texts blindly repeat phrases from earlier editions, many are including information from the new studies on tongue-tie.

Books by oral surgeons and dentists, such as Oral Medicine by Sergio Gandolfo and colleagues (2006), devote a section to tongue-tie and recommend treatment in severe cases. Unfortunately, not all authors have explored the recent studies associating breastfeeding difficulties with tongue-tie and showing improvements in latch, sucking mechanics, and maternal nipple pain after frenotomy, and only mention tongue-tie as a possible cause of speech articulation problems. Stevenson and Hall (2006) in Human Malformations and Related Anomalies are one example, but as geneticists they can be forgiven.

Dr. Hazelbaker's book helps parents and professionals cut through the old myths and explores the current understanding about tongue-tie. It covers both what we know from modern research and the more personal experiences of those who have dealt with the condition in themselves and their infants. It is also honest about the areas where uncertainty still exists.

As the developer of the Assessment Tool for Lingual Frenulum Function, Dr. Hazelbaker has a wealth of personal and professional information about tongue-tie; she is a recognized expert in the field, a person who suffered with a tongue-tie until middle age, and a mother who struggled to breastfeed two tongue-tied infants and find treatment for them.

Catherine Watson Genna, B.S., IBCLC

Supporting Sucking Skills in Breastfeeding Infants, Jones and Bartlett, 2008

Selecting and Using Breastfeeding Tools: Improving Care and Outcomes, Hale Publishing, 2009

"THE GREAT ENEMY OF THE TRUTH IS VERY OFTEN NOT THE LIE - deliberate, contrived and dishonest - but the myth - persistent, persuasive, and unrealistic. Belief in myths allows the comfort of opinion without the discomfort of thought."

—John F. Kennedy

PREFACE

I DEVELOPED THE HABIT OF sitting beside my father on the long end of the dinner table, maneuvering my chair and body so I would go unnoticed for the 30 to 40 minutes it took to finish a family meal. My mother often chastised me from her position at the south end of the table, reminding me more than once to chew with my mouth closed – an utter impossibility for me.

Because it was such a trial, I often avoided chewing altogether. I didn't eat breakfast most mornings, and I rarely chewed gum. Dinner remained the central challenge. Fortunately, my mother had six other kids to chide and henpeck, which offered me some relief. At that time, I didn't know I was tongue-tied.

In the late 1980s, Chele Marmet pointed out my tight lingual frenulum during a Lactation Institute course on infant sucking problems. It was that moment that generated my fascination with the subject of tongue-tie. I was barely 31 and just beginning my master's degree in lactation consulting. Although I had been toying with the idea of writing my thesis on tongue-tie, I definitively decided on the topic after the birth of my fourth child, David, who, when he cried, showed off a classic heart-shaped tethered tongue.

Fortunately, our midwife clipped his lingual frenulum at 24 hours. Even though he was treated very quickly, I already had tender nipples and a bit of nipple-tip tissue breakdown and inflammation. Had I not had my midwife's support for early intervention, I could have had severely damaged nipples, with deep nipple-tip wounds within a few days. Luckily, I knew what the problem was and how to correct it, so I promptly enlisted her help.

The hereditary aspect of tongue-tie clearly presented itself six years after David's birth, when I gave birth to my fifth child and second son, Bryan. He also was tongue-tied, but his tie was less obvious than David's. His lingual frenulum looked like a thin tether just behind his tongue-tip and high up on his lower alveolar ridge. Our pediatrician came to the house after office hours and divided Bryan's frenulum quickly and easily, using a grooved spoon and a sharp pair of sterile surgical scissors.

As I look back on my student days during my master's program, I can't help wondering why I didn't have my frenulum clipped as soon as I found out I was tongue-tied. Part of me, I recall, was afraid of the extensive procedure (frenectomy) I thought I would need. Another part of me just didn't want to bother with it. After all, I had learned to deal with my speech articulation issues, chewing and breathing compromises, and dental hygiene challenges. I compensated for my sluggish tongue by over-articulating my words, holding my breath while I chewed, and doing double oral hygiene duty with frequent meticulous and vigorous brushing.

Years later, by happenstance, Sandra Holtzman, a Florida-based oral myologist who specializes in the preoperative assessment and postoperative treatment of tongue-tie in children and adults, contacted me via e-mail. We arranged a meeting the next time I traveled with my family to Florida for vacation. She assessed both my sons and then took a look at me. She strongly encouraged me to have my lingual frenulum clipped. She also outlined a speech therapy process for me to retrain my tongue.

Sandy and I agreed that a simple frenotomy, without anesthetic, followed by a six- to eight-week course of speech therapy, would constitute appropriate treatment. I asked my dentist, Dr. Roger Veith, to perform the procedure. Roger possessed years of experience performing simple frenotomies on infants and toddlers in his office. He needed to be convinced, however, to perform my frenotomy without anesthetic. He simply was not sure that adults had as little innervation of the lingual frenulum as their younger counterparts.

Finally, after doing some research, Roger felt certain that the adult lingual frenulum could be divided without anesthesia. He also confessed to being extremely curious to see how a simple division would work on a lingual frenulum as fibrous as mine. We planned the procedure together with Sandy.

Sandy flew into Columbus, Ohio, where I live, intending to stay for a few days to supervise my speech therapy. She videotaped the entire procedure while my husband took copious photos. The small treatment room felt crowded with the various other onlookers: dental professionals who had never seen an adult frenotomy. Some were merely curious; others were quite skeptical.

Roger made the first cut. I felt pressure but no pain. He made two more cuts. I felt nothing with the second cut. The third grazed the underside of my tongue and felt like a pinch followed by a little burning. I bled a few drops, which Roger dabbed away with a wet cotton gauze square. I then stuck my tongue out of my mouth for the first time in my life without straining. Sandy directed me to move my tongue left, then right; out, then in; up and down. Roger looked on, a big smile on his face. As I moved my tongue, it felt awkward and stiff, but free!

After a successful therapeutic course that strengthened my tongue muscles, corrected my articulation errors, and retrained my tongue for a proper swallow, I found myself sleeping more deeply, awakening refreshed and less tense. The frenotomy freed up more than my tongue; it also allowed my entire thoracic and neck areas to stop tensing as compensation for difficult chewing, breathing and speaking. The attendant jaw clench also disappeared. So did the tension headaches caused by the persistent clench. I was better able to keep my teeth clean. Suddenly, my dental checkups improved, as did my overall gum health.

I regretted waiting so long to pursue treatment. Ignorance-based fear kept me from acting. I also began to feel resentful that my pediatrician had failed to clip my frenulum when I was a newborn. So much difficulty could have been avoided if he had continued the tradition of routine assessment and treatment at birth. Fortunately, my midwife and pediatrician were well-informed and able to provide timely treatment for my sons.

Since the publication of my thesis in 1993, many excellent studies have been done on tongue-tie, allowing clinicians to base their current clinical practice on sound research.

These research efforts to end the tongue-tie myths generated throughout time and perpetuated during the mid to latter 20th century have helped change the global dialogue from one of intense criticism of treatment for tongue-tie to one of grudging acknowledgment that tongue-tie has a negative impact on breastfeeding and should be managed and treated for optimal clinical results. Unfortunately, however, in the first decade of the 21st century, resistance to timely treatment of tongue-tie in all circumstances is nearly as strong as it was in the latter half of the 20th century.

That is why I wrote this book.

INTRODUCTION

FROM WHENCE THE CONTROVERSY?

THE RECOGNITION OF TONGUE-TIE as a problem may be older than Moses. In the book of Exodus, Moses said, "I am slow of speech and of a slow tongue." (Greene in Catlin and De Haan, 1971, p. 548). Moses allegedly received a frenotomy and was then able to speak plainly. The next easily found reference to tongue-tie appears in Pechey's A General Treatise of the Diseases of Infants and Children, written in 1697. Pechey wrote, "The mid-wife at birth must put her finger into the mouth and cleanse it from all filth and see whether the child be tongue-tied or no." (In Cullum, 1959, p. 497). Cullum also quotes The Nurses' Guide, or the Right Method of Bringing Up Young Children (by an Eminent Physician). The 1729 manual states (Cullum, 1959, p. 497):

> Concerning such defects as children often bring with them out of their mothers' womb into the world which ought to be rectified with all speed ... Very often the membrane under the tongue is so short and strait that it hinders the child from sucking and puts him in a condition of never being able to speak distinctly all his life, but these inconveniences are easily removed by a slight incision.

As cited in Cullum (1959), Petit (1742) and Jussieu and Berdot (1751) do not seem to share the Eminent Physician's enthusiasm for treating tongue-tie. Cullum notes that Petit reported two cases of death following division (incision) of the lingual frenulum (without citing method or circumstance), and Jussieu and Berdot "noted that congenital absence of the tongue does not render speech, taste, or deglutition impossible" (p. 497).

Professor Desessartz's 1760 statement that "nurses are imbued with the false idea that not an infant is born without this trouble" confirms these prior notions. (Cited In Wallace, 1964, p. 527). Several authors cite the 1776 remarks of Nils Rosen von Rosenstein, who agrees with the naysayers preceding him, stating:

> When children do not suck well, our old women say that they are tongue-tied and pretend that the bridle ought to be snipped with a pair of scissors. I have never as yet seen any child's tongue tied ... should an operation be judged necessary, it ought never to be done with the nails but performed by some experienced man, otherwise one of the blood vessels near the tongue might easily be opened and the blood flow from it. (Wallace, 1964, p. 527; Catlin and De Haan, 1971, p. 549; and Cullum, 1959, p. 497).

This assertion is in direct conflict with Theobald's 1764 statement that "it may be necessary to cut the bridle of the tongue and this is usually done by nurses and midwives with their nail" (as cited in Wallace, p. 527). Interestingly, only twelve years separate the two pronouncements, which, made prior to the institution of thorough scientific methods, supported one opinion or another about tongue-tie's treatment.

The waxing and waning of opinion about the impact tongue-tie has on feeding and speech – and even the condition's actual existence – remains the foundation of the passionate dialectic that influences today's opinions on the subject. No wonder controversy continues to run rampant.

For example, when I completed my master's research in 1993, I could locate only one pediatrician in my city who knew how to perform a frenotomy and was willing to do so. My dentist, however, had been taught how to perform them in dental school, had done so many times, and had no reservations about the procedure. He became my go-to primary practitioner when a baby needed to have his or her frenulum clipped. Sixteen years later, several pediatricians, as well as a number of dentists, ENTs, and oral surgeons, perform frenotomies. I hope this practice is here to stay rather than being the waxing phase of another cycle of opinion.

A reading of the modern literature on frenotomy indicates that there is no legitimate reason to withhold treatment of tongue-tie in an infant, child, or adult. The resistance to performing such a simple surgical procedure as frenotomy boggles the mind when so much research demonstrates its effectiveness and safety.

Nonetheless, resistance sometimes can be quite vehement, as several lactation consultants can testify. Some are in a position to lose their jobs should they provide their clients with research-based information that is contrary to the beliefs of the attending physician.

One lactation consultant was threatened by a pediatrician at her hospital. He felt so strongly that her information about tongue-tie was incorrect that he warned her not to say another word about it to any patient at the hospital or he would have her brought up for review and would push to have her fired. Unfortunately, she is not alone. Many other lactation consultants report that they have received job threats from physicians should they even breathe the words tongue-tie and frenotomy to a patient.

A mere opinion based on waxing and waning cycles fails as a rational basis for denying the necessary intervention to those who need it. At times, it may seem that doing nothing will "first, do no harm"; however, such is not the case when a tongue-tied baby is having difficulty obtaining nourishment from the breast or a tongue-tied child cannot swallow solid foods properly, keep his teeth clean, or speak plainly.

Even though the actual incidence of tongue-tie is still a matter of some debate, tongue-tie is common enough that many lactation consultants and other health care providers have seen it and/or worked with babies, mothers, and others affected by it. Regardless of the rate of incidence, the vast majority of health care providers and researchers agree that tongue-tie does exist. (Brinkman, Reilly and Meara, 2004; Lalakea and Messner, 2003b). The "grand controversy," which has simmered down to an interesting and compelling dialectic, now centers on the exact impact tongue-tie has on feeding, speech, and other morphofunctional issues; when and how it should be treated; and how to best impart this information to the uninformed.

Unfortunately, public knowledge lags behind the research. In 1994, a colleague told me it takes about ten years before new research findings become common clinical practice. I certainly hope not. When resistance to clipping frenula was at its highest, affected individuals and their families often got caught in the middle. They were assaulted by opposing recommendations, left on their own to make a wise and informed decision regarding treatment, and then had to search out practitioners on their own.

Melissa eagerly shared her story, which clearly illustrates this horrendous situation.

> Our epiphany came when Kyla was six months old. One of my La Leche League Leaders had awoken in the middle of the night wondering if anyone had ever checked Kyla's tongue. At the next La Leche League meeting, we were all dumbfounded by the obvious heart-shaped indent in the middle of her tongue. Tears filled my eyes as we finally realized that this tongue-tie was the cause of the excruciating pain I had been living. Kyla's frenulum was too far forward, preventing her from curling her tongue around my nipple to suck properly. Rather than focus on the fact that all the experts (including one midwife, three doctors, two lactation consultants, and five La Leche League Leaders) had all neglected to observe this very obvious condition (which can easily be treated immediately following birth!), we tried to focus on correcting it. Trying to find someone to perform the procedure [frenotomy] in a timely fashion was proving to be difficult. A simple clip of the frenulum was preventing us from enjoying the most natural of all mother-child bonds.

The mere fact that Melissa continued to breastfeed for six months with such severe pain is miraculous. Most mothers cannot persist in the face of such difficulty. Who could blame them? Melissa believed that breastfeeding brought her daughter important benefits, and she was willing to endure the pain she was experiencing to ensure her baby's well-being. Unfortunately, Melissa was failed by a support system that, while well-intentioned, did not think through all of the issues that could be causing her problem. Tongue-tie should have been one of the first things the professionals considered when Melissa's pain did not go away with proper positioning and latch-on technique.

Unfortunately, Melissa's story happens more often than most of us suspect or would like to believe. The forces that prevent the re-establishment of routine and simple treatment of tongue-tie, while nonsensical, are most likely complex and multifaceted. Some, if not most, seem to reside in the psychological and emotional realm. With all of the well-done new studies available on the subject, few objections could fairly be considered scientific.

Ignorance plays a role. Before and into the 1950s, routine assessment for tongue-tie occurred during the general newborn exam. In the late 1950s, about the year of my birth (1957), this assessment was dropped from routine practice. As a result, my tongue-tie remained intact. And although it is always appropriate to change clinical practice when new information about a subject or procedure becomes available, it appears that the decision to stop assessing for and treating tongue-tie in the early postpartum period was based largely on opinion and fear rather than science. Whatever the reason, routine assessment and treatment of tongue-tie were relegated to the dustbin of medical procedures.

Physicians then stopped learning about tongue-tie in school. Soon, what appeared in medical textbooks and what was taught in medical training was that tongue-tie made no physiological difference and was a nonmedical issue. Simple frenotomy became a lost art. The view that tongue-tie either did not exist or, if it did, caused no problems, gained popularity despite the contemporaneous research showing that tongue-tie did, in fact, have a negative impact on feeding and speech articulation. To this day, doctors and nurses still are led to believe that not only is the treatment of tongue-tie unnecessary, but also constitutes the practice of "bad" medicine. Case closed.

Some practitioners are aware of tongue-tie but have been taught that the condition will resolve on its own or that the simple performance of frenotomy puts the infant at risk for infection, scar-tissue formation, permanent impairment of speech and language development, or even hemorrhage resulting in death. These myths persist even when sound research shows that none of them is true.

So what's a parent to do?

Education based on well-performed research seems to be the solution to this attitude problem. Although it isn't the parents' duty to provide this education, they may be the only ones in a position to do so. If the parents are fortunate, the physician will listen and respond by expanding his or her repertoire.

When resistance is high, parents may have to simply choose a practitioner who is more knowledgeable and responsive to their needs. This choice may require them to switch doctors, travel, or seek out a practitioner from a different specialty – a naturopathic doctor, dentist, oral surgeon, or midwife – to perform the frenotomy. Despite the old-fashioned unspoken (and sometimes spoken) rule that patients should do whatever their doctor tells them, we now know that being well-informed and willing to choose a physician who is both well-educated and supportive is a patient's right.

WHY SHOULD WE CARE?

With all of the research demonstrating the superiority of breastfeeding for the baby and the mother, Western culture still fails to elevate breastfeeding to its rightful place at the top of the health enhancement strategies list. Formula feeding by bottle still remains the Western paradigm; therefore, any complication with breastfeeding is met with the advice to switch to formula feeding by bottle. After all, the thinking goes, what's the big deal? Babies do fine on formula.

In actuality, the premature weaning that results from this practice is no small matter. Apart from the possible speech problems the affected child may experience or the orofacial imbalance effects from bottle-feeding, the probability of the child's experiencing health problems from artificial feeding is extremely high (Cunningham, Jelliffe and Jelliffe, 1991; Walker, 1993; Wang and Wu, 1996).

Artificially fed babies (not just those prematurely weaned because of tongue-tie) are hospitalized fifteen times more often than breastfed babies in the first four months alone (Cunningham, 1979) and ten times more often for bacterial infections (Cunningham et al., 1991). Artificially fed babies have two to seven times the risk of juvenile diabetes (as many as 26 percent of cases are ascribed to artificial feeding) (Mayer et al; 1988, Hammond-McKibbon, Karges, Gaedigk, and Dosch, 1997), three to five times the risk of Sudden Infant Death Syndrome (Harper and Hoffman, 1988; and Mitchell et al., 1991), three times the risk of inflammatory bowel disease (Whorwell, Holdstock, Whorwell, and Wright, 1979; Koletzko, Sherman, Corey, Griffiths, and Smith, 1989), six times the risk of diarrhea (Howie, Forsyth, Ogston, Clark, and Flory, 1990), two to five times the risk of bronchitis and pneumonia (Paine and Cable, 1982; Cunningham, 1979; Wright, Holberg, Martinez, Morgan, and Taussig, 1989; Cesar, Victora, Barros, Santos, and Flores, 1999), a substantially increased risk of asthma (Oddy et al., 1999); three to five times the risk of ear infections (Saarinen, 1982; Teele, Klein, and Rosner, 1980), and six to eight times the risk of childhood lymphomas (Davis, Savitz, and Graubard, 1988; American Academy of Pediatrics, 2005).

They get sick more often than breastfed babies at a ratio of 21:8 (Cunningham, 1979; Wilson et al., 1998). Their IQs can be as much as 8.3 points lower (Lucas, Morley, Cole, Lister, and Leeson-Payne, 1992). This figure is estimated to be twice the IQ differential of those children affected by lead poisoning (Needleman et al., 1979; Bellinger, Stiles, and Needleman, 1992; Min et al., 2009). At worst, their increased risk of death from respiratory and intestinal infections, circulatory diseases, meningitis, heart disease, and cancer, even in industrialized nations, makes formula feeding a high-risk health behavior.

In addition, society minimizes and even dismisses the later-developing issues associated with tongue-tie, despite their severity. The casual, almost tongue-in-cheek, mention of the inability to "French kiss" or lick an ice-cream cone makes light of the underlying problem: Those affected cannot move their tongues around their mouths enough to perform even the Activities of Daily Living that most of us take for granted.

Orofacial defects, which also may arise from the cessation of breastfeeding and may be regarded as trivial by the medical community, in fact, matter a great deal. Although virtually ignored by health practitioners except those who specialize in their treatment, orofacial defects and dysfunction can have a great impact on the affected person, potentially leading to, at worst, airway collapse and asphyxiation. Orthodontia, rather than being thought of as a correction for a dental disease known as malocclusion, has become a rite of passage, first for teenagers and now for "tweens." The financial impact also can be substantial, as every parent who has struggled to pay for palate expansion and orthodontia knows far too well. We must take these problems seriously; they are diseases that could potentially develop as a result of tongue-tie and should therefore be considered significant risks.

The fear of treatment is no longer a valid excuse for not intervening. The risks of "clipping" the lingual frenulum cited in the old literature no longer apply when an experienced practitioner performs the frenotomy. Gone are the days when one had to worry about bleeding to death, infection, tongue-swallowing, suffocation, relapse, and scar tissue formation. Several of these cited risks were unproven and highly doubtful, anyway. Frenotomy is simply not as risky as some authors have led us to believe, and, when weighed against the risks of premature weaning or development of problems later in life, its minor risks pale in comparison to the benefits.

And although "there is no consensus regarding the indications, timing or method of surgical repair for ankyloglossia" (Klockars, 2007, p. 1321), that consensus is emerging, thanks to the rigorous efforts of multiple researchers who have dedicated years to studying the tongue-tie phenomenon. True, we need more studies; many specific questions need to be answered. But it is no longer possible for a naysayer to point to the literature and say, "See, I told you so. Tongue-tie never needs to be treated."

WHY THIS BOOK?

This book takes the reader on a journey through the literature, past and present, related to tongue-tie issues and controversies; reflects on areas of prior dispute; and, based on the research from the last fifteen years, assists the reader in coming to a new understanding of tongue-tie.

Chapter One defines tongue-tie within the total framework of ankyloglossia and its various manifestations, while adhering to the age-old Conceptual Definition of tongue-tie, first framed more than two millennia ago. This chapter distinguishes the Conceptual Definition of tongue-tie from its various Operational Definitions and discusses the role these Operational Definitions play in expanding our understanding of tongue-tie. Chapter One also includes a brief examination of tongue-tie as a syndrome of its own, presenting incidence statistics in various populations.

Chapter Two addresses the embryological and fetal development of suck-swallow-breathe. This morphofunctional foundation provides the background against which tongue-tie and its impact can be thoroughly understood and appreciated.

Chapter Three presents the normal anatomy and physiology of the tongue and of infant suck, focusing on the tongue's unique role. This chapter also includes an examination of tongue-tie and ankyloglossia as a sign/symptom of congenital anomalies; it does not address the anomalies themselves, but views tongue-tie within this larger physiological frame.

A discussion of the impact tongue-tie has on infant feeding, swallowing, oral toilet, airway integrity, speech, and orofacial/dental development appears in Chapters Four and Five. Extensive citation of the literature supports the assertions made, with an emphasis placed on the role tongue-tie plays in breastfeeding difficulties. Photos (with brief commentary) of the various presentations of tongue-tie and its impact on orofacial development appear in a special section between these chapters.

Chapter Six addresses the tongue-tie assessment process, emphasizing function over appearance. A presentation of the development and use of the Assessment Tool for Lingual Frenulum Function (ATLFF) and the Tongue-Tie Assessment Protocol (TAPP) appears alongside that of the more abbreviated forms of assessment found in the literature. This chapter discusses the strengths and weaknesses of each process and the common pitfalls of assessment, including the ability or inability of any given assessment process to help the clinician make a differential diagnosis. This chapter also identifies problems associated with developing a standardized treatment decision rule.

Chapter Seven thoroughly presents the various treatment options, with an emphasis on frenotomy. This chapter clarifies the types of treatment available (frenotomy, frenectomy, frenuloplasty, stripping, clipping, laser, and others), the safety and efficacy of each method, and the indications for choosing one particular method over another. A discussion of the need for postoperative treatment, such as suck training and speech therapy, follows.

This chapter also answers common clinical questions about the postoperative treatment course: How is suck-swallow-breathe disorganization handled in the infant? How is tongue weakness corrected? How do you feed the infant after tongue-tie correction? What happens if you delay treatment? What therapeutic methods assist with postoperative recovery and the re-establishment of optimal tongue function in all age groups?

The Afterword examines any remaining objections to the routine assessment and treatment of tongue-tie in infancy. It proposes areas for further contemplation, especially where controversy still strongly asserts itself. It also suggests areas for future research and proposes strategies for making health care providers and the public more familiar with tongue-tie.

Each chapter closes with a Chapter Takeaway. This segment is designed to provide an accessible summary for readers whose exposure to the more technical aspects of the tongue-tie discussion has been limited. Professional readers may choose to share the summary information with adult clients who may be facing an immediate decision about surgical intervention and therapy, either for a child or for themselves. Such a nutritious snack may be all that is needed to sate a parent's need for information.

Appendix A provides brief answers to frequently asked questions. Appendix B lists various resources for parents and professionals, including organizations that provide breastfeeding help and contact information for practitioners willing to perform frenotomies, especially for posterior ties. Appendix C provides historical information on the development of the Assessment Tool for Lingual Frenulum Function, instructions for the assessment process, and an up-to-date assessment chart. Appendix D provides finger-feeding instructions; a glossary and extensive bibliography round out the book – arming the reader with the tools to better inform the skeptical colleagues who are least likely to read this volume. In addition, the citations can serve as a foundation for written institutional policies.

It is time for a change – one that will enable all tongue-tied individuals to easily receive the care they need. I hope this book will finally put to rest the myths and misunderstandings that still define the topography of this subject's landscape. There is no benefit to keeping the old arguments alive. The last 15 years have produced more good literature on tongue-tie than the preceding 100 years of inquiry. We now have answers: good ones. Now that we do, minds need to change so that clinical practice also can change.

CHAPTER ONE
DEFINITION

ONE SUNNY MARCH DAY, my daughter Jessica's friend Joe came to visit. As we talked about what we were currently doing, I mentioned that I was revising my master's thesis into this book. He asked what it was about and when I told him tongue-tie, he screwed up his nose, squinted his eyes, and cocked his head a little – the same quizzical expression I'd encountered countless times before when I referred to tongue-tie.

"What's tongue-tie?" he asked.

I paused. Should I give him the "tour" or provide the simplest possible description and let him decide how much more he wanted to know? I chose the latter and pointed to the area under my tongue. "There's a membranous attachment right here that can sometimes cause problems with tongue movement if it's too short or tight."

He moved his tongue around in his mouth as if trying to imagine what tongue-tie would feel like. "Really? That can cause a problem?" His eyebrows arched as he looked at me expectantly.

Jessica, used to such bewildered curiosity, chimed in. "It can cause problems with breastfeeding and speech. Thank goodness Éva [her daughter] wasn't tongue-tied like my brothers. Each had his frenulum cut when he was a baby."

"Frenu-what?" Joe asked.

"That's the name of the membrane: fren-u-lum." I answered.

"And they cut them with a knife?"

"No. With a scissors. Sterile, of course. Or a laser."

"Does it hurt?"

"Well it didn't hurt me, and I had mine cut without anesthetic when I was 42 years old. It appears that a simple procedure doesn't hurt, but if an extensive procedure has to be done, the area can be sore for a few days."

"And then what?"

"And then, if it's done early in infancy, usually the baby will only need to breastfeed, and the tongue gets stronger with the exercise of breastfeeding alone. Sometimes, a baby will need some therapy, and if the person is older, as I was when I had my frenotomy, speech and oromuscular therapy may be necessary. It's amazing how such a seemingly small thing can cause such big problems."

Joe seemed a bit taken aback. "I have never heard of such a thing. Is it common?"

"It's not uncommon. It affects about three to four percent of all people."

I imagine that similar conversations commonly occur in the offices of lactation consultants, physicians, and speech therapists the world over, at least those "in the know."

It isn't such a big deal that the average person doesn't know what tongue-tie is. Most nonprofessionals don't. Unfortunately, however, there are far too many clinicians who also don't possess sufficient knowledge about tongue-tie, probably because of their lack of exposure to the problem. Were tongue-tie more prevalent, more straightforward, better understood and, perhaps, viewed as dangerous, everyone would be in the loop.

Some think that the controversy over tongue-tie's definition prevents us from reaching a common understanding about assessment and treatment. That isn't true. The professional community knows what tongue-tie means, and we have for several hundred years, but what we have failed to do in all that time is formulate a standardized assessment process and treatment decision rule based on what we already know.

ETYMOLOGY

At some unknown point in history, the term ankyloglossia was coined and used to describe a condition wherein the tongue was anchored to the mouth in some extraordinary manner. The Greek word ankylos is a combining form or prefix that means crooked, bent or fixed. Over time, it has come to mean stiffness or fusion of a joint (ankylosis). Glossa, also from the Greek, means tongue. Combining the two words into one, ankyloglossia, we understand the term to denote fusion of the tongue to the floor of the mouth, causing the tongue to appear crooked or bent.

The history of the use of the slang term tongue-tie is unknown. As an easier-to-pronounce synonym, its use has become more and more popular, although it was most likely used in popular parlance long, long before now.

Webster's Revised Unabridged Dictionary, 1913 edition (Porter, Ed.; as cited on http://everything2.com) provides a primary definition of tongue-tie: "Destitute of the power of distinct articulation; having an impediment in speech, esp. when caused by a short fraenum." William Shakespeare used the term tongue-tied in many of his plays and sonnets, implying that the individual was unable to speak or was struck dumb.

According to the 1990 edition of Mosby's Pocket Dictionary of Medicine, Nursing, and Allied Health (Anderson and Anderson, Eds.), ankyloglossia is "an oral defect, characterized by an abnormally short lingual frenulum that limits tongue movement and impairs the speech." A more recent version of a popular medical reference, Dorland's Pocket Medical Dictionary (2001, p. 48), defines ankyloglossia as "tongue-tie." This same dictionary defines tongue-tie as "abnormal shortness of the frenum of the tongue, interfering with its motion" (p. 846). This simple definition, expressed multiple ways, appears frequently in the recent literature.

All the ways in which the tongue is anchored abnormally to another structure of the mouth can be described as ankyloglossia. The tongue may be fused to the palate, the cheeks, the lateral gums, and/or the lateral frenula. Partial ankyloglossia denotes that an incomplete fusion of structures has occurred between the tongue and anywhere else in the mouth. Tongue-tie has come to specifically denote that the underside of the tongue is abnormally anchored to the floor of the mouth by its midline frenulum. Throughout this volume, I use tongue-tie rather than the more formal ankyloglossia because of its newfound (or newly rediscovered) specificity.

Despite this limited but representative sample of dictionary definitions, concerns still arise regarding the standardization of tongue-tie's definition (Lalakea and Messner, 2002; Segal, Stephenson, Dawes and Feldman, 2007). This concern seems to revolve around the fear that we will once again clip lingual frenula without having a legitimate reason to do so. That fear is grounded in the absence of a standardized treatment decision process, rather than the lack of a standardized definition. Clinicians want an objective treatment decision rule so they can feel comfortable and confident recommending surgical intervention. As recently as 2007, in their literature review on the topic, Segal et al, concluded that the "lack of standardized criteria for diagnosing ankyloglossia is one of the Canadian Pediatric Society's main criticisms of research on this condition" (p. 1028).

THE DEFINITION "CONTROVERSY" OVER TIME

Once upon a time, the definition of tongue-tie was considered the biggest controversy connected to the phenomenon. Author after author noted his or her concern over the controversial nature of tongue-tie's definition. In the past, the definition of ankyloglossia varied from observer to observer, as did the terminology used to label the problem, as exemplified by these quotes presented in Cullum's 1959 article (p. 497):

> In 1729, An Eminent Physician described tongue-tie as a short, straight membrane under the tongue that "hinders the child from sucking and puts him in a condition of never being able to speak distinctly all his life."
>
> In 1776, von Rosenstein, the First Physician to the Swedish King, considered an infant tongue-tied "if the child when it shrieks does not carry its tongue up to the palate or to the outside of the lips and the point of the tongue not be round but cloven."

> And in 1794, a prominent English surgeon, William Moss, said, "A child's being tongue-tied will impede and hinder his sucking freely. When that happens, he may be observed to lose his hold very often, and when he draws the breast he frequently makes a chucking noise."

Nearly two centuries later, one pediatric textbook makes an unusual distinction between tongue-tie and ankyloglossia, describing tongue-tie as "a condition in which the maxillary labial frenulum is attached closely to the crest of the alveolar ridge." It then claims that this is a common condition that reverses itself as the child grows, but that if the frenulum is unusually prominent and the tongue appears notched at the tip, then ankyloglossia is present (Avery and First, Eds., 1989, p. 1190). This book clearly confuses one condition with another; the maxillary labial frenulum is the piece of tissue that attaches the upper lip to the upper gum, not the piece of tissue that anchors the tongue to the floor of the mouth.

Another textbook suggests that tongue-tie or "short, thick, frenum of the tongue" could prevent a child from properly protruding his tongue, but that treatment would not alleviate speech problems (Arena, Ed. 1969, p. 195). This author erroneously concludes that tongue-tie is normal in infants because it disappears as they grow.

In the Pocket Picture Guide for Nurses: Pediatrics, Booth and Wozniak (1984) concur with Arena. They state:

> Tongue-tie (ankyloglossia). A short lingual frenum is present which extends to the tip of the tongue, and prevents tongue protrusion. Surgical intervention is seldom necessary as this anomaly is rarely responsible for difficulties in sucking or speech. (p. 82)

This statement accompanies a picture of a young tongue-tied child whose tie is so severe that today an informed clinician would recommend immediate surgery.

In Oral and Maxillofacial Surgery, Archer (1975) expands the definition of tongue-tie to include involvement of the genioglossus muscle. He asserts that the frenum and/or genioglossus muscle must be short enough to restrict tongue motion to qualify as ankyloglossia. Horton, Crawford, Adamson, and Ashbell (1969), a group of plastic surgeons, agree with Archer by including involvement of the genioglossus muscle in the definition. They take it one step farther, however, and describe degrees of involvement. Using the term "partial ankyloglossia," they discuss mild involvement, a mucous membrane band, to severe involvement, where both the frenulum and the genioglossus fibers are fibrosed. Complete ankyloglossia is described as complete fusing of the tongue to the floor of the mouth.

Some writers focus on tongue protrusion as a criterion for defining tongue-tie. Using the term "inferior ankyloglossia," Hussey (1974, p. 735) partially defines it as an inability of the child to protrude his tongue over the lower gum. Huggins (1986) suggests that frenular tightness prevents protrusion over the lower lip. She changes her view slightly in her book's 1991 edition by commenting that the tongue-tied baby may not be able to extend his tongue far enough to latch on to his mother's nipple. Marmet, Shell, and Marmet (1990, p. 117) use the term "short frenulum" and define it as an inability of the infant to extend his tongue over the lower gum line, which then inhibits normal sucking motion.

Browne (1959), Notestine (1990), and Tuerk and Lubit (1959), refer to the tongue-tied child's impaired ability to lift his tongue-tip to the hard palate. Notestine provides the most multifaceted definition of the three: "A short frenulum is defined as a frenulum that is attached at or near the tip of the tongue, at or near the crest of the gum pad, feels tight to palpation, and contributes to nipple distortion and pain" (Notestine, p. 114).

Fleiss, Burger, Ramkumar, and Carrington (1990, p.128) define ankyloglossia as "an abnormally short, thick, or fibrosed lingual frenulum ... which may fuse, or 'tie', the tongue to the floor of the mouth." This simpler definition paints a clear picture. Such descriptive language enables the reader to easily visualize the problem.

Researchers and writers are coming closer and closer together in their descriptions of the phenomenon. Amir, James, and Beatty (2005, p. 243) define tongue-tie as a "congenital oral anomaly in which the lingual frenulum is abnormally short and may restrict tongue-tip mobility." Similarly, Breward (2004, p. 298) describes tongue-tie as a lingual frenulum that is "tight, short or attached near the tip, impeding tongue movement."

Coryllos, Watson Genna, and Salloum (2004, p. 1) use descriptive language that hearkens back to earlier definitions of tongue-tie: "The bottom of the tongue is tethered to the floor of the mouth by a membrane (frenulum) so that the tongue's range of motion is unduly restricted." Geddes and Langton et al. (2008, p. e188) define tongue-tie as a "short lingual frenulum that results in restricted range of tongue movement such as limitation of the forward protrusion of the tongue and/or lateral mobility of the tongue."

As a rule, researchers and clinicians who work with older children and adults, tend toward a simpler definition primarily involving functional characteristics (Parida, 2008; Defabianis, 2000; Fernando, 1998). This definition from Klockars (2007, p. 1321) serves as an example: "The abnormally short lingual frenulum may result [in] varying degrees of tongue mobility."

Watson Genna (2008) uses morphofunctional language to define tongue-tie:

> Ankyloglossia is caused by insufficient apoptosis during prenatal differentiation of the tongue from the floor of the mouth. The cells that attach the tongue to the floor of the mouth normally regress from anterior to posterior, leaving a small remnant of attachment called the lingual frenulum. If the lingual frenulum is too inelastic, too short, failed to regress and extends along the underside of the tongue, or is placed too close to the gum ridge, tongue function will be restricted. (p. 181)

This manner of defining by the use of developmental description allows readers to appreciate the significance of tongue-tie and envision the role it plays in restricting normal tongue function.

Several authors use visual criteria to supplement functional criteria in describing tongue-tie (Behrman, Vaughan and Nelson, 1987; Paradise, 1990; Summitt, 1990). Hillan (2008) enhance their definition of a tight lingual frenulum inhibiting movement of the tongue by adding the criterion of a heart-shaped tongue-tip due to notching at the tip's midline. Hogan, Westcott, and Griffiths (2005) suggest that tongue-tie can be diagnosed and classified in severity by the extent to which the lingual frenulum occupies the underside of the tongue. Griffiths (2004) uses a similar system in addition to other visual qualities, such as the thickness of the frenulum and the shape of the tongue-tip.

In the past, many authors used visual anatomic criteria alone to describe and therefore define tongue-tie (Greene, 1945; Gunther, 1970; Lau and Ong, 1983). One such error persists: the necessity of a heart-shaped appearance to the tongue. Although the classic heart-shaped appearance upon lift or protrusion occurs in nearly half of all cases of tongue-tie, the other 50 percent of tongue-ties do not exhibit this particular form.

We must be cautious when using anatomical descriptors as definition. Anatomical descriptors do not accurately tell the physiological story. For example, a lingual frenulum may be shorter than the mean but be very elastic, allowing the tongue to complete its full range of motion. The tongue, in this case, looks tied but doesn't act tied. We are primarily concerned with how tongue-tie impairs normal physiology; therefore, our definition must be primarily one of function rather than appearance.

The above quoted tongue-tie descriptions serve as very good examples of an Operational Definition: the observers describe the specific qualities or impact of tongue-tie. In other words, in an effort to be specific, they tend to define the phenomenon by how it behaves. They describe the qualities of the "elephant," such as its strong odor, long trunk, little ears, big flat feet and tough gray hide, rather than use the simpler and broader "big mammal found in Africa, India and zoos." The tendency of observers to get lost in the details may lead one to think that no standardized definition of tongue-tie exists and that no two observers can agree. Although important and appropriate for enhancing our understanding of a phenomenon, an Operational Definition is too limited to serve. Resting just under the weight of the details in an Operational Definition is the Conceptual (and very much standardized) Definition of tongue-tie.

After completing an extensive literature review to establish an Operational Definition for my research study, I opted for a clear and concise Conceptual Definition that allowed both common and rarer qualities left unacknowledged and/or unknown by many authors writing before 1993 to emerge. I defined tongue-tie, or partial ankyloglossia, as impaired tongue function resulting from a tight and/or short lingual frenulum, which may or may not involve fibers of the genioglossus muscle. This definition guided the development of the Assessment Tool for Lingual Frenulum Function (Hazelbaker, 1993).

THE CONCEPTUAL DEFINITION OF TONGUE-TIE

For hundreds of years, tongue-tie has been conceptually defined: shortness and/or tightness of the lingual frenulum affects, to varying degrees, the proper function of the tongue. Just like the Velveteen Rabbit was made real by love, tongue-tie has been "made real" by giving it a name after first observing its existence as an operating phenomenon. Acknowledgment precedes definition. A thing is named only when it is observed to be meaningfully different from that which already exists, in this case, restricted tongue motion seen in some as different from tongue motion as experienced by most. Rather than being a trifle, this tidbit of philosophical contemplation goes a long way.

At some time in our past, perhaps our ancient past, it became evident that some people couldn't use their tongues in the way others could. Perhaps they were ridiculed, or ostracized; perhaps they experienced a compassionate acknowledgment of their difficulty. But, then, someone decided to investigate – to find out why such a problem existed. Perhaps he or she examined an affected person's mouth and discovered that the tongue could not move for one reason or another. Maybe that first examiner identified the lingual frenulum as the problem, but maybe some other investigator, later in time, identified another, more exact reason. We do not know when tongue-tie was first "diagnosed."

We must stop asserting that we do not yet know what tongue-tie means. Early citations prove that we have had a notion of tongue-tie for a very long time. This knowledge of tongue restriction due to an abnormal lingual frenulum, as described over and over in public writings, demonstrates that tongue-tie has a conceptual basis and therefore a Conceptual Definition. Today, we stand strongly and well supported on that Conceptual Definition.

It's time we stopped getting hung up on the definition "controversy" and started identifying tongue-tie's specific characteristics so that we can formulate a standardized treatment decision rule. Forming such a rule demands that we know when we should cut, when we should do therapy, or when we should choose to stand back and let Nature take her course. We learn this through informal and formal observation. Such observations require the use of Operational Definitions.

OPERATIONAL DEFINITIONS

An Operational Definition is a "process" defining the steps of measurement of a thing that already has been conceptually defined. For example, a researcher might want to determine the degree to which tongue motion could be restricted by using a valid measuring tool like a set of calipers to measure tongue lift in both normal and affected subjects. He or she might also measure the length of the lingual frenulum when the tongue is lifted and the extent to which the lingual frenulum occupies the underside of the tongue. Using these three sets of measurements, the investigator could draw some conclusions about the interrelationships existing among them, thereby helping to quantify normal lift and restricted lift, normal frenular length and short frenular length when the tongue is lifted, and normal and excessive frenular dimension along the tongue underside's anterior to posterior axis.

Well-constructed Operational Definitions play a key role in tongue-tie research. Tongue-tie, because it involves so many aspects of physiology, is a complex phenomenon. Operational Definitions provide a basis for measuring such complexity. Although we can simply and conceptually define tongue-tie as a limitation of tongue movement caused by an abnormally short and/or tight lingual frenulum, the ways in which tongue movement can be impaired and the degree to which they are can vary from individual to individual and also may differ in various age groups, possibly worsening over time. Operational Definitions serve to quantify these variations.

The first step in delineating an Operational Definition involves understanding the conceptual aspects of the "thing" being Operationally Defined. Griffiths (2004) conceptually understood that tongue-tie possibly has an impact on infant attachment to the breast because the condition interferes with normal range of tongue motion. This fact prompted him to ask the mothers of his cohort babies to report on their latch. Based on their accounts, he chose to stipulate compromised latch-on as an indication for surgical treatment of his breastfed tongue-tied subject babies. By default, latching difficulty became part of his Operational Definition. Although such a design runs the risk of excluding babies not experiencing latch problems, this study further quantifies latching difficulty as a symptom of tongue-tie. Griffiths further described how tongue-tied infants latch differently from normal infants.

A fine-tuned understanding of complex phenomena takes years and years of observation; we are fortunate that the observations of many clinicians and researchers in the last hundred years have moved us to a sufficient enough understanding that we can make some definitive pronouncements about tongue-tie's impact and treatment. Multiple studies, examining and describing different aspects of tongue-tie, have collectively generated a consensus regarding the general characteristics of tongue-tie's impact and the efficacy of both frenotomy and frenectomy. New information should emerge as studies, such as that presented by Coryllos and Watson Genna et al. (2004) on posterior ties and Palmer's (2005) information on airway obstruction, continues to emerge.

Identifying all the aspects of tongue-tie will take time and much more observation – both informal, as in the case histories presented by many authors, and formal, as in the numerous well-designed research studies performed during the last ten years. The emerging consensus is obvious; the dramatic, hand-wringing controversy appears to be nearly over. Researchers may choose to use different Operational Definitions for their studies; one may use tongue protrusion, another may use tongue elevation, and a third may use changes in progressive tongue contraction. These Operational Definition variations pose no problem; they provide us with details about the tongue-tie phenomenon.

WHAT'S NORMAL GOT TO DO WITH IT?

Researchers and clinicians actually never disagreed about the Conceptual Definition of tongue-tie. They haggled, and still do, over the concept of normal. Those who claim that tongue-tie does not exist do so because their conceptualization of normal includes a broader range of frenula presentations than those of their clinical counterparts in other fields. Based on the research, one could make the argument that these individuals are ignorant of the issues that arise when a lingual frenulum prevents a tongue from functioning in certain ways. Even tongue-tie experts still hotly discuss among themselves the degree to which tongue-tie interferes with normal functioning, although the line of demarcation is getting sharper and thinner.

A problem occurs when defining normal. Exactly what individuals do we include when we segregate normal from abnormal when it comes to tongue movement? Tongue-tie's Operational Definition then becomes somewhat of a circular issue, and therein lies the crux of the remaining tongue-tie definition "controversy"; we have yet to establish what is precisely normal. Not so long ago, Williams and Waldron (1985) stated that:

> The term tongue-tie implies some abnormality, a condition outside of the range of normal anatomic or functional capability ... but ... before any cause and effect relationship between tongue-tie and oral motor dysfunction or speech disorders can be established, an objective and replicable system of measurement for lingual form and function must be defined. (p. 353)

Fletcher and Meldrum (1968) mirror the statements of Williams and Waldron:

> Impressionistic judgments rather than quantitative data continue to dominate descriptions of lingual morphology. ... This counters a basic biological tenet which asserts that before physiological effects may be attributed to any anatomical condition, an accurate description of the anatomy must first be provided. (p. 382, 389)

During Fletcher's time, a dearth of exacting studies created room for a variety of opposing opinions regarding tongue-tie, thereby creating a polarizing controversy. Despite the fact that recent studies have moved us out of polarization and into consensus-building and that study after study shows that tongue mobility is, in fact, increased by surgical intervention, we cannot say with certainty where the borderline between normal tongue motion and tongue motion that is restricted by tongue-tie actually lies. Although this argument seems moot to the tongue-tie treatment enthusiasts, it isn't. When quantifying the impact of any illness or disease, one always compares the offender against what is generally thought to be normal or, at least, acceptable.

We may think we clearly know what is normal in the case of tongue-tie, but our inability to arrive at a standardized treatment decision rule demonstrates that we have yet to fully differentiate normal function from abnormal function. For example, what does tongue mobility actually mean? When an individual sticks out his or her tongue, how far should it be able to protrude? How far should it lift in the mouth and should the chin follow? How much does the tongue need to lateralize in order to effectively move food around the mouth for optimal mastication or to clean the teeth? What degree of movement allows a baby to effectively transfer milk from the breast? From the bottle?

A few studies have attempted to operationally define tongue-tie for the purpose of finding the fine line between normal and abnormal. Every factor formulated for the Assessment Tool for Lingual Frenulum Function (Hazelbaker, 1993) arose out of this form of careful observation and measurement. In my study of infants under 6 months, I observed the various tongue movement qualities of extension, lift, lateralization, peristalsis, cup and spread in a sample size deemed appropriate for my research design. Each baby was compared against the rest to describe an average range of tongue movement. In the case of the tongue lift, the average infant was able to easily lift his or her tongue to mid-mouth without moving the jaw upward. This factor became the reference for normal range of tongue motion during tongue lifting. I then identified degrees to which babies did not exhibit this same range of motion. These deficits became references for restricted tongue lift.

Similarly, Fernando (1998) formulated her parameters of abnormal tongue-function, indicating the presence of tongue-tie, based on previously identified descriptions of motion for optimal speech production, feeding, and oral toilet in older children and adults. Her Tongue-Tie Assessment Protocol (TAPP) reflects the care she took in identifying these deviations. Kotlow (1999) identified several indictors of fully functional tongue movement in children and adults. They include such aspects of tongue function as its ability to easily sweep the upper and lower lips, and to retrude without causing the lingual frenulum to blanch. He correlated these movements with the length of the free portion of the tongue to design a frenotomy decision rule.

Fletcher and Meldrum (1968, p. 390) endeavored to answer the questions surrounding the relationship that exists between lingual mobility and speech proficiency. They performed two rounds of measurements using different instruments to determine the range of motion of the tongue in a group of 11- and 12-year-old children. Their first measuring device proved to be unreliable. The second, a modified Boley gauge with an attached caliper, was reliable. In the second group, the research team was able to quantify restricted range of motion and then correlate it with speech articulation errors.

Geddes et al.'s recent studies (Geddes, Kent, Mitoulas, and Hartmann, 2008; Geddes, Langton, Gollow, Jacobs, Hartman, and Simmer, 2008) used ultrasonography to identify normal tongue motions in breastfed infants and deficits seen in tongue-tied babies. In the first of the two studies listed here, they observed tongue movements in a cohort of happily and effectively breastfeeding infants. This study confirmed that breastfed babies place their tongues over the lower gumline and cup the tongue around the breast teat to form a seal. Although this study shows the typical progressive contractility of the tongue, it disconfirms the notion that tongue "peristalsis" is the primary mechanism for milk removal. Rather, it demonstrates that intra-oral negative pressure is largely responsible for milk removal.

In the second study examining sucking in tongue-tied babies, Geddes' team imaged the infants' sucking pre- and post-frenotomy. Their imaging confirmed suspicion that tongue-tied babies used a different sucking action than normal babies, and that action then converted to normal postoperatively. Using their Operational Definition of normal sucking established during the first study, Geddes and her team were able to exactly identify functional deficits in tongue-tied babies in the second study.

There is no doubt that more study needs to be done. Researchers must ask a multitude of questions to quantify tongue-tie's many manifestations. Tongue-tie studies must proceed, keeping in mind the Conceptual Definition of tongue-tie and those aspects of tongue-tie already identified through previous study. By doing so, researchers can formulate optimal Operational Definitions.

IS TONGUE-TIE A SYNDROME?

Dorland's Pocket Medical Dictionary (2001, p. 800) defines syndrome as "a set of symptoms occurring together; the sum of signs of any morbid state; a symptom complex." Do the complicated nature of tongue-tie and the myriad ways in which tongue motion deficits present in the tongue-tied individual earn tongue-tie the designation of syndrome? It's true that tongue-tie often occurs in tandem with other midline defects that accompany various syndromes. Several researchers now assert that tongue-tie also can be heritable as an autosomal dominant trait. If we were to expand our conceptualization of tongue-tie as a syndrome, would it help us to understand the phenomenon better? How much more likely would tongue-tie be taken seriously if it were viewed from this expanded conceptualization?

Since tongue-tied individuals sometimes also exhibit other "minor" midline issues such as a high-arched palate and a prominent labial frenulum, is it possible that unseen or unrecognized midline issues also accompany tongue-tie? My first son, David, was born with a "classic" tongue-tie. He also presented with a high-arched palate and a prominent labial frenulum. He had severe excessive salivation issues as a young child and was diagnosed with unspecified Attention Deficit Disorder when he was older. His psychiatrist also has suggested strongly that David has a rapid-cycling form of Bipolar Disorder. Both of these mental issues are midline, limbic system manifestations.

Is tongue-tie part of an as-yet-unknown or unnamed syndrome and therefore an indicator of these problems, or does the presence of the tie prevent the full development of other aspects of midline function? Does the spreading of the palate under the morphological influence of the tongue put into motion optimal midbrain physiology that may be disrupted when the tongue is tethered? Although this may end up being a chicken-egg issue, these are questions worth asking. Our rapidly burgeoning interest in tongue-tie nearly guarantees that these questions will be answered in the future.

INCIDENCE OF TONGUE-TIE

According to Fletcher and Meldrum (1968), the incidence of tongue-tie is conjectural. Williams and Waldron (1985) assert that the lack of a standardized definition prevents the capture of meaningful prevalence statistics. No doubt, incidence statistics depend upon a careful examination of normal. The point of departure from normal can then be clearly seen, revealing incidence. We have as yet to find that clear point and so, for now, we must content ourselves with a range of incidence statistics dependent upon the Operational Definition of tongue-tie used in each research study.

In both this and the last century, only a few studies were conducted to ascertain the epidemiology of oral anomalies, including tongue-tie, in certain populations. In 1945, DePorte and Parkhurst reported an incidence of tongue-tie in their population as 99 out of 3,180 children – a rate of about 32 per 1,000 (3.2 percent). Their study was conducted with children born in New York State outside of New York City, between 1940 and 1942. This prevalence rate matches more recent reports. Cinar and Onat (2005) found an incidence of 2.02 percent in their study population, a ratio of 1.7:1 boys to girls. Friend, Mincer, Fong, and Carruth (1990) reported a higher incidence of 8.3 percent in their study cohort; 6 percent of boys and 2.3 percent of girls were tongue-tied.

Sedano (1975) found a much lower rate of 0.1 percent, or one per 1,000, in his sample of 6,180 Argentinean children. In this study, tongue-tie was found equally often in boys and girls. He cites a Chilean study, Oral and Genetic Studies of Chileans by Witkop and Barros (1960), which found an incidence of 0.2 percent in their study population.

These figures seem shockingly low as compared to the prevalence statistics reported in several subsequent studies, making one wonder about the Operational Definitions used by the various researchers. Sedano used a simple screening procedure, requiring the individual to lift their tongue toward the maxillary central incisors. If the tongue did not lift higher than the labial commissures and the lingual frenulum appeared thick, the individual was reported as having tongue-tie. Sedano was also looking at a general population of children, not just those experiencing a problem of one kind or another. His statistics may be skewed in one direction because of an inadequate screening procedure or may be representative of incidence in a general population of children in that age group. Without a standardized screening process, we cannot tell which is which.

Fernando (1998) reports an incidence of 6.58 percent in her study cohort. One hundred-ninety-six of 1,290 children of various ages were sent to her for evaluation. These children were referred because of other observed problems; we therefore could not consider this statistic generalizeable. Ballard, Auer, and Khoury (2002) found an incidence of 12.8 percent in their cohort of outpatient babies experiencing breastfeeding difficulties. However, of the all of the inpatient babies screened for tongue-tie, 3.2 percent were classified as such. This tells us that tongue-tied babies may experience greater difficulty with breastfeeding than their non-tied peers, but only gives us a sense of the possible incidence of tongue-tie in a general population of babies.

Marchesan (2004) notes an overall incidence of 9 percent in her study cohort of 1402 people who ranged in age from 5 to 62 years. All individuals in the study were being evaluated for speech or myofunctional difficulties. Slightly more than half of those identified as being tongue-tied were female, a departure from most studies that have found a significantly higher percentage of affected males. An interesting new study, just in press, found a male to female ratio of exactly 2:1 for anterior ties but the reverse for posterior ties. This same study found an incidence of 6% posterior ties and 94% of anterior ties in their total study cohort of 341 tongue-tied babies. (Hong et al., 2010).

Sawyer, Taiwo, and Mosadomi (1984) studied Nigerian children. Ankyloglossia was seen about equally as often in boys and girls, but the actual prevalence of the condition was low. In a sample size of 2,203 children, prevalence was 0.2 percent, or two per 1,000. Lomcali (1987, p. 124) states that ankyloglossia is "reported to affect a little more males than females"; however, it is not clear who reported this finding. Amir and James et al. (2005) found a 1.7:1 male-to-female ratio. Hogan et al. (2005) report a similar figure of 1.6:1 male-to-female ratio. They also found an overall incidence of 10.7 percent in their study cohort. Klockars, looking at inheritance patterns for tongue-tie, found a nearly 4:1 male-to-female ratio in his study of a single family. Fifty percent of all family members spread over three generations were tongue-tied.

Of the handful of studies looking at inheritance, two report a 40 percent incidence of known family history, (Cinar and Onat, 2005; Fernando, 1998), and one reports a 21 percent incidence of family history (Ballard et al, 2002). Is it possible, as suggested by Klockars' 2007 study, that inheritance may play a larger role in the manifestation of tongue-tie than once thought? Many people do not know what their family history is and may find out only when their own diagnosis is made. Since we now have several generations of non-treated tongue-tie, tracing family history may be easier.

SUMMARY

Depending on how one looks at it, one could say the above figures represent an uncommon or common phenomenon. After all, a statistic of three out of 100 does not seem to be that important, yet an epidemic refers to a phenomenon that affects only three percent of any population. We take epidemics very seriously. Everything is relative.

Incidence statistics depend upon definition and assessment criteria. Nezu (1987) clipped 40 to 50 percent of lingual frenula of babies seen in her clinic between 1977 and 1980. When a more carefully considered assessment protocol was created, the incidence of clipping dropped to one to two percent. Nicole's story illustrates the need for assessment standardization.

Both of Nicole's boys were tongue-tied, but each exhibited different aspects of the phenomenon. Nicole's firstborn latched reasonably well and was gaining slowly with the help of top-off feeds of formula, but Nicole's nipples were so severely damaged that one was almost entirely missing from her breast. It took six months before an accurate diagnosis was made. Fortunately, this first baby received a frenotomy; unfortunately, Nicole did not receive postoperative support to help retrain her baby's sucking. Eventually, however, Nicole's feeding problems resolved.

Nicole's second baby was evaluated for tongue-tie only because she requested that the midwives do so. He could stick out his tongue well, but within a day of his birth, Nicole was once again in severe pain. The baby gained well and so Nicole's midwives repeatedly told her to latch the baby on deeper to resolve the breastfeeding problem. Nicole, now much more knowledgeable on the subject of tongue-tie, suspected he was tongue-tied because his function was compromised enough to cause her nipple pain, but he had no visible signs.

At five weeks, Nicole decided to have him evaluated by a more experienced clinician, who verified that her infant had a rarer type of tongue-tie, one that is difficult to visualize. The baby's frenulum, which was underneath the mucous membrane, was clipped. Nicole and her second son also experienced some challenges after the procedure; once again, she did not receive optimal postoperative surgical support, and so their recovery period was a struggle. Eventually, like his brother, this baby also became an excellent breastfeeder and went on to breastfeed for several years.

This story illustrates the problems with assessment that correspond to an inadequate conceptual and operational understanding of tongue-tie. Had all the clinicians involved in Nicole's care known that tongue-tie presentation appreciably varies, they would have made appropriate treatment suggestions more promptly. Instead of thoroughly assessing tongue range of motion, the clinicians relied on secondary manifestations to determine the presence of tongue-tie – and that prevented an accurate and timely diagnosis. A standardized treatment decision rule based on a conceptual tongue-tie definition paired with information garnered from the use of Operational Definitions will prevent future such scenarios.

CHAPTER ONE TAKEAWAY

1. The definition of tongue-tie is restricted tongue mobility as a result of a short and/or tight lingual frenulum. This Conceptual Definition of tongue-tie has existed for as long as our written records extend and persists to this day without change.

2. Clearly defining tongue-tie helps clinicians distinguish it from other kinds of sucking issues in the newborn and other kinds of dental, speech, or airway issues in older individuals. The ability to make these distinctions helps people receive timely and targeted assistance, saving them from months or even years of suffering.

3. The supposed controversy about tongue-tie's definition is actually confusion about the borderline between normal and abnormal tongue range of motion, which has prevented clinicians and researchers from generating a standardized treatment decision rule. Consensus about when to treat surgically and when not to is emerging as scientific inquiry continues.

4. The Operational Definitions of tongue-tie which include specific qualifications or additions to its Conceptual Definition are for the purpose of research. An Operational Definition serves as a model for the thing being studied for the purpose of testing hypotheses. Each new study provides more information about the thing being studied. Operational Definitions, although somewhat different from the Conceptual Definition, allow us, ultimately, to understand the concept better and how it works in the real world.

5. Although new information garnered through research using Operational Definitions of tongue-tie may cause our understanding of it to change over time, those changes will largely be nuances rather than stark contrasts and will be for the purpose of refinement. For example, the identification of posterior ties further refines our understanding of tongue-tie's manifestation without diluting or expanding its Conceptual Definition.

6. The definition of tongue-tie is a functional one buttressed by visual elements of presentation. Using only appearance qualities to make a diagnosis causes clinicians to miss some ties or to overdiagnose and overtreat.

7. The incidence of tongue-tie varies from about 2 to 12 percent, depending on the population under study and the Operational Definition of tongue-tie used for the study. Its incidence in the general population may be less than one percent, however, good incidence studies have yet to be performed.

CHAPTER TWO

ORIGINS

ANNALISE, A NURSE AND lactation consultant, tells this story that illustrates some of the challenges faced by professionals and parents:

> Last year I saw the worst tongue-tied baby I have ever seen. This baby's frenulum was so tight his tongue curled under and had no lift at all. I went to the M.D. who was caring for the baby in the hospital and told him about the baby's tongue and asked him if he would take a look and determine if the baby needed an ENT consult. He went ballistic. He said that the tongue had nothing at all to do with breastfeeding. Babies could breastfeed without a tongue because it was all done with the lips. I thought at first that he was kidding, but he wasn't. He was so ignorant of sucking issues. I told him that if he did not believe it was a problem, we would follow the mom until she could get with her pediatrician. He ranted about how his daughter was an ENT physician, and he knows tongue-tie is not a problem during breastfeeding because she told him so. He then went to my manager and wanted me fired or reprimanded. He told my partner [in the lactation department] that if I continued to tell parents about tongue-tie, I would be banned from seeing any of his patients, and they would get no breastfeeding help on the days that I worked.

The astounding and unfortunately pervasive ignorance about infant suck and sucking issues is responsible in part for the untenable advice given to mothers to prematurely wean their babies. It is not known how many primary care physicians and other clinicians truly understand normal sucking and how to quantify deficits. As illustrated in the story above, it's clear that some have no knowledge whatsoever. A typical assessment involves sticking a gloved finger in the baby's mouth and if the baby responds by sucking on it, their suck is considered adequate. Those who deal with babies in any capacity ought to know more.

MORPHOGENESIS

Infant survival depends on successful feeding. Successful feeding depends upon successful completion of both the embryological and fetal stages of human development. Despite the fact that embryos and fetuses can be highly vulnerable, Mother Nature has a way of ensuring proper development most of the time. Sometimes things go wrong; tongue-tie represents one of those things. Although considered a minor and relatively uncommon anomaly, tongue-tie has such a profound impact on the affected individual, especially related to feeding and subsequent eating, that it requires serious consideration. Nearly as much as more "severe" issues, such as cleft palate, which currently receive far more clinical attention.

Like cleft palate, tongue-tie has an impact on all three aspects of infant feeding: suck, swallow, and breathe. Optimal infant feeding depends upon the exquisite timing of suck–swallow–breathe. As Wolf and Glass (1992) state:

> Three processes – sucking, swallowing, and breathing – are the cornerstones of infant feeding. Not only are these processes related functionally as they come together in bottle and breast-feeding, but they are related anatomically. The anatomical structures responsible for sucking, swallowing, and breathing are physically in close proximity and overlap in function, with some structures having roles in the life-sustaining processes of both feeding and respiration. The close proximity of these structures, the interrelated nature of their functions, and the dual role some structures play in providing oxygen and nourishment to the body often underlie the feeding problems of infants. (p. 3)

To best understand how tongue-tie disrupts infant feeding, it is necessary to take a developmental journey, starting with embryology and finishing at the end of the first postpartum month, when a particular infant's suck–swallow–breathe style has fully emerged.

EMBRYOLOGY

Embryological development embraces the period of gestation from conception to gestational development week 8. During this short but intense period, multiple organismic foundations develop, including those of the head and neck. Embryological development creates a dance of transformation. From a more primitive form rises and develops a more sophisticated form. The movement of masses of cells and/or tissues prods the further development of other tissues. So it is with the structures that play a role in suck, swallow, and breathe.

In week 1 post conception, the fertilized ovum wends its way into the uterine cavity, steadily progressing toward its new home in the uterine endometrium. By about days 7 to 10, the fertilized egg, now a blastocyst, tucks itself into a cozy nook near the uterine fundus. The sealed-off conceptus now morphs into the generative structures that will soon become the embryo and its various nutritional sources.

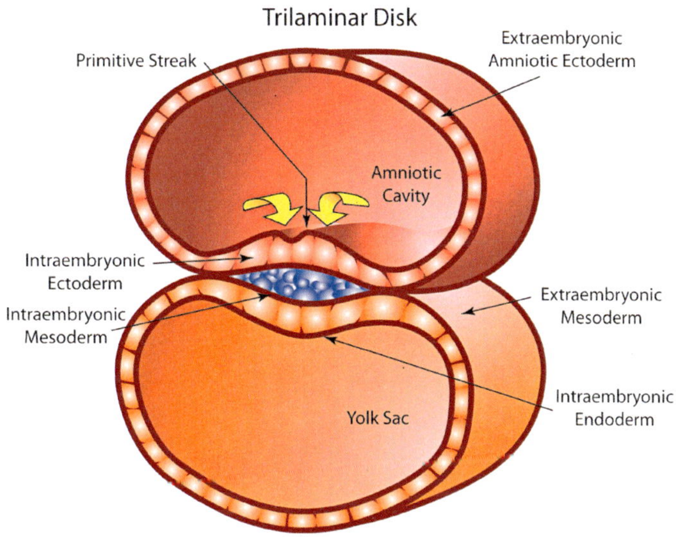

Figure 2-1. Trilaminar disk in cross-section.

© 2010 Alison K. Hazelbaker. Reprinted with permission. Artist: Paul Hughes.

The embryo, as we generally visualize it, forms from an embryonic disk, which starts as two layers and gradually becomes a three-layered structure. These three layers give rise to the various cells, tissues, and organs (Brookes and Zeitman, 1998). The ectoderm births the epidermis and the nervous system; the mesoderm the smooth muscle, connective tissue, and blood vessels; and the endoderm the epithelial linings of the respiratory and digestive systems, and its associated glands.

The germ layer that gives rise to the various tissues of the head and neck forms from the bilaminar embryonic disk, making it trilaminar. On the dorsal side, the neural plate arises from the ectoderm; on the ventral side, a tube that will eventually become the gastrointestinal tract arises from the endoderm. The mesodermal layer formed between these other two layers will give rise very quickly to its fledgling structures (Avery and Chiego, 2006). (See Figure 2-1.)

In week 3, soon after the layering of the embryonic disk, the neural plate, which is the mother of the central nervous system formed from ectoderm, births the neural folds and the neural crest. The neural plate first becomes the neural groove as its lateral edges rise dorsally and eventually come together at the midline with progressive closure at the cranial and caudal ends. This action gives the embryo its characteristic curved shape. (See Figure 2-2.)

This newly formed neural tube then closes. Three dilations, or vesicles, at the cranial end form and will become the various regions of the brain: forebrain, midbrain, and hindbrain. The forebrain eventually develops into the cerebral hemispheres and the diencephalon; the midbrain becomes the structures of the limbic system and the midbrain; and the hindbrain morphs into the pons, cer-

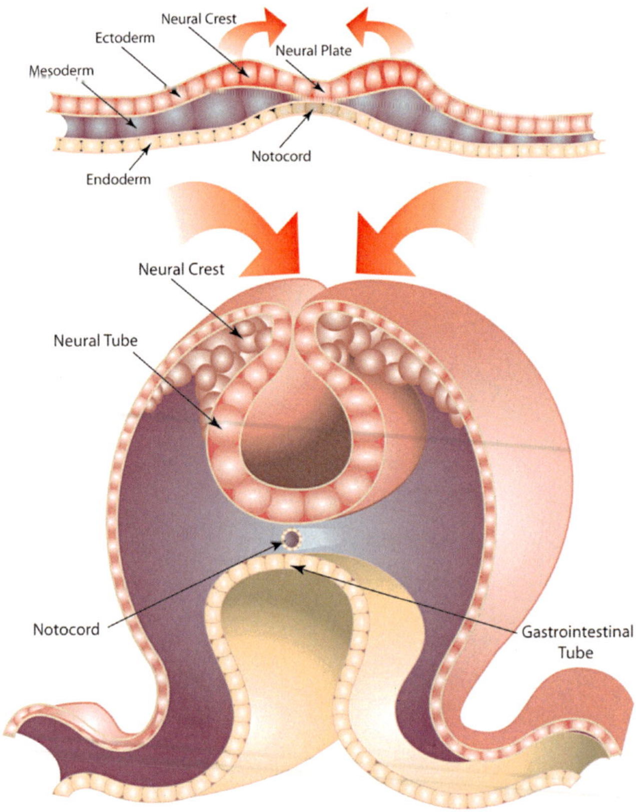

Figure 2-2. The neural tube and its crest. The neural crest gives rise to the dorsal root ganglia of the cranial and spinal nerves, and various cartilage, muscle and connective tissues in the head and neck region. The lumen of the neural tube gives rise to the ventricles of the brain and the cells of its thickened epithelial wall become the neuroblasts that eventually become the white and grey matter of the spinal cord.

ebellum, and medulla. The lumen of the neural tube gives rise to the ventricles of the brain, which become continuous with the spinal cord. The cells of the thickened neural tube wall epithelium give rise to the neuroblasts, which become the white and grey matter of the spinal cord. These same neuroblasts eventually mature and become the neurons.

The neural crest's neuroectodermal cells form a cell landscape on the surface of the brain and spinal cord that will become the dorsal root ganglia sensory pathways of the cranial and spinal nerves. The neural crest also contributes to the formation of various cartilage, muscles, and connective tissues in the head and neck region as they migrate from the dorsal surface to the ventral surface.

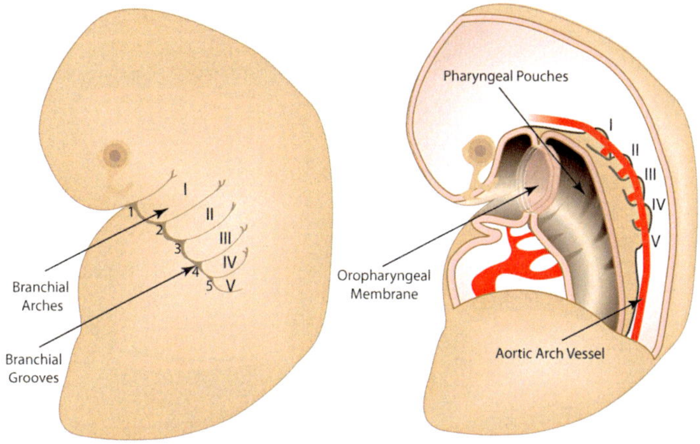

Figure 2-3. The branchial arches and their respective grooves, pouches, and blood supply.

The primitive human being rapidly develops greater and greater sophistication as the days glide into weeks. The two ends of the curved tube that is the primitive embryo fold in on themselves. This embryonic infolding, occurring in week 4, allows the formation of various pre-structures: the dorsal yolk sac is incorporated into the embryo as the primitive gut; the infolding at the newly formed head region becomes the oropharyngeal membrane; the heart moves inferiorly, allowing a pit to form between it and the brain just above the first tissue (branchial) arch (Avery and Chiego, 2006). This pit soon becomes the stomodeum and, ultimately, the oral cavity. At its deepest, the oropharyngeal membrane forms the back of this cavity, only to rupture in week 5, making the oral cavity continuous with the tubular foregut. This newly formed structure eventually becomes the combined food passage and airway.

At the same time, arches form ventrally that give rise to the various tissues that comprise the face, mouth, and pharynx.

ARCHES, GROOVES, AND POUCHES

The face and oral structures develop during embryonic weeks 4 to 7, courtesy of the tissue (branchial) arches derived from the neural crest cells that develop in the primordial pharynx floor. In one short week, the first of six pairs of branchial arches emerges and can be observed. Subsequent to that event, the other five pairs emerge in the following days and weeks. These stacked, parallel arches play an important role in oral and facial development and contain muscle, nerve, blood vessel, and skeletal elements. (See Figure 2-3.)

The muscles of mastication develop from the first branchial arch. In week 5, muscle cells begin their migration, arriving at their various destinations by week 6. They begin to replicate and differentiate into the masseters, medial and lateral pterygoids, and the temporalis muscles. The trigemi-

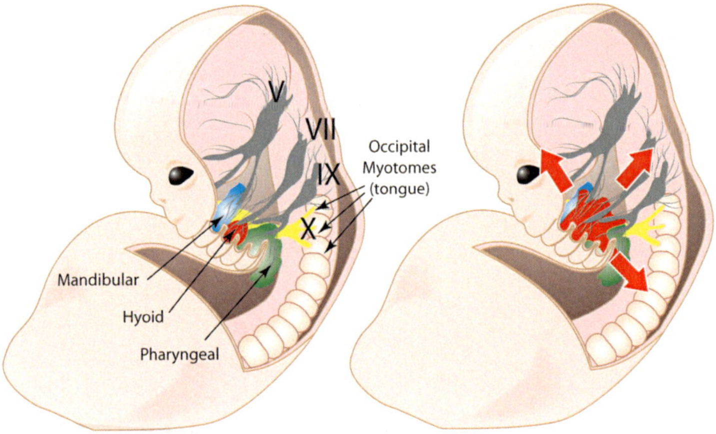

Figure 2-4. Development of the muscles and nerves from the pharyngeal arches. The muscles migrate as they develop, sometimes in multiple directions, spreading and differentiating. The nerve develops and migrates with the muscle mass. Notice the tongue muscle mass development and migration (yellow) starting at the occipital myotomes. The hypoglossal nerve (XII) develops and migrates along with this mass.

nal nerve (CN V), – the resident cranial nerve supplying the first branchial arch – innervates these developing muscles, the skin of the lower face, the anterior tongue mucosa, floor of the mouth, gingiva, and the mandibular teeth. This arch also gives rise to the maxillary artery and part of the external carotid artery.

The second of the pharyngeal arches, also known as the hyoid arch, develops into the latero-posterior tongue body, the facial muscles, the facial vessels, and aspects of the hyoid bone. Its resident cartilage, Reichert's cartilage, forms the basis for much of the stapes and contributes to the malleus and incus. Week 7 finds the facial muscles rapidly spreading, sheetlike, into the facial area accompanying the branching facial nerve. This task is completed in the early fetal period.

The third branchial arch gives rise to the greater horns of the hyoid and its inferior body. The root of the tongue develops from this arch as well. The glossopharyngeal nerve (CN IX) supplies this arch and reaches out to supply the forming stylopharyngeal and upper pharyngeal constrictor muscles, as well as the posterior third of the forming tongue. Both the mesoderm and the neural crest tissues give rise to aspects of the carotid artery; the common carotid and, subsequently, the internal carotid form from the branchial arch artery, and the carotid body arises from the neural crest and is innervated by the glossopharyngeal nerve. (See Figure 2-4.)

The superior laryngeal branch of the vagus nerve serves the fourth branchial arch, from which arises the thyroid cartilage, the cricothyroid, the pharyngeal constrictor muscles, the palatopharyngeus, the levator veli palatini and uvular muscles, and the palatoglossus muscle of the tongue. The muscle cell migration proceeds posteriorly, then spreads simultaneously caudally and cephalad to form the continuous semi-tube that characterizes the fully formed throat. Its artery develops into the aortic arch and contributes to the right subclavian and brachiocephalic arteries.

The fifth arch lives a short life, disappearing almost as soon as it develops.

The cricoid and laryngeal cartilages, and intrinsic laryngeal musculature arise from the sixth arch, whose nerve supply comes from the recurrent laryngeal nerve, a branch of the vagus. Its nutritional supply via the sixth artery later forms the pulmonary arteries and the temporary ductus arteriosus so important to fetal life. Postnatally, the ductus arteriosus becomes the ligmentum arteriosum.

Ectoderm coats the anterior surfaces of the arches and the interior surface of the second arch. The oral epithelium emerges from the ectoderm of the first and second arches. Endoderm lines the interior surfaces of arches three through six. The gastrointestinal tract and its glands arise from this primordial issue. At the potent core of the arches, within the mesoderm, lie the elemental tissues for the blood vessels, muscles, nerves, cartilages, and bones of the face, which will differentiate into these various structures in concert with one another.

The mandible is the first structure to develop as the medial ends of the mandibular prominences of the first branchial arch merge. As the mandible begins its formation, the maxillary prominences also make their move medially, followed closely by the medial nasal prominences. The surrounding mesenchyme proliferates to form the medial and lateral nasal prominences, which in turn become the primitive nasal sacs. This newly generated nasal cavity is separated from its sister oral cavity by the oronasal membrane, which ruptures at the sixth week and becomes the primitive choanae. From this point on, the nasal and oral cavities are directly communicating neighbors.

At first, the developing tongue occupies this space with little room for other structures. The cavity is bounded in front by the primary palate, which, as it develops and rises, becomes the permanent dividing structure between the nasal and oral cavities.

TONGUE

The tongue organ forms from the lingual primordium, which arises from branchial arches one to four in week 4 to 5, each arch contributing specific aspects of the primordial structure. Mesenchymal proliferation of the pharyngeal arches generates multiple swellings on the floor of the mouth. Bordered by bilateral lingual swellings, the tuberculum impar rises up from the midline of the mandibular process. The lingual swellings merge with each other and with the tuberculum impar at the midline, forming a larger mass, which then gives rise to the mucous membrane of the anterior two-thirds of the tongue.

The mesenchyme of arches two to four form a copula (arch two-generated) and hypobranchial eminence (arches three to four-generated) that merge to create a large mass. This posterior mass becomes the root of the tongue and its overlying mucosa. The sulcus terminalis, a V-shaped demarcation, forms the line between the mobile tongue body and the anchored tongue root. (See Figure 2-5.)

The tongue muscles arise from the myoblasts generated in the bilateral occipital myotomes concurrently with the other muscles of the orofacial and pharyngeal areas. The muscle cell masses migrate forward into the newly formed oral cavity floor where the lingual primordium has begun developing. The nerve cells that form the hypoglossal nerve migrate together with the myoblasts. Both infiltrate the lingual primordium in week 5 and push the lingual primordial tissue to develop into the tongue mass of differentiated and mature striated muscle, fully completing their developmental task in fetal week 1. (See Figure 2-6.)

The ectoderm surrounding the still-developing tongue grows downward, allowing the tongue to separate from the floor of the mouth. This ectodermal tissue then degenerates to form the lingual sulcus and frees the tongue body for movement while gently anchoring it to the remaining surrounding oral and pharyngeal tissues. Incomplete degeneration leaves tissue behind that restricts the tongue's mobility to one degree or another. What we now call tongue-tie is the incomplete degeneration of ectodermal tissue at the apex of the tongue. Ankyloglossia results from a complete failure of downward ectodermal growth and its subsequent degeneration, preventing the tongue from differentiating from the mouth floor.

The complex innervation of the tongue organ owes its origin to the multiple generating locations of the organ. The anterior sensory innervation arises out of the generative first branchial arch, which is innervated by the trigeminal nerve. The fifth cranial nerve therefore serves the sensory needs of the anterior two-thirds of the tongue. The posterior one-third of the tongue's sensory innervation arises from the same generative third arch that is innervated by the glossopharyngeal nerve. Motor coordination comes from the hypoglossal nerve, which arises from the occipital somites, as do the myoblasts, which form the tongue musculature.

The epiglottis, a cartilaginous cum muscular flap that resides at the base of the tongue and plays a distinct role in airway protection, also arises from the hypobranchial eminence (Nanci, 2008). It receives its nerve supply from the glosspharyngeal and vagal nerves.

PALATE

The palate begins its development at the end of the week 5 somewhat concurrently with the tongue, completing its form by week 12 in the early fetal period. Mesenchymal masses merge toward the midline in an anterior-to-posterior sequence to form the primary hard palate by week 6. This portion of the palate comprises only that segment anterior to the incisive foramen. The palate posterior to this small opening develops from the secondary palate formed by two lateral horizontal palatine processes that grow and then fuse slightly before or during week 9.

The palatine processes formed by maxillary tissues of the maxillary processes grow medially

Number	Arch-Derived Structures	Groove-Derived Structures	Pouch-Derived Structures
I (Mandibular)	Trigeminal (V) nerve, muscles of mastication, anterior belly of the digastric muscle, mylohyoid, tensor tympani, tensor palatine malleus, incus, sphenomandibular ligament, Meckel's cartilage	External auditory meatus	Middle ear and eustachian tube
II (Hyoid)	Facial (VII) nerve, muscles of facial expression, stapedius, stylohyoid, posterior belly of the digastric muscle, stapes, styloid process, stylohyoid ligament, lesser cornu of hyoid, upper part of the hyoid body	Cervical fistula	
III	Glossopharyngeal (IX) nerve, stylopharyngeus muscle, greater cornu of the hyoid, lower part of the hyoid body	Cervical fistula	Palatine tonsil, thymus, inferior thyroid
IV	Vagus (X) nerve, laryngeal muscles, pharyngeal constrictor muscles, laryngeal cartilages	Cervical fistula	
V	Spinal accessory (XI) nerve, sternocleidomastoid and trapezius muscles		
VI			Superior parathyroid, ultimobranchial body

Table 2-1. Summary of structures that develop from pharyngeal arches, grooves, and pouches.

until they reach the lateral aspects of the growing tongue. The palatine processes then grow downward on either side of the tongue. During week 8 of development, the palatal shelves push against the tongue, forcing it down and forward in the oral cavity. This push accompanies and may, in part, be generated by the lifting of the upper facial complex. The shelves slide over the tongue, reorienting themselves horizontally. Palatal shelf elevation occurs in a flash – "as fast as the act of swallowing" – and prepares the palate for subsequent fusion (Avery and Chiego, 2006, pg. 55). (See Figure 2-7.)

The shelves grow medially, in large part due to the upward push of the now-broadened tongue.

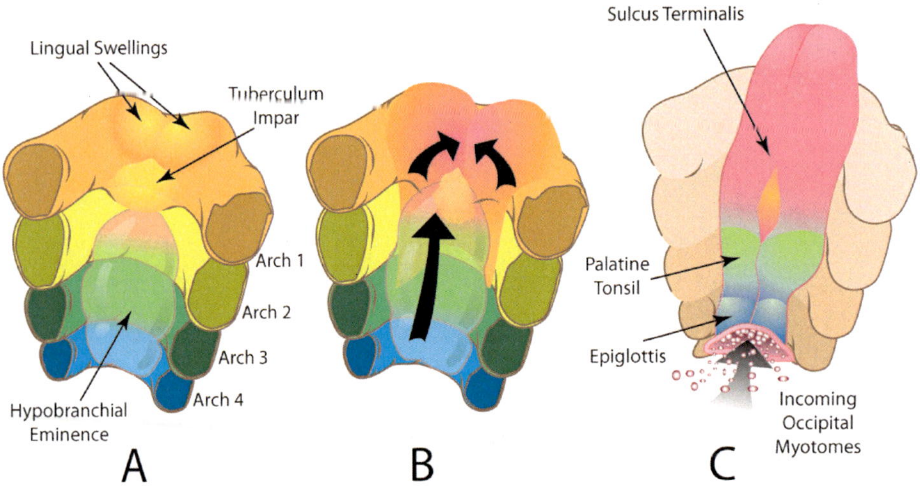

Figure 2-5. Tongue development. The tongue organ forms from the lingual primordium, which arises from branchial arches 1-4 in the fourth to fifth week. Each arch contributes specific aspects of the primordial structure. A. Mesen chymal proliferation of the pharyngeal arches generates multiple swellings on the floor of the mouth. Bordered by bi-lateral lingual swellings, the tuberculum impar rises up from the midline of the mandibular process. B. The lingual swellings merge at the midline with each other and with the tuberculum impar forming a larger mass, which then gives birth to the mucous membrane of the anterior two thirds of the tongue. The mesenchyme of the second through fourth arches form a copula (second arch generated) and hypobranchial eminence (third and fourth arch generated) that merge to create a large mass. This posterior mass becomes the root of the tongue and its overlying mucosa. C. A V-shaped demarcation, the sulcus terminalis, forms the line between the mobile tongue body and the anchored tongue root. The tongue muscles arise from the myoblasts generated in the bilateral occipital myotomes concurrently with the other muscles of the orofacial and pharyngeal areas. The muscle cell masses migrate forward into the newly formed oral cavity floor where the lingual primordium has begun developing.

Shelf fusion occurs anterior to posterior; its final step is the enzymatic breakdown of the midline epithelial barrier and its replacement with connective tissues between the right and left sides. As fusion proceeds, the palate lengthens. The muscular soft palate forms from the most posterior aspects of the palatine processes infiltrated by myoneural cells, which subsequently differentiate to form the muscular and neural components.

The nasal septum descends from the newly connected medial nasal prominences and fuses with the palatine processes, again moving sequentially anterior to posterior. This migration takes about the same amount of time as the similar march toward midline fusion taken by the palatine processes that form the bony hard palate. By week 12, this process concludes, forming a continuous roof to the oral cavity.

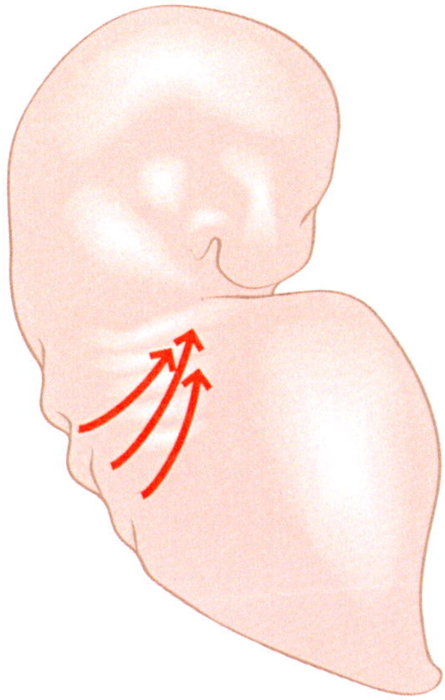

Figure 2-6. Tongue myoneural cells migrating from the occipital somites.

ESOPHAGUS AND RESPIRATORY TRACT

Week 4 is an exciting and busy time for the embryo. The primitive gut, now separated into foregut, midgut and hindgut, gradually differentiates into the glands and epithelium of the digestive tract, all derived from the endoderm. The pharynx, respiratory system, esophagus, stomach, duodenum, liver, pancreas, gallbladder, and biliary ducts emerge gracefully from their primitive state, all fed by the wellspring of the primitive circulatory system.

At about 26 days, the swallowing and respiratory mechanisms begin to develop along separate pathways. Respiration develops slowly in comparison to swallowing; early on, the fetus swallows amniotic fluid and, near term, is capable of swallowing nearly a wombful every two days.

In the foregut portion of the primitive alimentary tract, the gastropharyngeal isthmus divides the primitive pharynx from the stomach. The isthmus elongates to become the esophagus, courtesy of the mesenchyme and endodermal contributions of the caudal pharyngeal arches and the corresponding and infiltrating nerve supply of the vagus (CN X). Esophageal growth keeps pace with tracheal growth, the esophagus reaching its relative length by week 7.

The rapidly proliferating epithelium nearly obliterates the lumen of the esophagus this same week, only to break down in the subsequent week to recanalize it. The descending heart and lungs goad the caudally oriented growth of the esophagus, ensuring that it keeps the stomach at an appropriate position relative to these other visceral structures.

The esophagus' final arrangement of striated and smooth muscle has been laid down for its

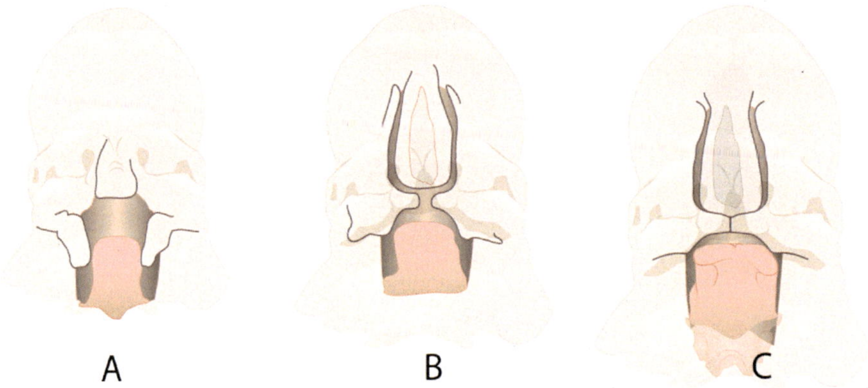

Figure 2-7. Palatal growth, coronal section. A. The tongue grows upward into the nasal cavity. Notice how the palatine shelves grow medially to contact the tongue. Concurrently, the tongue begins differentiating, growing alongside of the palatine shelves. B. In only one week, the palatine shelves have changed from a vertical orientation to a horizontal orientation and are growing medially on their way to creating a separate nasal cavity. C. The palatine shelves gradually fuse from anterior to posterior, forming the hard bony palate. Notice the shape and size of the tongue; it now fills the oral cavity. © 2010 Alison K. Hazelbaker. Reprinted with permission. Artist: Paul Hughes.

upcoming efforts of channeling swallowed amniotic fluid. The striated muscles of the upper one-third arise from the mesenchyme of the lower branchial arches. The smooth muscle of the lower two-thirds develops from the surrounding splanchnic mesenchyme.

The primitive pharynx, derived from the foregut, after giving birth to the branchial arches, gives rise to the laryngotracheal groove in week 4. This groove morphs into a diverticulum and differentiates from the primitive pharynx via the development of the separating longitudinal tracheoesophageal folds. The folds fuse, dividing this part of the tube into two longitudinal sections. This new separating divider is known as the tracheoesophageal septum. The now-bifurcated tube's dorsal portion becomes the esophagus; its ventral aspect further differentiates into the larynx, trachea, bronchi, and lungs over the next several weeks, further maturing during the fetal period (Arvedson and Brodsky, 2002).

Branchial arches four and six give rise to the cartilage and muscles of the larynx. The epithelium of the mucous membrane lining grows out of the endoderm at the cranial end of the laryngotracheal tube. The opening of this tube into the pharynx becomes the primitive glottis. Mesenchyme at this same location gives rise to paired arytenoid swellings. As these swellings migrate upward toward the tongue base, the primitive glottis opening changes shape from a small slit to a T. Rapid growth of laryngeal epithelium nearly blocks the laryngeal lumen, but recanalizes in the early fetal period at about weeks 10 to 11. (See Figure 2-8.)

The muscles, connective tissues, and cartilages of the trachea derive from the surrounding

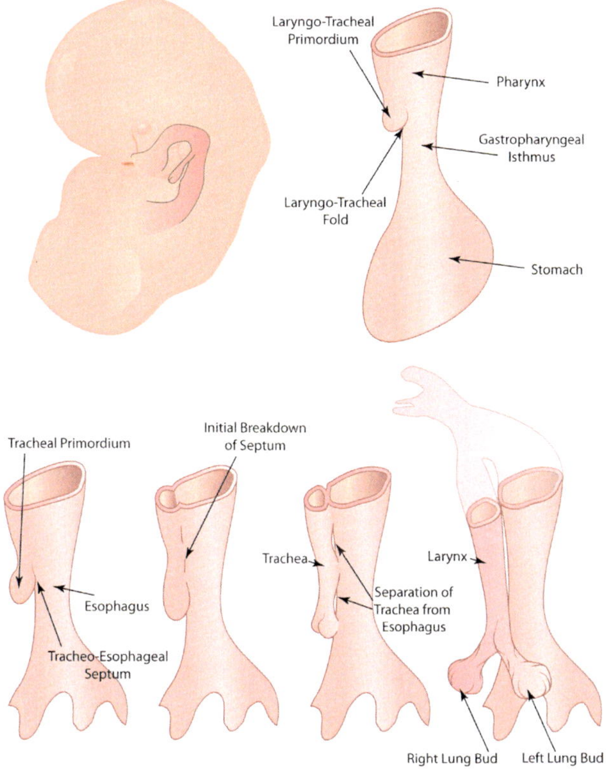

Figure 2-8. Developing larynx and trachea. The primitive pharynx, derived from the foregut, after birthing the branchial arches, gives rise to the laryngotracheal groove in week 4. This groove morphs into a diverticulum, and differentiates from the primitive pharynx via the development of the separating longitudinal tracheoesophageal folds. The folds fuse, dividing this part of the tube into two longitudinal parts. This new separating divider is known as the tracheoesophageal septum. The now bifurcated tube's dorsal portion becomes the esophagus; its ventral aspect further differentiates into the larynx, trachea, bronchi and lungs over the next several weeks.

mesenchyme. These cartilages eventually form a C-shape and give the near-circular shape to the larynx and trachea. As rapid growth continues, the lung buds form at the distal aspect of the tracheal primordeum, on their way to becoming the right and left bronchi. This asymmetrical bifurcation foreshadows the adult asymmetry of the mature lungs.

Lateral lung bud growth results in perforation of the right and left coelomic ducts, which double as primitive pleural sacs at their cranial aspect. Lateral growth of the septum transversum splits the coelomic ducts into an upper and lower portion, and then fuses with the ventrally growing pleuroperitoneal valves, forming the respiratory diaphragm and a floor for the lung "rooms" (Brookes and Zeitman, 1998).

Each lung or bronchial bud continuously branches until about week 17. At this stage, the lumina of the bronchi and bronchioles enlarge, and the finer structures of the lungs develop as vascularity increases exponentially. This stage is completed by about week 25. The last two stages of lung development during gestation give rise to primordial alveoli and mature the same, respectively. The lungs continue development for years after birth, but are capable of supporting life at about week 26. (See Figure 2-9.)

CRANIAL NERVES

Twelve pairs of cranial nerves develop during weeks 4 to 6 of embryonic life. Six of these twelve pairs play key roles in coordinating suck-swallow-breathe. Four of these nerves (V, VII, IX, and X) form in part from neural crest cells, which migrate into the primordial brain structures in weeks 3 to 4. Also,"Neuroblasts derived from superficial ectodermal placodes in the maxillomandibular region contribute to the ganglia of the trigeminal, facial, vagus and glossopharyngeal nerves" (Sperber, 2001, p. 44). By about week 5, the forebrain has bent forward relative to the central-orienting cranial-to-caudal axis, allowing the developing cranial nerves to penetrate into the tissues they innervate. These tissues simultaneously develop in the branchial arches and grooves.

In the following few weeks, the neural cells and generative cells of the tissues these nerves innervate migrate to their final destinations and proliferate and differentiate into their various structures. The nerves follow, lead, or simply accompany the muscle cell masses to their final destinations, growing and differentiating as they go. This "grow as you go" method accounts for the sometimes meandering pathways the nerves exhibit in the mature organism. Growth of the nerve influences growth of the forming tissue it innervates, and vice versa. Migration then becomes a rich generative milieu for the rapidly developing embryo. (See Figure 2-10.)

BLOOD SUPPLY

The basic blood pathways to the various body areas arise from the circulatory primordium and are established by the end of the embryonic period. As the heart develops, continuously becoming more complex as it differentiates into its more mature self, the circulatory system continues to grow and differentiate to meet the ever-increasing demands of the fetus. As each structure arises and matures, the vascular system simultaneously grows to provide the necessary nourishment via the blood, thereby sustaining continued growth and development of the structure.

FETAL DEVELOPMENT

SUCK AND SWALLOW

Sucking and swallowing mature at different rates in the fetal period. They are seen, but not necessarily together. As early as 12.5 weeks gestation, sucking and swallowing have been observed in fetuses, but they are not well-coordinated as a sequence at this very early stage of development.

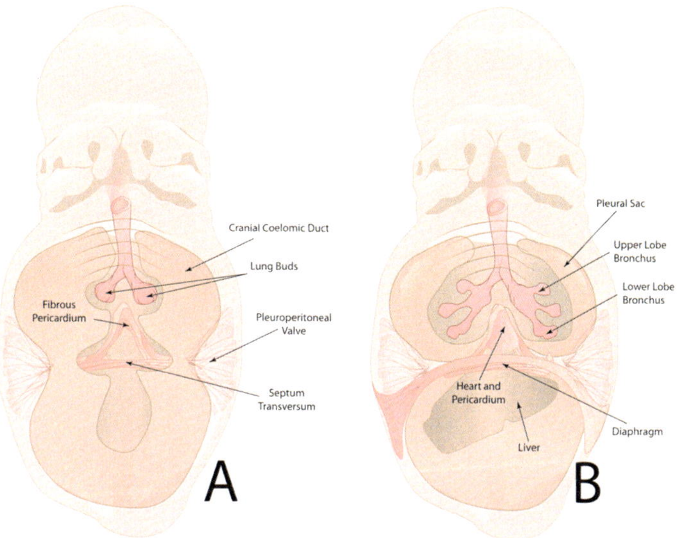

Figure 2-9. Lung development. A. The lung buds form at the distal aspect of the tracheal primordeum. This growth results in perforation of the coelemic ducts, which double as primitive pleural sacs at their cranial aspect. Lateral growth of the septum transversum splits the coelemic ducts into upper and lower portions and then fuses with the ventrally growing pleuroperitoneal valves forming the respiratory diaphragm and a floor for the lung "rooms." B. Each lung bud becomes a primary bronchus, which in turn branches into segmental bronchi. This branching continues until about week 17. As development continues, the lumina of the bronchi and bronchioles enlarge and the finer structures of the lungs emerge.

Sucking and swallowing as a coordinated pattern emerges between weeks 32 and 35. At about week 34, a stable rhythm asserts itself, enabling an infant who may be born at this age to oral feed without much compromise to caloric intake. This pattern reaches full maturity between weeks 39 and 40. At birth, the infant is fully capable of coordinating sucking with swallowing with breathing. If the infant cannot accomplish this complex sequence with ease, something has failed to mature or has disrupted synchronization.

Sources disagree about the exact timing of the emergence of sucking. Arvedson and Brodsky (2002, p. 30) report that "true suckling begins around the 18-24th [gestational] week." Suckling, according to them, is marked by a backward and forward movement of the tongue, with emphasis on the backward movement. According to Wolf and Glass (1992), sucking has been observed in utero between weeks 15 and 18. They describe these mouthing movements as immature sucks. Sperber (2001) asserts that intrauterine thumb-sucking occurs as early as week 16. This activity builds upon the muscular movements of the lips and tongue seen early in the fetal period.

Herbst (1983) suggests that the mouthing movements seen at week 24 may be a form of non-

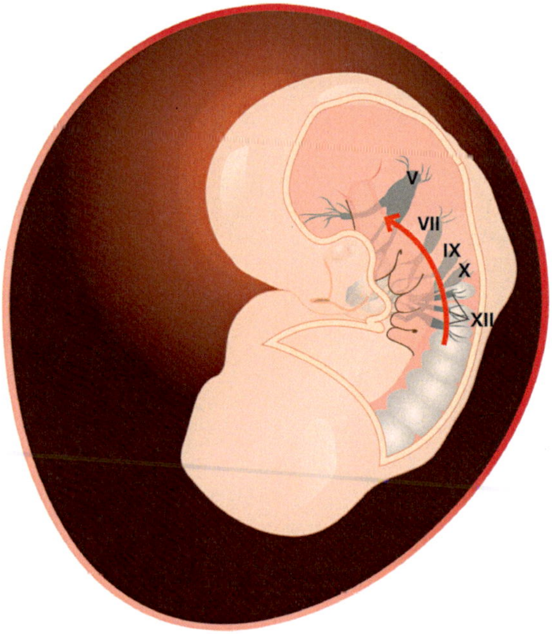

Figure 2-10. Cranial nerve migration. © 2010 Alison K. Hazelbaker. Reprinted with permission. Artist: Paul Hughes.

nutritive sucking. At weeks 27 to 28, random mouthing activities can be visualized. Several texts agree that by week 32 stronger sucking has been noted with a burst-pause pattern beginning to emerge. This more rhythmic activity matures into the burst-pause rhythmicity of the suck-swallow-breathe triad (Qureshi, Vice, Taciak, Bosma and Gewolb, 2002).

The pharyngeal swallow, an early motor response of the pharynx, is first seen between weeks 10 and 11 of gestation (Herbst, 1983). By week 12, this swallowing can be observed (Arvedson and Brodsky, 2002). The fetus begins to drink its amniotic fluid at this time. It is possible that this action of taking in amniotic fluid is a rehearsal for postnatal suck-swallow-breathe coordination. For certain, this swallowed amniotic fluid lays down the meconium in the gastrointestinal tract. By week 40, a full-term fetus is capable of swallowing 450 ml of amniotic fluid (about half of the total fluid volume) in a single day. During pregnancy, an imbalance in amniotic fluid circulation can be an indicator of an anatomical or physiological swallowing problem.

At 40 weeks, the fetus possesses an intact suck-swallow-breathe mechanism that forms the foundation for later feeding efforts, including a voluntary swallow. The maturation that occurs in the first month postpartum actually represents stylistic preferences or responses influenced by the infant's environment: rate of milk flow, hunger and satiety levels, breast size and shape, bottle-teat type, and other factors. The infant's ability to respond to environmental cues indicates the amount of volitional control built into the suck-swallow-breathe mechanism (Qureshi and Vice et al., 2002).

BREATHE

By gestational week 11, respiratory movements can be elicited by a stimulus, but rhythmic respiratory movements mature much later (Sperber, 2001). By weeks 19 to 20, the epiglottis is well-developed. Its ability to fully contact the soft palate emerges by week 23. This contact, along with other mechanisms, ensures patency of the airway and makes the coordination of swallowing with breathing much easier. At week 24, the lungs begin to produce surfactant – a lipid that maintains patency of the alveoli – thereby preparing the lungs to eventually take in air. Between weeks 26 and 29, the fetus begins to rehearse breathing by showing the beginnings of rhythmic respiratory movements. Breathing, however, is not fully coordinated with sucking and swallowing until week 37, and even then still may be somewhat erratic. By week 40, most infants beautifully coordinate suck with swallow with breathe, although some authors maintain that full coordination does not emerge until early in the postpartum period. Complete coordination may depend on the degree of myelination of the vagus nerve at the time of birth (Watson Genna, 2008).

WHAT GOES WRONG?

Avery and Chiego (2006) indicate that the face and palate are the most likely areas to malform. Their development depends upon exact timing and is therefore extremely vulnerable to external disruptions. According to Arvedson and Brodsky (2002), tongue abnormalities are relatively uncommon, especially those that interfere with feeding and swallowing. However, the dramatic incidence of tongue-tie both as a stand-alone condition and accompanying malformation underscores its significance. Most writers and researchers consider tongue-tie a minor anomaly, but one of note.

Insufficient apoptosis of the tongue during the stage of differentiation of the tongue from the floor of the mouth causes tongue-tie. “Apoptosis, or programmed cell death, is the fragmentation of a cell into membrane bound particles, which are then eliminated by phagocytosis by specialized cells” (Avery and Chiego, 2006, p. 6). Programmed cell death during the embryonic period eliminates obsolete or purposefully transient tissues to make way for ever-increasing differentiation and complexity.

The typical programmed cell regression under the tongue during embryogenesis leaves a small segment of tissue we identify as the normal lingual frenulum – an extension of the lingual oral mucosa that gently connects the tongue to the floor of the mouth throughout life. Failure of cell destruction can occur to one degree or another during this regression stage, leaving variable amounts of tissue behind, which accounts for the resulting erratic and confusing presentation of tongue-tie.

Tissues are most susceptible to defective development when they begin to differentiate in embryonic weeks 2 to 8. A defect in the development of a group of cells is considerably less damaging than a defect in an organ or organ system. The smaller and less complex the development, the less extensive the problem created, as long as that structure does not play a foundational role in the development of higher order and more complex structures. As a general rule, teratogens are least likely to create developmental problems during the first three weeks of pregnancy (Avery and Chiego, 2006).

Abnormal development results from both genetic and environmental factors, and is usually the byproduct of a combination of the two. In the case of tongue-tie, a clear genetic influence mediated by a mutated T-box transcription factor gene generates the anomaly. How the gene mutates has yet to be quantified. One lactation consultant from North Carolina reports a curious increased incidence of tongue-tie in babies conceived via IVF suggesting an as yet unknown epigenetic influence. The role of environmental teratogens as a mediating factor of tongue-tie is poorly understood but may influence mutation. Lately, experts in the identification and treatment of tongue-tie have seriously posed this question about possible epigenetic influences because they are seeing a rapid escalation of tongue-tie incidence as environmental and foodstuff pollution increases.

CHAPTER TWO TAKEAWAY

1. Tongue-tie occurs as a result of insufficient normal tissue degeneration during the embryological formation period of the tongue organ.

2. Tongue-tie can be inherited either as a minor anomaly of its own or in tandem with other signs and symptoms of various syndromes. Gene mutation may be responsible; environmental factors also may be implicated.

3. The tongue plays a significant role in assisting palatal development during embryogenesis and the early fetal period. Its ability to perform these functions depends on its optimal mobility.

4. Proper tongue development in this embryonic period lays the foundation for optimal physiological performance both during the fetal period and subsequent life outside of the womb.

CHAPTER THREE

PHYSIOLOGY: SUCK–SWALLOW–BREATHE COORDINATION DURING INFANCY

DEENA, AN R.N. AND INTERNATIONAL BOARD CERTIFIED LACTATION CONSULTANT from Israel, shares this personal story about her tongue-tied grandson.

> I suspected a submucosal tongue-tie on him when he was first born, but the breastfeeding was at first going fine, so I thought it best not to be a meddling, worrying grandmother. I did ask a friend and colleague to have a look, and she disagreed because he extended the tongue beyond the gumline. I still was not happy with [the situation] because I observed that when he cried his tongue didn't elevate to the roof of his mouth. A week after his birth, my daughter developed sore nipples. Another colleague who I asked to see my daughter felt it was just [poor] positioning. After my daughter developed mastitis and candida, I convinced her to have her son's tongue checked and treated by a dentist to whom I refer. He clipped the tongue. Things somewhat improved, but my grandson needed another treatment two weeks later. After that, things progressed well and, to date, he is 14 months and still breastfeeding. He is developing beautifully!

Deena refers to a "hidden" tie not easily visualized, but easy to feel when the practitioner performs a thorough intra-oral assessment. Deena used her knowledge of sucking physiology to assess her grandson's situation, which eventually led to the appropriate treatment of his condition and a successful breastfeeding and developmental outcome. Understanding what a newborn can and should do at breast or on a bottle serves as a foundation for picking up on feeding abnormalities due to tongue-tie.

The suck–swallow–breathe triad should be intact and fully operational at term; its development begins in the fetal period and extends into the first month postpartum. Tongue-tie can have a negative impact on suck-swallow-breathe in the neonatal period in two ways. First, it can influence the course of events during gestation that will then manifest as feeding difficulties in the early postnatal period. Second, it can further disrupt optimal function by hindering orofacial and throat development that relies on proper tongue mobility.

NORMAL INFANT SUCK-SWALLOW-BREATHE COORDINATION

ANATOMY

Numerous structures – orofacial, pharyngeal, esophageal, and respiratory – play a role in the mature suck-swallow-breathe sequence. Typically, the structural system is divided by geographical landmarks. Six compartments form embryologically: the nose, the oral cavity, the pharynx, the larynx, the esophagus, and the trachea/lungs. All serve together as the anatomical framework for suck-swallow-breathe. The pharynx can be divided further into three anatomic areas: the nasopharynx, the oropharynx, and the hypopharynx.

Until about 4 to 6 months of life, the normal increased anterior-to-posterior dimension of the infant skull, in combination with the baby's short neck, keeps the oral and pharyngeal structures apposed. This arrangement increases the ability of the infant to exquisitely time breathing and swallowing, ensuring that he or she stays well-oxygenated during the active phase of his or her feeds.

As the infant develops more upright posture and muscular control, the neck elongates, the posterior tongue drops into the gradually emerging oropharynx, and the larynx and hyoid lower with the elongation of the neck. The epiglottis and soft palate end their intimate neighborly relationship. At this developmental stage, some tongue-tied babies begin to have difficulty with swallowing coordination; the early closely apposed structural arrangement served as compensation for functional bolus control provided by an optimally mobile tongue.

Infants prefer to breathe through the nose until they are about 6 months old. The nose, therefore, plays its most significant role, easing respiration during early infancy. The two nasal passages of the nose open into the shared compartment of the nasopharynx. The nasal septum divides the nose vestibule into halves, each one bordered by the nasal turbinates. The bony and soft palates serve as the floor to the nose and nasopharynx respectively. The cranial base forms the posterior wall of the nasopharynx.

The lips allow ingress to the oral cavity. The mandible and maxillae create a solid bony frame for this cavity. The mandible serves as a connecting structure for the mouth floor musculature. The bony hard palate and muscular soft palate form the roof, and the cheeks serve as the cavity walls. The tonsillar pillars mark the open posterior aspect of the oral cavity and serve as a gateway to the pharynx.

The oropharynx, which forms as the neck elongates in mid-infancy, resides between the nasopharynx and the hypopharynx. The descending hyoid bone pulls the tongue root back into the pharynx to form its anterior wall. The middle and inferior pharyngeal constrictor muscles form the posterior

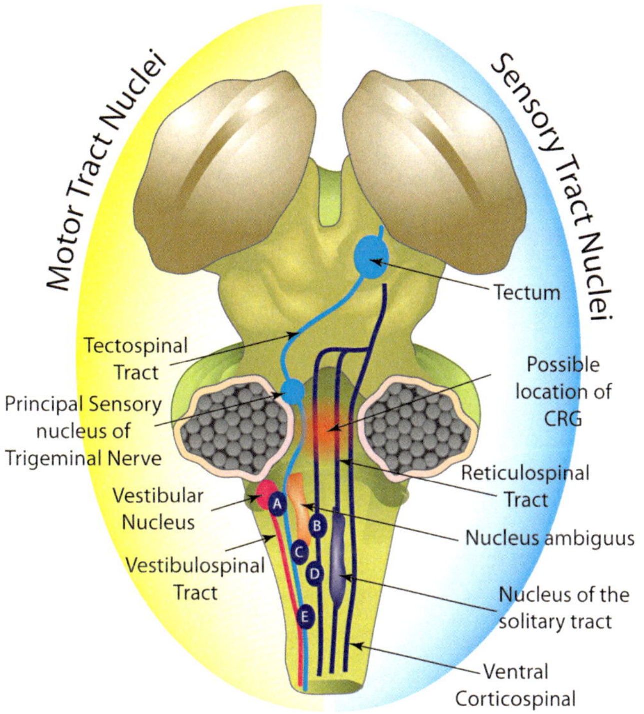

Figure 3-1. Brain stem control of the suck-swallow-breathe mechanism.

and lateral walls; the upper boundary is the soft palate, and the inferior boundary is the tip of the epiglottis.

The epiglottis is the upper landmark of the hypopharynx; the false vocal folds of the larynx and the upper esophageal sphincter serve as its posterior landmark. The middle and inferior pharyngeal constrictor muscles form its posterior and lateral walls, and the upper larynx and epiglottis its anterior boundary.

The upper esophageal sphincter forms the upper boundary of the esophagus, and the lower esophageal sphincter its lower boundary. This tubular compartment takes its shape from the arrangement of muscles that form its walls throughout its length.

The larynx, a complex structure comprising cartilage, muscles, and ligaments, performs a triple role of protection, respiration, and phonation. Its cartilages include the epiglottis, thyroid, cricoid, arytenoids, cuneiform, and corniculate. These cartilages provide the larynx its firm but relatively elastic protective form. The thyrohyoid and thyrocricoid ligaments provide positional stability. Its intrinsic muscles form the vocal folds and aid respiration and phonation. The epiglottis serves as its upper boundary and the trachea its lower boundary.

An impressive array of parallel cartilage rings connected by ligaments form the trachea, the hallway to the extensive series of "rooms" of the lung. The trachea branches into the bronchi and bronchioles that serve as secondary and tertiary pathways to the individual lobes and lobules of the lungs, which are only one aspect of the complex greater respiratory mechanism.

MUSCLES AND NERVES

The suck-swallow-breathe sequence acts very much like a system of its own, with a complex array of structures and functions working together to achieve the goal of bringing nourishment of both food and air into the human organism. This foundational nutritional mechanism matures into mastication and swallowing, using the same structural and functional components. Such a complex system requires complex wiring. Six cranial nerves work together to coordinate the sequence, with assistance from various cervical and thoracic level nerves. Two primary nerve tracts in the brainstem coordinate afferent and efferent signaling, and the cortex provides executive control. (See Figure 3-1.)

The trigeminal (CN V), facial (CN VII), glossopharyngeal (CN IX), vagus (CN X), spinal accessory (CN XI) and hypoglossal (CN XII) nerves comprise the main supply for the mechanism, assisted by cervical nerves one through six and a few thoracic nerves. The brainstem nerve tracts providing input from the brain consists of the nucleus of the tractus solitarius (NTS), the site of afferent control, and the nucleus ambiguus (NA), the site of efferent control. Both the trigeminal and hypoglossal nuclei assist the NTS and NA. Adjacent to the primary nuclei in the medulla resides an area of rhythmic control. Wolf and Glass (1992, p. 15) refer to this area as the "central rhythm generator" (CRG); Corbin-Lewis, Liss, and Sciortino. (2005, p. 36) refer to it as the "central pattern generator" (CPG).

Volitional control originates in the cortex by way of the pontine and subcortical structures of the midbrain. Although the brainstem serves as primary regulator of suck-swallow-breathe in infancy, maturation of this system allows the emergence of volitional control, allowing the older individual to coordinate aspects of the suck-swallow-breathe mechanism with other physiological functions; e.g., speaking.

The trigeminal nerve (CN V) serves as the sensory input mechanism that initiates and modulates sucking via ongoing input from the oral mucosa; the soft palate during swallowing; and the nose, as air flows in and out. It provides motoric innervation to the muscles of mastication, which include the masseter, temporalis, and medial and lateral pterygoids; the mandibular depressor muscles, which include the anterior belly of the digastric, geniohyoid, and the mylohyoid; and to one palatal elevator, the tensor veli palatini. In a way, the trigeminal serves as a masterful ongoing feedback mechanism that allows for optimal modulation of suck-swallow-breathe coordination.

The facial nerve (CN VII) controls motor coordination of the lip muscles, which include the levator

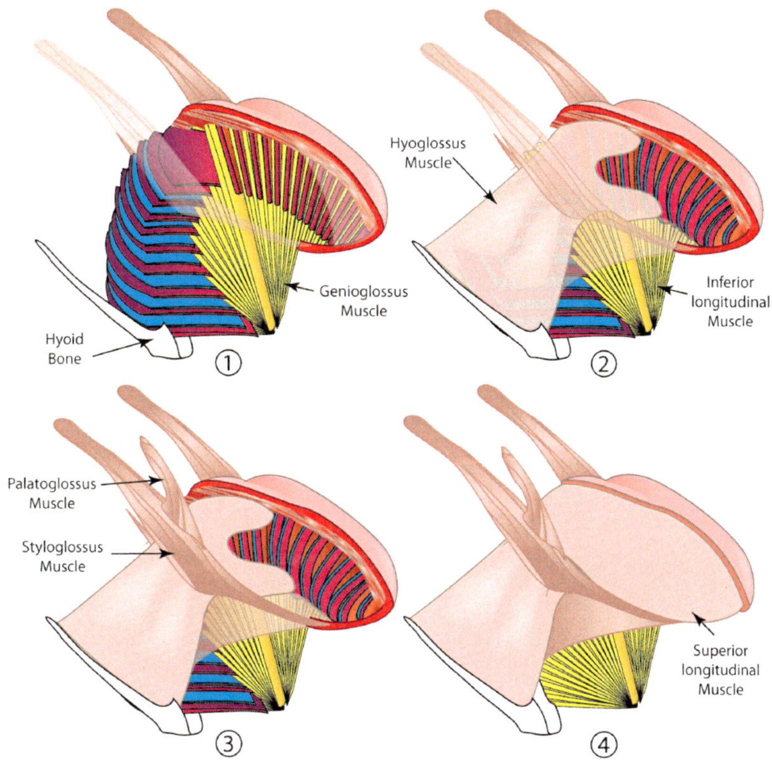

Figure 3-2. The layering of the tongue musculature deep (1) to surface (4). In view one the blue and purple represent the inner musculature. ©2010 Alison K. Hazelbaker. Reprinted with permission. Artist: Paul Hughes.

and depressor anguli oris; the levator labii superioris; the depressor labii inferioris; the superior and inferior incisivus labii; the superior and inferior orbicularis oris; and the facial mucles, which include the risorius, the buccinator, the zygomaticus, and the mentalis. It supplies taste sensation for the anterior two-thirds of the tongue and mediates sensory input from the middle ear, which assists with spatial orientation.

The glossopharyngeal nerve (CN IX) also accounts for the taste sensation in the posterior one-third of the tongue and is partly responsible for the sensory feedback of the carotid sinus. It provides both sensory and motor innervation to the pharynx – specifically the superior constrictor muscles, the palatoglossus, the palatopharyngeus, and the stylopharyngeus – thereby mediating and modulating the swallow reflex in the upper portion of the pharynx.

The vagus (Wanderer) nerve (CN X), so named because it innervates multiple structures throughout the body – some at great distance from its origin in the midbrain – plays a key role in several functions directly involved in the suck-swallow-breathe sequence, and also peripheral to and supportive of it. This nerve provides motor input to the pharynx, larynx, and esophagus while it mediates the sensory aspects of the pharynx, larynx, trachea, tongue, and lungs. Acting as a major modulator in the parasympathetic mode for lung, heart, and digestive function, the vagus nerve responds to both internal and environmental cues to modulate the various organ functions for which it is responsible.

The spinal accessory nerve (CN XI) acts in concert with the vagus nerve, innervating the motor functions of the pharynx and larynx. It also ensures good mediation of motor control of the sternocleidomastoid and trapezius muscles, both of which play a supportive function in providing postural stability for the suck-swallow-breathe mechanism.

The hypoglossal nerve (CN XII) serves only one organ–the tongue. It mediates motor function of this complex set of muscle fibers. It also assists in lowering the mandible and elevating and moving the hyoid anteriorly via the action of the geniohyoid and mylohyoid muscles. The tongue organ, complex in its structure, deserves special attention.

The cervical nerves assist the cranial nerves by controlling motor function for the paramedian muscles between the mandible, hyoid, and shoulder girdle. Optimal movement of these muscles keeps the airway patent through postural stability. In addition, cervical nerves three to five provide motor input to the respiratory diaphragm. (See Table 3-1.)

TONGUE

As a result of its embryological configuration, the tongue can be functionally divided into oral and pharyngeal components. Its tip, blade, dorsum, and sides comprise its oral portion; its root, extending from the circumvallate papillae to the hyoid bone, comprises its pharyngeal portion. A set of muscles oriented in multiple directions allows the tongue organ to rapidly change its shape and position, making it highly mobile. (See Figure 3-2.)

PHYSIOLOGY

The intrinsic muscle fibers of the tongue orient longitudinally, horizontally, and vertically. One longitudinal set of fibers, the superior longitudinals, originates at the root of the tongue and inserts just posterior to the tip. Some fibers insert into the lateral tongue margins. When contracted, these fibers elevate the tip and create a concave depression on the tongue's surface. The inferior longitudinals originate at the hyoid bone and in the root of the tongue. They terminate in the tip. Contraction of these fibers depresses the tongue tip and shortens the body of the tongue.

The transverse fibers lie between the longitudinal fibers and arise from the midline septum, extending laterally to the tongue edges. Contraction of these fibers causes the tongue to narrow and elongate. Vertical fibers, found mostly in the tip, flatten the tongue when contracted. These fibers travel through the entire tongue thickness from surface to underside.

The extrinsic fibers form three pairs of muscles: the styloglossus, the hyoglossus, and the genioglossus. Each of the styloglossus pair originates at a styloid process and inserts into the lateral margins of the posterior tongue. They raise the posterior tongue when contracted, or retract the tongue when it is protruded. The hyoglossus pair originates at the greater cornu of the hyoid bone

Nerve	Muscle	Action	Result
Facial (VII)	Superior and inferior orbicularis oris muscles, superior and inferior incisivus labii	Provides anterior seal of lips	Bolus containment
Facial (VII)	Buccinator, risorius	Reduces area of lateral sulci and tenses cheeks to contain bolus within the limits of the teeth and gums	Bolus control
Hypoglossal (XII)	Genioglossus, intrinsic tongue muscles	Depresses tongue-tip and creates midline channel	
Trigeminal (V)	Masseter,medial pterygoid temporalis,Lateral pterygoid,anterior belly of the digastric	Raises and lowers the mandible	Mastication
Hypoglossal (XII)	Geniohyoid,mylohyoid	Lowers mandible	
Facial (VII)	Levator anguli oris,depressor anguli oris, levator labii inferioris, zygomaticus, mentalis	Moves lips in coordination with tongue and jaw	
Facial (VII)	Superior and inferior orbicularis oris	Reduces intra-oral sulci gape to increase negative pressure gradient	Bolus propulsion
Trigeminal (V)	Buccinator		
Hypoglossal (XII)	Intrinsic lingual muscles, genioglossus	Creates midline channel of tongue, allows progressive contraction of tongue	
Vagus (X)	Levator veli palatine, musculus uvulae	Elevates velum	Velopharyngeal closure
Trigeminal (V)	Tensor veli platini	Tenses anterior velum and opens auditory tube	
Glossopharyngeus (IX) **Vagus (X)**	Superior constrictor, horizontal fibers of the palatopharyngeus	Creates Passavant's pad on posterior pharyngeal wall, moves lateral pharyngeal walls medially	
	Palatoglossus		
Hypoglossal (XII)	Mylohyoid, geniohyoid, cervical plexus	Elevates and anteriorly displaces the hyoid bone	Hyolaryngeal elevation
Trigeminal (V)	Anterior belly of the digastric muscle		
Vagus (X)	Interarytenoids, lateral cricoarytenoid, thyroarytenoid, thyrohyoid, aryepiglottic	Adducts vocal folds inverts epiglottis	Laryngeal protection
Vagus (X) **Glossopharyngeal (IX)**	Superior, middle, and inferior constrictors; stylopharyngeus, salpingopharyngeus	Progressively contracts and elevates pharynx	Pharyngeal elevation and constriction

Table 3-1. Deglutition muscles, muscle activity, and innervation

and also inserts into the lateral aspects of the posterior tongue. The tongue depresses and retracts when this muscle pair contracts.

The genioglossus pair originates at the interior surface of the mandible. Its fan shape reveals the progressive length of its fibers: shorter anteriorly, the fibers inserting into the intrinsic muscles; and longer inferiorly where it inserts into the body of the hyoid bone. The mid-length fibers insert into the dorsum of the tongue. The genioglossus moves the tongue in various ways. Contraction of the anterior fibers causes the tongue tip to retract and depress. If these same fibers contract on only one side, the tip deviates laterally to the uncontracted side. When the anterior and middle fibers contract at the same time, the tongue surface forms a groove. When these fibers act alone, the posterior tongue pulls forward, protruding the tip. Contraction of the inferior fibers pulls the hyoid up and forward – a necessary position that protects the airway and allows passage of the bolus during the pharyngeal phase of the swallow.

The final pair of extrinsic muscles – the palatoglossae – elevates the posterior tongue when the soft palate is held in an elevated position. When the tongue rests in the oral cavity, this same muscle pair lowers the velum. The palatoglossae originate from the lateral aspects of the posterior tongue and insert into the soft palate. This pair is innervated by both the vagus and glossopharyngeal nerves, unlike the other tongue muscles that are all supplied by the hypoglossal nerve (Corbin-Lewis and Liss, 2005).

The tongue takes up room in the oral cavity, enabling it to fulfill its function both as a preparatory and transport organ. The fatty cheek pads, prominent in early infancy, brace the lateral edges of the tongue, helping to stabilize it for bolus formation. The oral cavity increases in size relative to the tongue as the individual grows and matures; maturation of tongue function generated by complete range of motion during the infancy period ensures optimal preparatory and transport efforts later on, without the extra buttressing provided by surrounding structures.

To ensure optimal pressure changes throughout the feed during sucking, the tongue organ plays a key role in generating a seal of the oral cavity – first through the tongue-tip placement that wraps around the underside of the breast-nipple or bottle teat, and secondly by way of the apposition to the soft palate that seals off the posterior cavity during the milk expression phase. As the jaw drops during the milk expression phase, the tongue depresses posteriorly, allowing negative pressure to increase, drawing milk out of the breast or bottle.

The tongue also plays a significant role in propelling the bolus into the pharynx, initiating the swallow. A retraction movement of the posterior tongue, coupled with posterior tongue depression, creates a ramp and a backward thrust of the bolus from the ramped tongue.

The swallowing center of the brainstem regulates tongue-base movement, but the tongue also can respond to voluntary control mechanisms.

The foundational understanding of the normal suck-swallow-breathe sequence was put into place decades ago. The use – first of radiological studies and currently of ultrasound – have helped quantify the sequence (Ardran, Kemp, and Linda, 1958; Bosma, Hepburn, Josell, and Baker, 1990; Geddes, Langton et al., 2008; Hayashi, Hoashi, and Nara, 1997; Hedberg, Nyqvist, Farnstrand, Eeg-Olofssom, and Ewald, 2001). Additionally, new techniques have enabled researchers to plot the nerve pathways and nucleic connections between the various aspects of the sequence (Corbin-Lewis et al., 2005).

The suck-swallow-breathe sequence is a developmental reflex, not to be confused with a simple involuntary reflex, e.g. rapid leg extension when the knee is tapped just below the kneecap. A developmental reflex includes both voluntary and involuntary components, and is a complex set of individual movements and responses of various structures that eventually link during the fetal period to form a schema or programmed response.

In the early postpartum period, suck-swallow-breathe manifests as a neurobehavioral program of response when certain stimuli are presented to the infant. According to Watson Genna, all mammals, including humans, have a neurobehavioral program for sucking (2008, p. 1). This program will manifest in a sequence of behaviors that culminates in breastfeeding. Ransjo-Arvidson et al. report that the following human sequence directly after birth leads to the first breastfeed when unimpeded (as cited in Watson Genna, 2008, p. 1):

1. Hand-to-mouth movements
2. Tongue movements
3. Mouth opening
4. Focusing on the nipple
5. Crawling to the nipple
6. Massaging the breast to evert the nipple
7. Licking
8. Attaching to the breast

Both tactile and olfactory cues help the infant achieve successful contact with the nipple. Self-attachment is the norm, and mother assistance, other than providing proximity and positional stability, is not necessary. Infants quickly build on their first experience of attachment by experimenting with tongue and lip movements, and sucking pressures. Some learning will be optimally adaptive; some will not. Some compensations serving as adaptive in the short term, but maladaptive in the long term, will require intervention to normalize. Drugs interfere with the normal behavioral sequence. Skin-to-skin contact, as in Kangaroo Care, can reestablish the sequence (Watson Genna, 2008).

REFLEXES

Reflexes for infant feeding are developmentally associated wiring and communication schemas or programs elicited by specific sensory inputs that assist the human organism to appropriately respond to and sustain life. Reflexes can be adaptive or protective. The oral reflexes associated with infant feeding include the adaptive responses of rooting, sucking, phasic bite, tongue protrusion, and the transverse tongue reflex. Protective reflexes include cough and gag. Adaptive reflexes disappear, or integrate, as the infant develops, becoming the foundation for more mature skills. Protective reflexes serve an ongoing function and are mature at term birth. (See Table 3-2.)

SUCK–SWALLOW

Arvedson and Brodsky (2002) remind us:

> Swallowing results not only in transporting food to the stomach, but also in clearing the mouth and pharynx of secretions, mucous, and regurgitated stomach contents. Thus, the function of swallowing is nutritive as well as protective of the lower airways. (p. 14)

Thirty-one muscles must be coordinated by six cranial nerves and several cervical nerves by way of a complex interaction of signaling in both the brain stem and cerebral cortex to create a safe and efficient swallow. The complexity of coordinating swallowing and breathing accounts for the recruitment of so many nerves and muscles.

Swallowing is typically divided into four phases: oral preparatory, oral, pharyngeal, and esophageal. In young infants, the proximity of the tongue base to the larynx nearly blends the oral and pharyngeal phases into one. (See Figure 3-3.)

Although the act of swallowing once was thought to be voluntary during oral preparation and reflexive during the other three phases, Wolf and Glass (1992, p. 26) state that swallowing "contains features of voluntary and reflexive behaviors throughout all phases." The authors indicate that the oral preparatory phase also is known as the lingual transport phase, and is the period in which food is processed for easier swallowing. During this phase, the food is macerated and liquefied to a certain consistency, and then gathered into a bolus in preparation for its release into the pharynx for swallowing.

In young infants, this food processing is known as sucking; in older infants, oral preparatory processes may be either sucking or chewing. This phase is and should appear to be one continuous act, indicating that the infant has optimal physiological function that enables him or her to keep the milk or food bolus cohesive and mobile.

The trigeminal nerve carries sensory information from the mandible and from the various touch and pressure receptors of the hard palate and oral mucosa to modulate sucking and chewing action. Taste sensation is carried through the facial and glossopharyngeal nerves. Motor output occurs as a result of the action of the trigeminal nerve, which controls the jaw movements, and the hypoglossal nerve, which controls the tongue muscles.

During this phase, the tongue plays a crucial role. After mouth opening occurs, the tongue extrudes to either accept the food or to latch on to the breast-nipple or the bottle teat. During sucking, the latch stabilizes the breast or bottle teat in the mouth, creates a seal around it; progressive contractile movements then initiate a sequence of pressure changes that moves the bolus progressively from the high positive pressure area (anterior tongue against palate) to the low pressure area (dropping pos-

Adaptive Reflexes	Protective Reflexes
Rooting reflex: The head turns or orients toward a touch near or on the lips. Some babies root to touch anywhere on the head. Rooting appears to be a seeking motion with the mouth. Multiple nerves mediate the root: The trigeminal, facial, hypoglossal, and spinal accessory nerves all play their respective roles. Rooting integrates between 3 and 6 months. By then, sucking is well-established and rooting behavior is no longer required.	**Cough reflex**: Expulsion of material from the upper airway triggered by chemoreceptors in the larynx and the subglottic space. Sensory stimuli travel to the brain stem via the interior branch of the superior laryngeal nerve, which is a branch of the vagus nerve. This reflex serves the organism throughout life.
Tongue extrusion reflex: The tongue protrudes when stimulated at its anterior edge, especially at the tip. The trigeminal, facial, and hypoglossal nerves play key roles mediating tongue extrusion. This reflex integrates between 4 and 6 months and sets the stage for taking in foods other than milk.	**Gag**: Touch to the posterior tongue or at certain spots in the pharynx elicits the gag. The gag reflex prevents swallowing an object that would obstruct the pharynx. The glossopharyngeal nerve and branches of the vagus nerve govern this reflex, which persists throughout life.
Phasic bite reflex: When the lower gumline is touched, the infant responds by closing the gums together in a "biting" movement followed by a rapid release. The trigeminal nerve mediates both sensory and motor aspects of this response. The phasic bite serves as the foundational action for later chewing. By 9 to 12 months, this reflex integrates because the normal infant has established efficient chewing motions.	
Transverse tongue reflex: The tongue-tip follows a stimulus placed at its lateral edge. The transverse tongue reflex assists with moving a bolus from side to side for mastication. Both the trigeminal and hypoglossal nerves mediate this response. It integrates between 6 and 9 months.	
Sucking reflex: Stimulation to the roof of the mouth elicits a latch of the tongue (or seal) against the teat followed by progressive contractions that both traction the teat in the mouth and create intra-oral pressure changes to help gather and direct the milk bolus, moving it from an area of high pressure to lower pressure in a sequential manner. The sucking reflex involves the trigeminal, facial, glossopharyngeal, vagus, hypoglossal, and spinal accessory nerves with assistance from cervical nerves one through six.	

Table 3-2. Feeding reflexes

terior tongue) where a vacuum has been generated. As the posterior tongue rapidly drops, the anterior tongue remains in contact with the hard palate, slightly changing the degree of positive pressure exerted by it. In accordance with Boyle's Law, the milk then moves from the high pressure to low pressure area via a push-pull force.

To assist this intra-oral pressure, the lateral tongue remains in contact with the buccal fat pads and with the soft palate at its posterior border. As the dorsum of the tongue elongates and drops to create space in the posterior oral cavity, the soft palate quickly moves anteriorly, followed by a rapid swing in a backward and upward direction. The soft palate closes off the nasopharynx, rapidly increasing the oral-pharyngeal space, which pulls the bolus backward. The posterior tongue then serves as a ramp that moves back to touch the pharyngeal wall, thereby mechanically dumping the bolus into the pharynx.

At the same time the dumping occurs, the hyoid bone moves upward toward the base of the tongue, pulling the larynx up and assisting laryngeal vestibule closure. The epiglottis, a cartilaginous structure that projects from the tongue-base, gracefully drops over the laryngeal additus, specifically over the aryepiglottic folds, in part as a result of the upward and anterior movement of the hyoid. The epiglottic drape over the laryngeal vestibule shields it from the oncoming bolus as it opens the velleculae to the dropping bolus. (The velleculae are wedge-shaped spaces formed by the anterior wall and lateral musculature of the pharynx and the lateral edges of the epiglottis.)

In the next phase, the posterior-inferior tilt of the epiglottis over the laryngeal vestibule diverts the bolus unilaterally or bilaterally. When the bolus splits roughly in half, each half drops into the ipsilateral pyriform sinus and then rejoins its mate just before entering the open esophagus.

The push–pull originated by the tongue's progressive contractile forces continues in this third phase of swallowing. With the help of the pharyngeal constrictor muscles and their progressive contractile movements that generate positive pressure behind or above the bolus, and negative or low pressure in front or below the bolus, the bolus makes its progressive and rapid descent toward the esophagus. (See Figure 3-4.)

The rising larynx becomes smaller in diameter, making its vestibule smaller, as well. The closure of both the true and false vocal folds further ensures that the dropping bolus will not enter the airway. The laryngeal shift anteriorly and superiorly places traction on the upper esophageal sphincter, signaling it to relax and allowing an esophageal "gape" to occur. The now-open upper esophagus receives the reunited bolus, initiating the fourth phase of the swallow. The bolus's journey requires only one second from the initiation of phase two through phase three, thanks to the combined efforts of the vagal branches, and the glossopharyngeal and hypoglossal nerves.

In this final phase of swallowing, the now truly peristaltic contraction of the esophagus propels the bolus downward toward the stomach, continuing the push–pull of the changing pressure gradient aspects of the previous three phases. The upper esophageal sphincter (or cricopharyngeal sphincter) closes after the bolus moves through at the proximal end of the "food tube." The lower esophageal sphincter (or cardiac sphincter) opens to receive the bolus and admit passage into the stomach. Along its length, as the bolus enters the top of the tube, the muscles are inhibited, followed by a proximal-to-distal excitation that initiates the cephalocaudal movement of the bolus.

Both the inhibitory and excitatory signals are carried to the esophageal muscles by the vagus nerve. The upper portion of the esophagus and the cricopharyngeus are composed of striated (voluntary) muscle; the lower end and the cardiac sphincter are smooth muscle. Both types of muscles respond to the motor signals of the vagus nerve during the end-phase of swallowing. Any bolus that originates lower, however, such as an air bubble, moves along the lower esophagus due to involuntary action locally controlled by segmental ganglionic reflex arcs rather than by the brain. This action is known as secondary or tertiary peristalsis.

The superior laryngeal nerve of the vagus provides the sensory innervation of the criocpharyn-

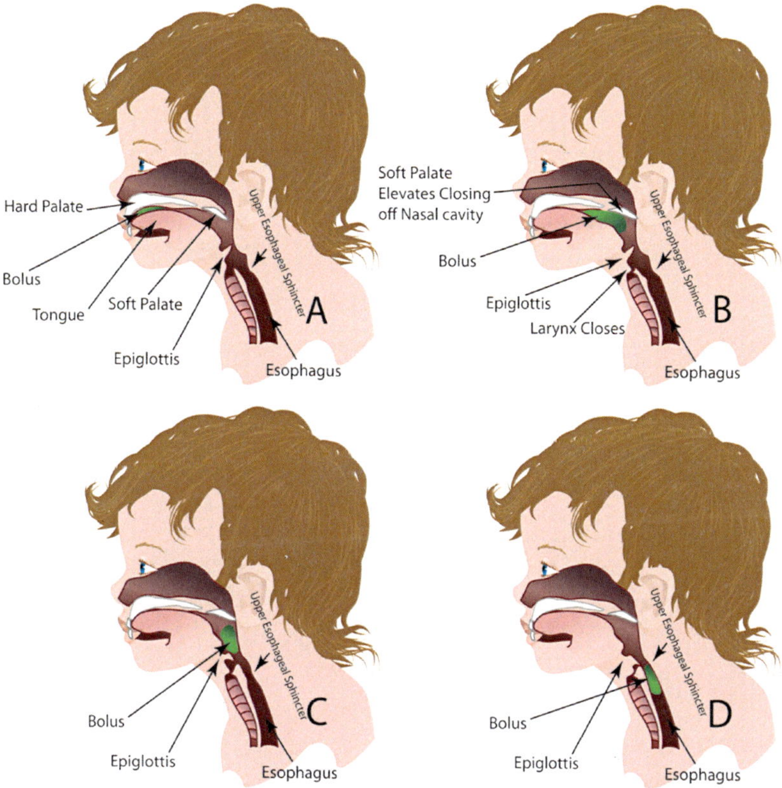

Figure 3-3. The four phases of swallowing. A. Oral preparatory phase: The bolus enters the mouth and is prepared for swallowing by the teeth and the tongue. B. Oral transitory phase: The tongue moves the bolus to the pharynx through its progressive contractile motion. The bolus drops into the vellecular space. The vocal folds remain open and the Upper Esophageal Sphincter remains closed. C. The pharyngeal phase: The soft palate elevates closing off the nasopharynx. The hyoid bone moves anteriorly and elevates closing the vocal folds and tipping the epiglottis down. The bolus drops into the bi-laterial pyriform sinuses and then drops into the Upper Esophageal Sphincter as it opens. The pharyngeal muscles progressively contract to help move the bolus during this stage. D. The esophageal phase: The tongue, epiglottis and hyoid return to resting position as the bolus passes into the esophagus. Once the bolus passes through the Upper Esophageal Sphincter, it closes, the soft palate drops back down, and the laryngeal folds reopen. Esophageal peristalsis moves the bolus down to the stomach.

geus and the upper esophagus. The thoracic branches of the vagus (via the recurrent laryngeal nerve) innervate the lower esophagus and the cardiac sphincter. Deep pressure or touch to the esophageal mucosa or mechanoreceptors from the descending bolus can affect action.

In addition to the pressure gradient forces, three assisting forces propel the bolus during these four phases: gravity; the momentum of the bolus, which is dependent upon its consistency and

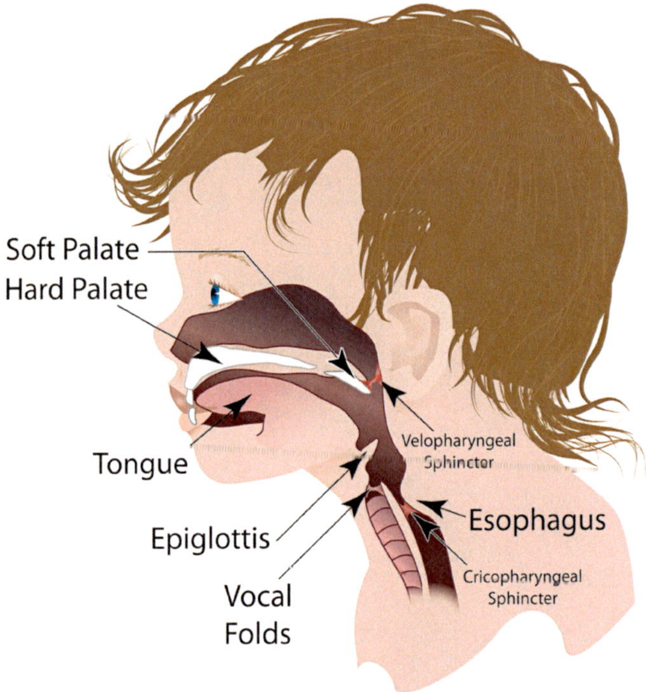

Figure 3-4. Valving of the upper aerodigestive tract generating the push-pull of changing pressures. The gentle seal of the lips constitutes the first valve, the firm tongue seal against the breast or bottle along with its progressive contraction constitutes the second valve, the velopharyngeal sphincter constitutes the third valve, the tongue base in relationship to the posterior and lateral pharyngeal walls constitutes the fourth valve, the mobile epiglottis and closed or open laryngeal vestibule constitutes the fifth valve and the opened or closed cricopharyngeal sphincter constitutes the sixth valve. © 2010 Alison K. Hazelbaker. Reprinted with permission. Artist: Paul Hughes.

viscosity; and the mechanical force of the backward thrust of the posterior tongue that initiates the pharyngeal swallow (Corbin-Lewis et al., 2005; Logemann, 1998; Wolf and Glass, 1992).

Three types of receptors help modify and modulate swallowing: chemoreceptors, baroreceptors, and temperature receptors. Some regions are highly sensitive to targeted input and some are organized in a field-like arrangement. A large number of receptors must be stimulated to elicit a swallow. The type of stimulus that triggers motoric response varies from area to area. Sensitivity, intensity of stimulus required, and types of receptors all play their roles in determining how and to what degree each area responds. Because of this variability, multiple boluses may collect in the vallecular space before a swallow is initiated. Typically speaking, the larger the bolus, the sooner the swallow reflex is triggered in the sequence. However, texture and temperature play a role as well, generating great variability in the timing of the swallow reflex.

BREATHING

To some people, the word apnea raises the hairs on the back of the neck. However, the effective and well-timed normal swallow includes a brief suspension of breathing, or apnea, as a mechanism to protect the airway during the pharyngeal phase. In the normal individual, a puff of expelled air precedes the apnea, the swallow proceeds, and then a complete expiration occurs. As the individual takes the next "bite," he or she inspires, preparing for the next swallow.

In the young infant, the proximity of the epiglottis and the soft palate ensures that the infant can perform nearly continuous breathing while sucking. The suspension of the expiration during the pharyngeal phase is substantially shorter, accounting for the '***hnh ... hnhhhh***' sound made during an optimally rhythmic sucking burst.

Poor teat choice or a too-rapid flow of breast milk can compromise this rhythmicity, contributing to longer episodes of apnea that may well extend over a period of several sucks and cause sucking bursts to shorten, compromising feed efficiency and reducing overall oxygen saturation. This same tendency can be observed in children and adults who learn to stop breathing while they chew, only to perform several complete respiratory cycles to catch up.

Breathing, governed by the vagus nerve, requires optimal timing efficiency of the other five cranial nerves to ensure that it continues as feeding occurs. Optimal timing allows breathing to proceed as follows:

1. The individual takes in a breath either via the nose or mouth.
2. He or she may continue to breathe while chewing. In infancy, during the active phase of the feed, the baby takes in one breath as he or she moves the bolus of milk from the breast to the oropharynx for the swallow.
3. As the bolus enters the vestibule of the pharynx, an initial expiratory puff precedes the breath suspension that protects the airway as the bolus moves over and past the laryngeal opening.
4. Once the bolus, now in the hypopharynx, is lower than the larynx, the individual fully expels that breath, and the entire sequence begins again.

Not all swallows are accompanied by a full breathing cycle. Sometimes more than one swallow can occur on one breath. These swallows usually comprise smaller boluses, which may even collect in the vellecular space or the pyriform sinuses before the third phase is completed and expiration occurs. As long as these swallows are well-timed with events that protect the airway and do not compromise oxygen saturation, they are considered normal. Milk feeding can occur as a 1:1:1 ratio of suck to swallow to breathe, but variations occur from baby to baby, with some taking one swallow per two or more sucks, and breathing occurring anytime during the suck-swallow cycle (Geddes and Kent, 2008). Individual styles develop during the first month postpartum. We do not yet know if these styles persist through life.

TONGUE-TIE AND SYNDROMES

Tongue-tie appears as a symptom of various syndromes. Garcia Pola, Gonzalez Garcia, Garcia Martin, Gallas, and Leston (2002, p. 59) indicate that "a short lingual frenulum has been associated with progressive systemic sclerosis and with Urbach-Wiethe's disease (lipoglicoproteinosis)." They go on to state that tongue-tie may be more common in individuals born with either Turner's syndrome or Klinefelter's syndrome. No hard evidence exists supporting increased incidence in individuals with these syndromes; however, neck abnormalities indicating pharyngeal arch derivation occurs in Turner's syndrome, making tongue abnormalities a possible scenario.

Infants born with Beckwith-Wiedemann syndrome and Opitz syndrome may have tongue abnormalities, including ankyloglossia. Tongue-tie may present with cleft mandible, oromandibular-limb hypogenesis, and orodigitofacial syndrome. Major symptoms of orodigitofacial syndrome includes hypertelorism, laryngotracheal abnormalities, and hernias. All three types of this syndrome may present with lingual abnormalities. Type II orodigitofacial syndrome is also known as Mohr's syndrome.

Klockars (2007) reports that tongue-tie can be found in the rare van der Woude syndrome, also the result of genetic mutation. This syndrome most commonly manifests as lingual pitting and cleft palate/lip. The incidence of tongue-tie in individuals with this syndrome is unknown.

Mukai, Mukai, and Asaoka (1991) found a significant incidence of epiglottal and laryngeal deviation accompanying ankyloglossia, which, when left untreated, contributed to Sudden Infant Death Syndrome. They postulate that this triumvirate of symptoms may represent a heretofore unidentified syndrome.

Because tongue-tie long has been considered a nonentity, it is possible that its presence as a sign or symptom of various syndromes has been ignored or underreported. Perhaps future study will include a serious consideration of tongue-tie and ankyloglossia as a manifestation of gene mutations and chromosomal abnormalities.

THE GENETIC CONNECTION

Ann's fourth child, a daughter, was born tongue-tied. At the time, Ann did not know how to identify its presence, so no surgical treatment was undertaken. Ann used very careful management for the duration of their breastfeeding experience. Subsequently, she learned that her brother was tongue-tied and had had his frenulum clipped at birth. Ann also had two grandchildren born tongue-tied. Stories like this abound, but the degree to which inheritance plays a role has yet to be quantified.

Klockars (2007), one of the few researchers performing a "family tree" study of tongue-tie inheritance, specifies that tongue-tie is an autosomal dominant trait, says:

> Obvious candidate genes causative for non-syndromic ankyloglossia include TBX22 gene, a T-box transcription factor gene mutated in X-linked cleft palate and ankyloglossia

> and LGR5, an orphan G protein-coupled receptor, associated with neonatal lethality and ankyloglossia in mice. (p. 1323)

Björnsson, Arnason, and Tippet (1989) studied the same family tree for more than 10 years, finding a consistent pattern of X-linked cleft palate, sometimes accompanied by ankyloglossia in two branches of the tree. Mutation of the TBX22 gene causes the condition. Multiple studies undertaken by this and other research teams (Forbes et al., 1996; Gorski, Adams, Birch, Friedman, and Goodfellow, 1992; Ivens et al., 1988) refined the mapping.

Braybrook et al. (2001) found six different mutations in the TBX22 gene in families presenting with cleft palate and ankyloglossia. In a subsequent study analyzing the condition in two other families, Braybrook et al. (2002) found novel missense and insertion mutations that resulted in cleft palate and ankyloglossia. Marcano et al. (2004) found a range of phenotypic presentations resulting from the TBX22 mutation. Individuals in this study presented with cleft palate, ankyloglossia, or both, suggesting that some cases of ankyloglossia occur as a distinct aspect of this range of mutations.

Our understanding of the genetic underpinnings of tongue-tie remains in its infancy. To arrive at a greater understanding of the genetic influences and their susceptibility to environmental factors, more study must be initiated. In addition, the influence of key environmental factors that may change the endocrine environment during pregnancy requires further study. Some researchers suspect that the startling recent sharp upward surge in midline defect incidence may be associated with disruption of endocrine receptors that, in turn, affect gene expression.

CHAPTER THREE TAKEAWAY

1. The suck-swallow-breathe sequence involves 31 muscles, 6 cranial nerves, and at least 3 cervical nerves. The complexity of this mechanism derives from the dual role these tissues and structures play in the physiology of eating and breathing.

2. As a model for the general physiology of swallowing, there are four phases of the sequence: oral preparatory, oral, pharyngeal, and esophageal. Sucking and mastication comprise the oral preparatory phase.

3. According to Boyle's Law, movement occurs from an area of high pressure to one of low pressure. The swallowing mechanism operates under this basic principle of physics. The food bolus travels along the pathway via the changing pressure gradients that serve as a push-pull mechanism for the bolus. The tongue plays a key role in both initiating and implementing this pressure gradient sequence.

4. The posterior tongue also plays a crucial role in mechanically propelling the milk or food bolus into the pharynx – influencing both the direction and the momentum of the bolus.

5. Tongue-tie interferes with the tongue's fundamental role in initiating and controlling the subsequent phases of the swallow. Compromises to the entire suck-swallow-breathe mechanism can occur as a result, setting the stage for compromises in swallowing and airway patency later on.

CHAPTER FOUR

IMPACT: BREASTFEEDING AND BEYOND

MARY GRACE LANESE, A LONGTIME COLLEAGUE and experienced International Board Certified Lactation Consultant, shares this story:

> Two doctors with whom I work have been instrumental in the establishment of a birthing home in the poorest of the poor rural area of southwestern Haiti. I have been involved in developing breastfeeding protocols and procedures for the birthing home, Maison de Naissance. In March of 2005, two weeks prior to my second trip there, I received a frantic phone call from their midwife overseer. A mom had just brought in three-month-old twins for well-baby care. One twin (Sandana) was thriving; the other (Sandanie) was near death from dehydration and starvation failure to thrive. She had not gained a single gram since birth.
>
> The medical student in attendance was desperate to make a diagnosis and implement a treatment. By satellite communication, he and I talked frequently, and he was able to follow my directions, teaching the mother to hand-express her milk and feed Sandanie by cup following her breastfeedings. Two weeks later, the night I arrived in Torbeck [Haiti], I was able to assess Sandanie's latch. There was no electricity in that location, so the assessment occurred by candlelight and flashlight. Sure enough, a tight frenum!
>
> We had no instruments. Two days later, a family doctor arrived with some instruments. The next day, we walked about three miles through what is left of the jungle there to the

> family's pitiful woven-reed hut. Of course, white men and women walking through the countryside drew a lot of attention and we soon felt like the Pied Piper. The frenum was clipped outside on a rickety old table with chickens, dogs, pigs, and roosters weaving between our legs. Sandanie was put immediately to breast and her mother's eyes grew big as saucers. The latch was ideal.
>
> The next day, we returned to weigh Sandanie. She had gained 40 grams overnight. She continued to gain 40 grams per day for months. When I visited again, the twins were brought to see me, and they are now the same size, although small for three-and-a-half-year-olds. Now we are just praying that they survive to five years and beyond.

In developing nations, where women depend on breastfeeding to keep their babies alive, a story like this moves us to determined action. In developed nations, where, in the minds of the society in general and health care professionals specifically, bottle-feeding still constitutes an acceptable, if not preferable, means of infant feeding, deep concern takes a backseat. If a baby can bottle feed, the thinking goes, who cares if he or she is tongue-tied? Because of ignorance, successful breastfeeding once again comes in second place.

This ignorance is explainable, in part, by the historical lack of research about the impact of tongue-tie on infant feeding. Only since 1993, largely due to the push for research-based information from the lactation field, have several researchers cared to ask the question of how tongue-tie affects breastfeeding, No study, however, specifically addresses the negative impact tongue-tie may have on bottle-feeding.

Breastfeeding has become the central issue related to tongue-tie, but it is merely the first marker of tongue-tie related problems. Later problems may manifest if this first marker is not addressed, although feeding problems alone constitute a significant reason to buttress and justify early surgical intervention.

TONGUE-TIE AND FEEDING

It's no wonder that so little has been written about tongue-tie's impact on feeding. Before bottle-feeding became prevalent, clinicians observed the impact of tongue-tie on breastfeeding and acted based on those observations. The references of the time, which included textbooks and various opinion-based clinical articles, took it for granted that frenotomy corrected the problem. The effects of tongue-tie were most likely common knowledge, even though several popular physicians of the time doubted their significance.

The growing popularity of bottle-feeding in our culture during the first two-thirds of the 20th century created amnesia regarding the tongue's role in infant feeding. Research slowed, and a new standard of normal emerged as a result. Danny's story illustrates this new way of looking at issues related to tongue-tie.

OLD NOTIONS

Danny slid easily out of his mother with a few strong pushes. The doctor gently laid him on his mother's tummy, and he soon was searching for her nipple. He latched on well, but his mom noticed an unusual feeling. However, his twin brother was busy preparing for his passage, and soon Danny's mom was having some strong contractions. During this time, the nurse began Danny's newborn exam. I was the baby companion designated to keep an eye on Danny while his mom continued her labor.

The assessment was conducted a few feet away from the mom's bed. As the nurse continued her examination, I noticed that Danny's lingual frenulum appeared short and a bit tight. I pointed this out to her and asked when the doctor would be in to check out the babies and do a quick frenotomy on Danny.

The nurse snapped, "Tongue-tie doesn't cause any problems. No doctor performs such a procedure anymore." I assured her that this was incorrect. She gave me that look – the one that screams distaste, annoyance, and outrage that I had forgotten my place. As soon as the pediatrician arrived and I pointed out the problem, he immediately clipped Danny's frenulum, much to the nurse's surprise. Two hours later, when Danny's twin brother, Dylan, appeared, both babies were put to breast. Danny nursed significantly better; his mom noticed the improvement, and Danny soon became a champion breastfeeder. Dylan was not tongue-tied and experienced no problems at breast.

The nurse's attitude in this true story represents current medical thinking about tongue-tie and feeding in many areas of the United States and abroad (Brinkman, Reilly, and Meara, 2004; Messner and Lalakea, 2000a). Many practitioners believe, as did their earlier counterparts in the 20th century, that tongue-tie either does not exist or has little to no negative impact on feeding.

Warden (1991) states that ankyloglossia does not present a problem during nursing. In his 1964 article "Minor Disorders in Infancy," MacCarthy says, "A short frenum is never a cause of feeding difficulty." Kummer (2005) contends that approximately 25 percent of tongue-tied infants have difficulty latching to the breast, but that "the majority have no early feeding problems" (p. 2). Wright (1995) says, "There may be rare instances in infancy where problems with feeding and suction can be helped by frenulotomy, but evidence for this is anecdotal" (p. 276). It is interesting to note that none of these writers reviewed or cited the available literature to support their statements.

Clinicians in a primary position to assist the tongue-tied baby and its family may reiterate these opinions rather than base their clinical approach on the most recent legitimate research that presents different conclusions (Brinkman et al., 2004; Griffiths, 2004; Messner and Lalakea, 2000a).

Only a handful of authors from the second half of the 20th century mention feeding difficulties resulting from a short and/or tight lingual frenulum. Observing the day-to-day impact of tongue-tie on their patients, they felt the need to share their findings for the benefit of other mothers and babies at a time when frenotomy had become unpopular or forgotten. Their voices largely have gone unheeded.

Today, the scenario is changing slowly, although more change would be welcome. Many good studies and increased clinical evidence support the claim that tongue-tie adversely affects feeding.

IMPACT ON BREASTFEEDING

The reader can find general comments about compromised breastfeeding in multiple early tongue-tie articles. Lomcali (1987) states, "It is reported that ankyloglossia is hindering the sucking function and forming nourishment difficulties." Oldfield (1959) acknowledges that tongue-tie often causes some difficulty in feeding. Green and Richmond (1962) vaguely assert, "Functional or neurologic impairment of tongue movements may interfere with normal feeding and speech processes." Ploude (1991) describes a case in which a baby was gaining slowly until its frenulum was incised or surgically corrected. This baby's older sibling had experienced the same difficulty. Walker (1989) reports that orofacial abnormalities, including a short lingual frenulum, can affect an infant's ability to properly latch on, suck, and get enough milk.

Nicholson (1991) presents an interesting case of one woman and her three children. Her descriptions of the three cases in one family help the reader understand the details of feeding compromise lacking in earlier articles on the subject. Using a table to compare this woman's three breastfeeding experiences, Nicholson notes that child #1 (not tongue-tied), did not have a problem at breast; children #2 and #3, (both tongue-tied), had difficulties. Child #2 wanted to stay on the breast almost constantly and experienced long-term growth problems. Its tie was not treated until after the third child's tie was clipped. Child #3, prior to treatment, experienced breastfeeding problems. The mother had sore nipples with child #3, but not with child #2; neither baby was able to adequately grasp and milk the breast tissue. After treatment, child #3's breastfeeding problem resolved, as did the mother's sore nipple condition. Had child #3 not been treated, a poor growth pattern, similar to that experienced by child #2, might have emerged. Clearly, there was a connection between tongue-tie and poor feeding in this family.

In their 1991 breastfeeding problem-solving manual, Mohrbacher and Stock write, "If the baby has difficulty staying on the breast or if the mother hears a clicking sound as [the child] nurses, these are signs that suction is being broken and the baby is not effectively milking the breast." They additionally assert that tongue-tied babies may gain weight slowly and be fussy at breast. Marmet and Shell et al. (1990) performed a retrospective study. Their article describes the impact tongue-tie has on breastfeeding; theirs is the first research article to do so in detail.

Interestingly, as early as 1794, Moss recognized feeding difficulties similar to those described centuries later by Marmet et al. (1990) and Mohrbacher and Stock (1991). What happened in the intervening years? Perhaps definitive writings from this interval were lost or destroyed. Perhaps tongue-tie related feeding problems were simply taken for granted; writing it all down might have been redundant.

The late-20th-century studies allude to or name the most common problems that manifest themselves in the tongue-tied breastfed baby, and sometimes with the bottle-fed baby: inadequate latch that interferes with milk transfer; insufficient milk intake and inefficient feeding due to inability to maintain an adequate tongue seal; poor tongue position; fussiness during feeds; poor growth pattern; and nipple-breast pain and damage.

IMPAIRED SUCKING

Optimal tongue mobility is the name of the game in normal individuals. With sufficient mobility, the observer will note:

- Proper tongue placement in the mouth. Proper placement sets the stage for optimal sucking and swallowing, and in turn influences progressive contraction of the tongue. Proper tongue placement also allows plenty of space for the formed breast teat and assists the tongue in generating good intra-oral pressure changes for optimal milk transfer. This oral spaciousness helps form a better dental arch, thereby ensuring better occlusal relationships between the teeth and jaws, which in turn affect the strength and tone of the pharynx.

- Progressive tongue contractility originating at the tip, which assists with milk removal, stabilizes the teat in the mouth, and forms and moves the bolus of food into the midline for swallowing during breastfeeding and bottle-feeding and consumption of solids. Additionally, this progressive contraction of the tongue generates the digestive reflex wave that moves nutrients and gases along the digestive tract, setting the stage for optimal motility along the entire digestive pathway and laying the foundation for the mature swallow.

- Tongue lateralization, tongue extrusion, and tongue retrusion that efficiently move boluses of milk or food around the mouth to prepare for the swallow reflex sequence and to masticate foods for easier swallowing. Complete range of motion of the tongue ensures better preparation of food for the digestive sequence. In addition, the individual will handle all types and textures of food better during mastication and swallowing as he or she grows and matures.

- Optimal tooth and mouth cleanliness. All movements of the tongue perform the oral toilet (teeth and mucous membrane cleaning.) Proper oral toilet prevents dental caries, gingivitis, and halitosis.

- Optimal oral-environment interactions. Tongue range of motion determines the degree to which the infant can engage with the environment through tongue play, hands-in-mouth activity, and oral examination of objects. Optimal psychosocial development depends in part on the sensory input that comes through the orosensory channel.

The efforts of the anterior and posterior portions of the tongue combine to achieve smooth, sequential sucking movements that manifest as progressive contraction. The anterior tongue elevation stabilizes the breast in the mouth, while the dropping and lifting of the posterior tongue during each wave creates intra-oral pressure changes that help draw milk boluses to the throat for swallowing (Geddes and Kent et al., 2008). Although the authors suggest that intra-oral pressure changes may be the primary action of milk removal from the breast, more study needs to be done to verify their results. Regardless, correct tongue action plays the predominant role in milk removal from the breast, aided by the positive pressure of the milk ejection reflex.

Tongue-tied babies have difficulty with some or all aspects of the suck–swallow–breathe constellation. Tongue placement plays the most significant role in feeding. Without proper tongue placement over the lower gumline, a coordinated suck resulting in effective milk transfer cannot occur. The tongue-tip initiates a progressive contraction action that generates peristalsis farther down. The wavelike gentle pressure exerted by the tongue along the entire length of the formed teat sets up a correct swallow sequence, helping direct the bolus properly into the upper throat. Successful completion of these aspects of suck and swallow helps protect the airway and contributes to efficient feeding. Tongue-tied babies exhibit minor to major compromises that may persist throughout life.

TYPICAL COMPROMISES TO NORMAL SUCK–SWALLOW–BREATHE IN THE PRESENCE OF TONGUE-TIE

Although there are variations in the presentation of tongue-tie – a tongue-tie "fingerprint" – general patterns emerge in both presentation and impact. By definition, tongue-tied individuals have a lingual frenulum that is either too short, too tight, or both. Some possess a lingual frenulum that is prominent, occupying the entire length of the tongue's underside and even creating a notch at its tip. Some have an elusive tie – one that tucks itself into or under the mucous membrane at the tongue base. Some are flirtatious; they stand out proudly but are thin and shimmer translucently.

Tongue-ties defy clean-cut categorization since they may demonstrate vastly different impacts, despite similar appearances. This slippery tendency creates a major problem when we try to quantify tongue-tie's impact in a standardized manner.

So let's look at tongue-tie from the general perspective of what is supposed to happen – and doesn't – when the tie prevents the tongue's optimal range of motion.

The tongue, when not in motion, rests just behind the midline of the superior alveolar ridge. This position pulls the tongue forward, allowing the nasopharynx to open fully, thereby creating a fully patent airway for optimal intake of air. During sucking, the anterior edge of the tongue shifts downward over the lower gumline, allowing room for the breast or bottle teat to enter and inhabit the oral cavity.

This position accomplishes several things. First, it maintains the optimally open space of the pharynx, making swallowing easier. Second, it places the tongue in an optimal position to create a primary seal around the breast or bottle teat. This seal plays a key role in generating the intra-oral pressure changes imperative for milk flow and transfer, especially during breastfeeding.

Third, this forward tongue position leads the anterior superior movement of the larynx as it shifts to make room for the opening esophageal sphincter and closes off its own open inlet to prevent aspiration of milk and food during a swallow. If the tongue is back in the pharynx, the larynx has no place to go. Fourth, the forward tongue optimally generates the progressive contractile motion so important for bolus formation and for triggering the proper chemoreceptors and baroreceptors that initiate the pharyngeal swallow. A scattered bolus provides incorrect sensory information to the involved nerves, making it difficult for them to organize the swallowing phase. Fifth, the properly elongated tongue, whose mid- to posterior dorsum drops as the bolus moves to the posterior oral cavity, both directs and mechanically propels the bolus into the pharynx, initiating this first phase of the swallow.

As hard as it is to imagine, the events and various steps of sucking, swallowing, and timed breathing occur so rapidly as to appear simultaneous – yet they are not. When things go well, the timing of these steps proceeds so smoothly that the resultant rhythmical feed sounds like a lullaby.

Tongue-tie interferes with proper tongue placement – sometimes so significantly that any attempt the individual makes to sequence these events is impossible. If the tongue is tethered, it cannot efficiently accomplish the necessary pressure changes that move the bolus properly to the back of the oral cavity. The poorly formed bolus then becomes misdirected, and a misdirected bolus threatens the airway.

Additionally, the compromised range of motion of a tied tongue prevents the necessary backward tongue-thrust that occurs as part of the initiation of the pharyngeal swallow. Reduced force during this aspect causes sluggish bolus movement, and this sluggishness contributes to mistimed rhythmicity between swallowing and breathing. Such mistimed coordination often results in gagging, coughing, and, sometimes, extended apnea.

Aspiration also may occur if the airway is too compromised. Airway compromise, at worst, is deadly. At best, uncoordinated timing in air intake shuts down the continued swallow as a protective mechanism. This inhibition causes food to back up in the vallecular space, and eventually will set off the cough and gag reflexes. The entire feed then ceases, and a wise person will refuse to eat any more, as tongue-tied infants and children so often do, much to their parents' dismay.

Respiration is king. It has to be.

Milder manifestations of tongue-tie may create only moderate compromise; the baby has to suspend respiration for a split-second longer while it swallows. This extra beat results in disturbances of timing, creating arrhythmicity. The baby may just pause to catch its breath like an out-of-shape runner. For the average infant, this catching-up poses a little extra calorie burn, but the otherwise-compromised infant – one who can't afford to spend extra calories, could lose weight, ultimately injuring his or her overall health.

If babies can't feed well at breast, they also won't feed well on a bottle – despite the popular, yet mythical, notion that bottle-feeding corrects all manner of sucking problems. And they won't be good feeders when they start solid foods because the underlying causes still exist; the swallowing and breathing issues remain and may worsen as long as the tongue remains tethered.

Untreated tongue-tie eventually will result in the development of compensatory behaviors that protect the airway and still accomplish the feeding task. Although breathing is king, feeding is queen; food also is necessary to sustain life.

Tongue-tied individuals may take smaller "bites." Either their feed will take longer, or they will feed more frequently to make up for their feeding fatigue. Conversely, they may gulp down their food, taking a big "bite" while they hold their breath for the duration of that swallowing cycle. Then, to compensate, they gulp in air just after the swallow and before the next big "bite." All of that air does not reach the lungs. Some is misdirected to the esophagus, which may still be slightly open at the upper esophageal sphincter as the gulping takes place.

Some hold their tongues posteriorly (Ardran et al., 1958; Geddes and Langton et al., 2008; Woolridge, 1986b). Placement of the anterior tongue edge behind the gumline inhibits progressive contraction, which in turn inhibits the generation of intra-oral pressure. These individuals also must take smaller "bites"; there isn't room in the pharynx for larger boluses because the tongue is in the way. Although posterior tongue placement seems as if it would further protect the airway, it, in fact, interferes with breathing by closing off the pharyngeal space and preventing the larynx from adopting its up-and-forward posture during the swallow. This particular habit of the tongue persists for a long time unless retrained. Individuals then may suffer later from airway occlusion and collapse. Apnea during sleep may be a sign that an individual has adopted this dysfunctional tongue posture.

A retracted tongue from tongue-tie nearly guarantees that the tongue humps somewhere in the mouth, most often near the juncture between the hard and soft palates. Along with jeopardizing progressive contractility, this humping inhibits correct positioning of the nipple in the mouth, creating a shallow and/or painful latch. The mouth must be a welcoming, open room for deep attachment to occur. Tongue humping takes up the available space where the breast nipple would go. The nipple gets caught between the hump and the palate and then may be damaged either by friction or compression (Geddes and Langton et al., 2008; Hazelbaker, 1993, 2003; Watson Genna, 2008).

Tongue humping also directly prevents tongue grooving and proper generation of intra-oral pressure, thereby decreasing milk removal and correct directing of the milk bolus. This increased disorganization generates a threat to the airway because of poor set-up of the swallowing step in the sequence of suck–swallow–breathe. As a result, tongue-tied babies more easily gag, cough, choke, and sputter, and are at risk for micro-aspiration. The suck–swallow–breathe pattern then becomes even more uncoordinated, forcing the baby to protect the airway with compensatory movements such as tongue thrusting, jaw clamping, and even greater tongue humping to slow the flow of milk.

Babies experiencing threat to the airway become fussy at breast; they pull off frequently, become fretful, wave their legs and arms about, fist, flare their nostrils, and cannot calm. Some tongue-tied babies experience so much feeding stress that they refuse the breast altogether.

The sides of the tongue, responding to the superior and inferior longitudinal muscles and the hypoglossal nerve, elevate to help create a trough-like groove down the midline of the tongue. This groove serves to form and stabilize a teat from the nipple and the areolar-breast tissue behind it, containing and directing the bolus of milk. Some tongue-tied infants form this groove well; others do not. A relative lack of groove that prevents the constant seal of the tongue against the breast can create a "chucking" sound with some or each attempted suck cycle. This periodic release of suction compromises milk transfer and feed efficiency, leading to extended feed length, possible weight gain compromise, and reduced milk supply.

Not all tongue-tied babies have poor tongue placement. Some can extend the tongue over the lower gumline even during gape, but cannot keep it there during sucking because the lingual frenulum's poor elasticity causes the tongue to retract during this phase of feeding. I termed this action (after Marmet et al., 1990) "snap-back" in my original research on tongue-tie (Hazelbaker, 1993).

Some babies have ties at the anterior edge of the tongue and at the ridge of the inferior gumline. This tie keeps the tongue placed forward, and this presentation of tongue-tie may render the best feeding result; the baby still is able to use the tongue reasonably well to extract milk. However, with this presentation, the clinician most likely will see slow feeding, impaired tongue lateralization, reduced tongue lift, and compromised tongue retrusion and extrusion. The mother may have a low milk supply (Hazelbaker, 1993). These babies are more likely to experience problems down the road when lateralization begins to play its most significant role during mastication, when the tongue must be free to manage solid foods.

Keep in mind that tongue mobility remains the goal of tongue-tie treatment. Surgical release garners this result. Secondary results, like better milk transfer, occur only when treatment restores optimal tongue placement, movement and strength.

MILK TRANSFER

An inability to use the tongue effectively to remove milk from the breast is an effect of tongue-tie cited in many past and current studies. Browne (1959) identified tongue-movement compromise leading to poor milk transfer as an effect of tongue-tie:

> Certain children are handicapped, occasionally very seriously, by being unable to get the tip of the tongue against the hard palate. In infants the effects are an inability to compress the natural or artificial teat, with a consequent slowing of feeding that at best is exasperating and at the worse produces starvation. (p. 952)

Marmet et al. (1990) provide one of the first modern detailed descriptions of tongue motion deficits that lead to insufficient milk transfer:

> The tongue may not be able to elevate or maintain extension sufficiently to produce the wave-like motion necessary for proper sucking. Trauma occurs with sucking due to friction on the nipples as the tongue is snapped back to the mandibular floor by the tight

> frenum – much like a rubber band that, when stretched, snaps back. This frictional movement can be felt during digital suck assessment. When the tongue cannot form the appropriate seal in the oral cavity, suction may be repeatedly released, producing a smacking sound. These behaviors usually produce ineffective sucking, which in turn may lead to insufficient milk drainage, mastitis, lowered milk supply, and consequent poor infant weight gain. ... When a clinical picture is consistent with all these findings and resists remedy by management and suck training techniques, a frenotomy should be considered. (p. 118)

Geddes and Langton et al. (2008) performed an elegant ultrasound study in which they measured milk transfer both pre- and post-frenotomy. Infants transferred significantly more milk in significantly less time after their tongue-ties were surgically released. This research team also endeavored to quantify milk volumes pre-and post-frenotomy. Although their sample size was small (six mothers), they found that the 24-hour milk productions of these mothers increased significantly, between 36 and 362 grams.

Other researchers cited milk transfer and the rate of same in their studies, although total milk volumes were not assessed. Griffiths (2004, p. 411) mentions "the continuous feeding cycle" due to reduced milk transfer. Hogan and Westcott et al. (2005) also mention continuous feeds in their sample. Some of these babies required top-up feeds by bottle to ensure adequate calorie intake. Fifty percent of the babies in the Wallace and Clarke (2006) study demonstrated continual feeding. In all three studies, rate of milk transfer improved after surgical correction.

Ballard and Auer et al. (2002) note that milk transfer can be so compromised that babies can fail to thrive. Half of the infants in a subcohort of their study population presented with Failure to Thrive; one had to be hospitalized with starvation-related fatty infiltration of the liver. Poor or slow weight gain as a result of poor milk transfer is an obvious outcome. And, of course, the hungry baby is a fussy baby unless the calorie intake is so low that the baby conserves energy by sleeping; some tongue-tied babies may become "content to starve." These latter babies can appear at first simply to fit into the "model baby" category. Parents do not know they should intervene, which worsens the problem.

If a mother senses or knows that her baby is hungry, she may resort to supplementing the baby or may be told to do so by her primary care provider. Although this may be a necessary step to ensure adequate infant growth and turn around a potentially disastrous weight-loss scenario, supplementation represents the proverbial "slippery slope." Correcting the tongue-tie as soon as possible remains the best clinical strategy if simple management fails to improve the situation quickly. Bottle-feeding does not always provide a satisfactory solution.

Engorgement constitutes a specific and very early sign of impaired milk transfer. Some tongue-tied babies cannot seem to get the milk-making system primed enough to keep it from shutting down from the back-pressure of retained milk. The development of engorgement naturally follows (as do other forms of milk stasis, such as plugged ducts). Although engorgement occurs most often as the result of mismanagement in the first few days, any baby of a mother experiencing engorgement ought to be checked for tongue-tie.

Melissa describes the horrible engorgement she endured in the first week postpartum, which added all-over breast pain to her ever-increasing nipple pain, and complicated her breastfeeding course. Melissa writes:

> Thank heavens for cabbage leaves and warm showers, where I was able to hand express enough milk so that poor Kyla had a fighting chance of latching on. My nipples disappeared into my rock-hard breasts.

Impaired milk transfer directly correlates with lesser total milk volumes. The infant drives the breastfeeding system via efficient milk removal. The system receives support in the first weeks from high endocrine levels, but, ultimately, how much milk the baby removes determines how much milk the mother makes. Despite its fundamental importance, this fact seems to elude many clinicians.

MILK SUPPLY COMPROMISE

A baby who cannot use its tongue correctly to remove milk from the breast will adversely influence the mother's supply to one degree or another (Prieto et al., 1996). Unfortunately, the full extent of this impact may become apparent only when autocrine control takes over for endocrine control at around week 12 postpartum (Daly, Kent, Owens, and Hartmann, 1996). At this late point, developing a full supply that has been impaired by tongue-tie becomes more of a challenge (West and Marasco, 2008), and at some point along the breastfeeding trajectory, given our current knowledge, perhaps impossible.

With the aid of her hormones, Mindy started out with a gushing supply of milk. Over time and gradually, her supply settled and then began to drop. After the third month, her previously abundant supply had diminished to the point of barely being enough to sustain her baby, Elijah. He started to drop off his growth curve and in a one-month period failed to gain any weight. With some timely management, Mindy's supply increased enough to sustain Elijah's weight gain, but she could no longer make enough milk to feed two babies. Some of this drop occurs organically and normally at the three-month mark, but, judging by her level of production in the first two months, Mindy could have had an overabundant supply for her entire lactation cycle had her baby not been tongue-tied. Several studies mention reduced supply as a result of infant tongue-tie, and rebounding supply as a result of surgical intervention (Coryllos et al., 2004; Geddes and Langton et al., 2008; Hazelbaker, 1993; Marmet et al., 1990). Most reports rely on reversal of weight gain deficits and feed dissatisfaction in the tongue-tied baby, paired with mother-reported changes in fullness of breasts, increasing sensations and signs of milk ejection, and increased level of thirst as indicators that milk supply has increased.

The Geddes and Langton study is the only one to measure milk intake of tongue-tied babies pre-

and post-frenotomy. As previously noted, data from this study show a significant increase in milk transfer and in total milk volumes as a result of surgical intervention, validating anecdotal reports that use other indicators of improvement.

LATCH

Both Hazelbaker (1993) and Watson Genna (2008) describe tongue bunching due to the tightness and relative positioning of the frenular attachment to the tongue. The bunching prevents the necessary spread of the anterior tongue in preparation for the curved tongue seal that creates good latch and subsequent good intra-oral pressure changes. The tongue tip plays a significant role in initiating the latch sequence. If it is anchored or bunched, it cannot perform this role efficiently or at all.

Watson Genna (2008, p. 181) asserts in her excellent and practical book on sucking problems that mouth gape also plays a huge role in the infant's ability to deeply attach to the breast. She suggests that the restricted tongue has a tendency to retract (hump) with a wide gape, making it impossible for the baby to place its tongue correctly over the lower gumline, subsequently being unable to grasp the breast for an effective seal. The obvious problem with this presentation is the prevention of a good latch. The tongue must be extended and dropped over the lower gumline to allow for deep attachment to the breast, which in turn contributes to efficient milk transfer.

Some tongue-tied infants latch well and transfer milk efficiently. Elasticity in the floor of the mouth may partially compensate for a restrictive lingual frenulum (Watson Genna, 2008.) However, most tongue-tied babies are less efficient than their non-tied peers (Geddes and Langton et al, 2008). Many researchers cite latch insufficiency in their studies. According to these studies, latch insufficiency is the most frequent tongue-tie-related breastfeeding difficulty. It therefore may constitute the most important measure of feeding efficiency and effectiveness in the tongue-tied breastfed baby.

In a review of 700 cases, Hillan (2008) notes that of the smaller cohort of 96 babies seen in 2006, 56 percent slipped off the breast. Of these babies, 85 percent had improved latch after frenotomy. The vast majority of these babies were older than one week – old enough to have settled into proper latch either spontaneously or with improved management. Eighty-eight babies of 2,763 in the Ballard and Auer et al. (2002) study presented with significant ankyloglossia. Sixty-three percent of them latched poorly. After frenotomy, 100 percent of these babies latched significantly better. Eighty-five percent of the Hogan and Westcott et al. (2005) sample experienced latching issues. Eighty-eight percent of the Griffiths' (2004) cohort experienced latching difficulties. Neither study, however, cite specifics of the latching compromise. Srinivasan, Dobrich, Mitnick, and Feldman (2006) used LATCH scores to measure improvement of infant latch at breast. There was a significant improvement of mean scores after frenotomy.

Of the Amir et al. (2005) study cohort, 44 percent cited breast attachment difficulties. Fifty-one percent of these mothers experienced improved latching following frenotomy. Dollberg, Grunis, and Mimouni (2006) found latch difficulties in their cohort. Wallace and Clarke (2006) found an 80 percent incidence of poor latch. More than half of these poorly attached babies also experienced continuous feeding.

Marmet et al. (1990) cite latch difficulties in their seminal article on the subject of tongue-tie. They were the first to specify the nature of latch problems seen with tongue-tie:

> The baby bites down on the areolar tissue with his gums to grasp the breast since his tongue either cannot reach or maintain position on the lower gumline or lip. ... In addition, the tongue may not be able to elevate or maintain extension sufficiently to produce the wavelike motion necessary for proper sucking. ... When the tongue cannot form the appropriate seal in the oral cavity, suction may be repeatedly released, producing a smacking sound. (p. 118)

Thick, fibrous frenula may create more problems than thin, elastic frenula (Coryllos et al., 2004; Hazelbaker, 1993). Watson Genna (2008, pp. 195–201) describes several latch alterations for tongue-tied babies that may improve their feed efficiency. Performing exercises to improve tongue placement and movement efficiency also may cultivate deeper attachment at breast.

In my study cohort (1993), all the tongue-tied babies had latch issues. Some were unable to take the breast deeply into their mouths, causing poor milk transfer and nipple-breast pain and damage; others were unable to maintain an appropriate tongue seal, periodically releasing suction. Until they underwent surgery, their milk transfer remained poor due to inadequate intra-oral pressure, compromised progressive contraction of the tongue, and too-slow and fatiguing feeding. Notestine, a dentist, notes latch issues as the primary reason for his clinical interest in treating tongue-tie (G. Notestine, personal communication, March 19, 2009), saying:

> My sister, Anita, was a La Leche League (LLL) Leader, and a three-week-old boy in the group was struggling to latch on. This was the third child of this mother, and she knew how breastfeeding was supposed to be – and this wasn't it! Her nipples were raw and bleeding, the child had been hospitalized with dehydration, he was being finger-fed around the clock. ... It was a nightmare for this mother, but she was very persistent and knew it could be better. The LLL group offered all their advice, lactation consultants were consulted, the pediatrician said to just give a bottle, which wasn't working either, and there was great frustration and despair. My sister asked me [as] a general dentist, to look and see if there was anything wrong with his mouth. I saw him, and as soon as he opened his mouth to cry, I could see that he was tongue-tied.

> Everyone said 'What's that?" I explained, and then I was asked to do something about it. Well, I never treated anyone younger than 50 without teeth, so the infant mouth was totally foreign territory for me! But the mom and the LLL group were so desperate that I prayed hard, clipped the frenulum, and hoped. The baby cried a little, there was very little bleeding, and he didn't die from my treatment! He was very hungry, so the mom put him to the breast, expecting the excruciating pain again, but she was ready to tough it out AGAIN. The look on her face when he started suckling was priceless. The total relief of a pain-free feeding made her cry with joy. It didn't hurt, he stayed on, he removed milk, he got a full belly, on and on and on. From that day, the frustration was over and he grew normally.

Bottle-feeding does not guarantee smooth, efficient feeding. It will help to resolve nipple-breast pain and damage, but so will good management and surgical intervention. Switching to bottle-feeding, as was suggested to the mother in the above example, may improve milk transfer, but mostly because of the constant flow of milk from the bottle through too-large teat holes. This strategy often results in a "drink or drown" phenomenon, removing any opportunity for the tongue-tied baby to pace his or her own feed. Mukai et al. (1991) found significant reduced oxygen saturation in a cohort of tongue-tied infants; sometimes the saturation levels were reduced to dangerous and life-threatening levels. Switching a baby to a bottle in cases like these would constitute a very wrong and potentially dangerous clinical strategy because of the further possible compromise to oxygenation from the continuous and too-fast flow (Mukai et al., 1991; Watson Genna, 2008; Wolf and Glass, 1992).

The Mukai et al. (1991) study is the only study that examines the level of oxygen compromise during breast or bottle-feeding in tongue-tied babies. This study significantly adds to our understanding of tongue-tie's impact on the infant's ability to get enough oxygen during the feeding process and may help us understand how these babies are affected in later life. The researchers observed that babies who experience significant drops in oxygen saturation often will refuse to latch on to the breast altogether. Although often mentioned in anecdotal accounts, this phenomenon seems to go unacknowledged in the literature as a whole. The Ballard and Auer et al. (2002) study makes only passing reference to it.

Unfortunately, most studies do not quantify the latch deficits seen in their sample populations. This detailed information would strengthen support for tongue-tie surgical treatment. Pointing out specific and concrete issues and how surgery improves the clinical picture enables practitioners to find a rationale for surgical intervention. Specifics also help clinicians individualize post-surgical plans.

Poor latch not only reduces milk transfer leading to milk supply reduction, but it also can be a significant contributor to nipple-breast pain and damage.

NIPPLE AND BREAST PAIN AND DAMAGE

Maternal breast and nipple damage can result from repetitive stress from the abnormal tongue movements typical of tongue-tie. A retracted tongue from a too-tight lingual frenulum bares the surface of the lower gum-ridge, setting off a reflexive bite when touched–an occurrence that compels the mother of a tongue-tied baby to describe latch as a sharp, biting sensation. The combination of absence or compromised progressive contraction of the tongue and the activation of the phasic bite reflex causes these affected babies to "chew" at breast (Hazelbaker, 1993; Marmet et al.,1990; Watson Genna, 2008). Some clinicians refer to this "chewing" as a piston-like jaw movement (as opposed to the swing-like movement of the jaw when the tongue can perform its tip-to-base progressive contraction). Additionally, Watson Genna (2008) notes:

> Pinching or biting sensations may occur due to excessive positive pressure from the tongue or jaws; friction (often described as feeling like sandpaper or a cat's tongue on the nipple) may be due to compensatory in-out movements of the tongue; and feeling percussive movement against the nipple may be due to excessive posterior tongue elevation. (p. 34)

Nipple soreness commonly results from tongue-tie-related tongue movement deficits or compensatory movements designed to protect the airway. A transcript from the La Leche League International 1991 Physician's Seminar (Gartner, Tanis, and Lawrence) mentions long-term nipple soreness that results in exquisite pain. Several other early studies cite nipple soreness and damage as ill effects of tongue-tie (Meintz-Maher, 1998; Minchin, 1985; Ploude, 1991; Walker, 1989). This common citation of nipple soreness prompted Messner and Lalakea (2000b) to state that nipple-tissue breakdown and pain alone justify clipping a lingual frenulum if the mother requests.

Many recent studies cite nipple soreness as a primary determinant of necessity for surgical intervention (Dollberg et al., 2006; Griffiths, 2004; Hillan, 2008; Hogan et al., 2005; Segal et al., 2007; Srinivasan et al., 2006). These studies might lead one to believe that tongue-tie always causes sore nipples. Yet, surprisingly, nipple soreness occurs less often than one might suppose. Segal et al. performed an extensive review of the available literature. They found that nipple soreness due to mismanagement occurs in 60 to 80 percent of the general population of breastfeeding mothers. The incidence of persistent nipple pain in mothers whose infants have tongue-tie ranges from 36 to 80 percent, depending on study construction.

In Ballard and Auer et al. (2002), only 36 percent of the mothers whose infants presented with significant tongue-tie experienced nipple soreness. In Hillan's 2008 study, during a three-year period, a range of 77 to 86 percent of mothers had sore nipples. Griffiths (2004, p. 411) indicates that 77 percent of his cohort had "painful, sore or bleeding nipples." Eighty-three percent of mothers in Hansen's 2005 study (cited in Hanson, MacKinlay and Manson, 2006) experienced nipple soreness. Hogan and Westcott et al. (2005) found an incidence of 80 percent nipple soreness in the tongue-tie group. But the same percentage of mothers in the control group also experienced nipple soreness.

Perhaps one is led to believe that nipple soreness occurs universally with tongue-tie simply because many of these studies use nipple and breast pain reduction as an outcome measure based on their Operational Definition of tongue-tie (Dollberg et al., 2006; Geddes and Langton et al., 2008; Griffiths, 2004; Hogan et al., 2005; Srinivasan et al., 2006). These measures may have skewed the incidence rate.

Its nonuniversal manifestation, however, demonstrates that nipple soreness fails to be a reliable sole indicator of the presence of tongue-tie and therefore should not be used as the lone diagnostic or surgical indicator. The absence of nipple soreness does not preclude tongue-tie, nor should one presume that persistent nipple soreness is always due to tongue-tie. However, nipple-breast pain and damage happen often enough with tongue-tie to warrant investigation if management alone fails to quickly resolve the issue.

No matter how often it occurs, persistent nipple soreness, uncorrectable through good management remains a compelling reason for clipping the lingual frenulum of a tongue-tied baby. The nipple-breast pain from tongue-tie ranges from a mild tenderness at latch to an excruciatingly sharp, stabbing sensation either during or after the feed that may stay at the same intensity or worsen as the feed progresses or ends (Hazelbaker, 1993, 2003; Srinivasan et al., 2006). Mothers often complain of a rasping or biting sensation during feeds (Hazelbaker, 1993; Marmet et al., 1990; Watson Genna, 2008). Or they may say that their nipples feel numb during the feed, only to "wake up," tingle, and burn within three to five minutes post-feed (Hazelbaker, 1993, 2003).

Some mothers report that this tingly-burning sensation lasts for up to an hour after feeding, only to be replaced by a mild to intense tender-achy feeling that never seems to resolve throughout the day (Hazelbaker, 2003). Some mothers experience bruising on the nipple-tips due to compression from the tongue against the hard palate, which traps the nipple (Geddes and Langton et al., 2008). I also have seen mild to severe bruises on the areola that correspond with the placement of the infant gums.

Often with tongue-tie, the nipple comes out of the baby's mouth in a compressed state. A compression "stripe" can be seen at the tip and/or along its shank. The nipple-tip or shank may appear blanched for up to several minutes post-feed due to the cutoff of circulation in the area (Hazelbaker, 2003). The Geddes and Langton et al. (2008) ultrasound study images this compression of the tongue against the hard palate.

Some people confuse this blanched appearance with other phenomena.

An article in the *Journal of Human Lactation* (Garrrison, 2002) suggested that mothers with this grouping of signs and symptoms had developed Raynaud's phenomenon. This may be so in some cases, but it appears more likely that they are experiencing what I term nipple compression syndrome. The infant's intra-oral tightness compresses the nipple-areolar complex, causing poor circulation (the blanched tip) and nerve inflammation (burning, stinging, and stabbing). Basically, the mother develops neuralgia of the breast. This nerve irritation, inflammation, and/or bruising accounts for the slowness of nipple and breast healing following frenotomy; the nerve and tissue trauma is so severe that time is required for complete healing (Dollberg et al., 2006; Hazelbaker, 2003).

Clinicians also may mistake this type of breast and nipple pain for thrush (a common yeast infection), resulting in the all-too-common practice of treating these symptoms with antifungal and topical steroid medications – an approach that will fail for obvious reasons. Thrush usually will respond to treatment within 24 to 48 hours. If a quick response does not occur, especially if the pain symptoms occur in the absence of other common symptoms such as flaky skin, angry red inflammation, iridescent infant mucous membranes, white spots in the infant's mouth, and/or a diaper rash, one must consider the possibility that the mother and baby have been misdiagnosed.

Nipple pain is the second-most-common cause of premature weaning after perceived insufficient milk supply (Woolridge, 1986a). It may well be the primary reason mothers of tongue-tied babies stop breastfeeding. And no wonder. What mother in her right mind would want to subject herself to severe pain for long? But some mothers do so because they are dedicated to breastfeeding. Melissa, who was profiled earlier, is one of these dedicated moms.

Melissa described her nipple pain in the first few days as "the toe-curling, slam-your-heel-on-the-floor kind of pain." This pain intensified as the days went by, with the pain of latch dovetailing with compression and friction pain that lasted the entire feed:

> Tears would stream down my face as I clenched my teeth and agonized over how we would overcome this obstacle. One night ... the pain was so bad I was throwing things across the room. Chris, my husband, was worried about my emotional well-being.

As well he should have been. But the solution to this type of situation is not to advise the mother to feed the baby formula by bottle, but to correctly diagnose the problem and initiate timely and appropriate treatment. In Melissa's case, all her daughter needed was to have her frenulum clipped – a simple procedure that should have been done quickly, soon after the initial symptoms materialized.

Tongue-tie also causes severe nipple damage, either immediately or over time. Good (1987) describes a case where the mother's nipples were bruised and sore:

> By day ten, her right nipple had a tear 1 cm wide by ½ cm deep, and she was able to see the red tissue inside her nipple. [She had her baby's frenulum clipped and nursed immediately after the clipping]. ... She anticipated a new sensation but what she actually felt was the absence of the old pulling, tugging, and friction on her nipple. Within two weeks, the purple discoloration of her nipples [and her wound] had vanished. The baby seemed to enjoy nursing more, as he fed for longer time periods and displayed newfound pleasure in sucking. (p. 154–155)

Tongue-tie also may contribute significantly to breast inflammation due to milk stasis. Breward (2004), Hansen et. al. (2006), and Coryllos et al. (2004) all mention mastitis in their studies. Because some tongue-tied babies do not transfer milk well, milk remains in the breast, setting the stage for milk stasis. Breast inflammation resulting from milk stasis and/or plugged or filled ducts creates another type of pain – one that produces a pinpoint discomfort in one or two ducts, or soreness that can extend from the nipple-tip back to the chest wall, sometimes involving the entire breast area. The key to resolution remains efficient milk removal – the task the baby accomplishes when it sucks correctly. Ongoing milk stasis can, of course, cause lowered milk supply through back-pressure inhibition.

Nipple or breast pain alone does not indicate presence of tongue-tie. But any baby causing nipple-breast pain and damage that does not improve with consistent deep attachment technique and proper management within a 24- to 48- hour period must be evaluated for the presence of tongue-tie. Because pain during breastfeeding tops the list of reasons for premature weaning, this significant symptom needs to be taken seriously. Preserving breastfeeding and the mother's comfort during breastfeeding takes precedence over many concerns – especially those that are ignorance-based or politically motivated.

FATIGUE

Babies come into this world as active participants in the feeding process and with the ability to transfer milk efficiently. A normal infant awakens for feeds, communicates clearly that he or she is hungry, and eagerly participates in the feeding process. An eager, hungry baby keeps his or her eyes open for a good part of each feed, and, in the first five minutes will transfer milk nearly continuously with long bursts of sucking, punctuated by very short pauses. As the baby becomes more and more sated, the bursts become shorter and the pauses longer.

As a baby feeds, his or her suck-swallow-breathe cycle occurs rhythmically and consistently throughout. Eventually, the baby either removes itself from the breast when entirely satiated, or can be removed easily by breaking his or her now-mild tongue-seal. This efficiency allows a baby to transfer milk while burning a minimal number of calories, leaving ample calories for growth.

Babies who must work harder to transfer sufficient quantities of milk may tire faster. This tendency may contribute to extended feed length and reduced milk transfer. Often, tongue-tied babies have to work harder to transfer milk. More often than not, they have disorganized bursts of sucking, demonstrating all manner of compensations to remove milk while protecting their airways. These compensations, coupled with reduced calorie intake, lead to muscle fatigue.

Watson Genna (2008, p. 25) states that the presence of clonus, or tremors, can occur because of tongue fatigue. In part, she attributes this fatigue to the recruitment of accessory muscles to assist with sucking. The compensatory muscle movements are "less ergonomic," contributing to reduced feed efficiency.

As the fatigue sets in, the feed becomes even less efficient. Often, these babies start to become disorganized within a few minutes of beginning to eat. They may close their eyes and dilly-dally, sometimes for an hour or more, to conserve energy. They may fall asleep during the middle of the feed or after a prolonged feed, but they cannot be put down without waking to demand the breast again. After a brief sleep, the tongue-tied babies may rally and repeat the process. This inefficiency and fatigue result in an all-day feeding marathon that still may result in insufficient calorie intake.

Griffiths (2004, p. 411) found that 72 percent of the babies in his study fed inefficiently, "became tired and fell asleep, but were still hungry, so slept only for a short time before waking to feed inefficiently again." Hogan et al. (2005) describe this same pattern, no matter what the feeding method. Both articles refer to this inefficient pattern as a continuous feeding cycle. Often, the misguided solution to continuous feeding involves "topping-off," or replacing breast feeds with bottle-feeding – a seemingly logical strategy for increasing the infant's caloric intake, but one that may fail because tongue-tie also can cause significant compromise during bottle-feeding.

IMPACT ON BOTTLE-FEEDING

McEnery and Gaines (1941) state:

> In the newborn infant, tongue-tie presents only a minor difficulty in taking the breast or bottle. In taking the bottle, there should be no trouble. In regard to the breast, especially if the nipple be short or retracted, there may be some difficulty, but this can be corrected by gentle massage of the mother's nipple, not after she has been delivered but in the last month of gestation. It is often because of a misunderstanding of the technique of nursing that the frenum of the tongue is cut. (p. 252)

Their view represents a popular misconception about breastfeeding management and about tongue-tie and bottle-feeding. Berg (1990b), in her article "Two Cases of Tongue-Tie and Breastfeeding," states that the incidence of treatment for ankyloglossia decreased with the increase in bottle-feeding because a baby does not need to use its tongue to compress the bottle teat to remove adequate amounts of milk. Over time, health care providers may have forgotten that tongue-tie inhibits proper tongue motion needed for any feeding method. With the elevation of bottle-feeding over breastfeeding as the preferred method in Westernized cultures, switching a breastfed baby to a bottle causes little discomfort to the conscience. Treating breastfeeding and bottle-feeding as the same process may be one explanation for the unpopularity of treating tongue-tie in breastfed babies, and the misperception about tongue use during bottle-feeding prevents clinicians from investigating more thoroughly when a bottle-fed baby experiences problems.

Although breastfeeding demands more from the baby in terms of coordination of the tongue, efficient bottle-feeding relies on proper tongue placement and mobility, as well. Bottle-feeders also need to pace their feeds, protect their airways, and set up the bolus of milk for an efficient swallow.

Meyer Palmer, author of the Neonatal Oral-Motor Assessment Scale, comments that suck-swallow-breathe coordination should be the same regardless of feeding method (Meyer Palmer, NOMAS Certification Course, 1995). In my experience, clinicians almost never perform a feeding evaluation on bottle-fed babies. As a result, choice of bottle and teat appears to depend largely on the relentless marketing tactics of manufacturers.

Rarely, if ever, do clinicians and mothers consider bottle-teat factors such as size of hole, number of holes, rate of flow with and without gravity assist, compressibility of teat, integrity of the material used to make the teat, and the skill of the baby. All of these factors must be evaluated when choosing the right teat for a particular bottle-fed baby, especially one who is tongue-tied.

In my clinical practice, I have worked with many bottle-fed babies who have been hooked up to apnea monitors for weeks. However, no feeding evaluations ever were performed before applying such an intervention, nor were any of the babies evaluated for feeding deficits at any time while on the monitors. One hundred percent of the time, these babies dramatically improved when an appropriate teat choice was made that enabled them to better control the flow and pace the feed.

While it may be true that the tongue plays less of an extraction role in bottle feeding, a tongue-tied bottle-fed baby may or may not have an easier time of it. Clinicians commonly see bottle-fed, tongue-tied babies who must protect their airways because they have little control over flow rate, swallowing, and breathing even when the bottle teat is changed to minimize rate of flow and maximize the infant's control. (Griffiths, 2004).

Lisa's baby, Joe, is a perfect example. As a means to bolster Joe's significant weight loss, the intervention chosen was to bottle-feed to increase his calorie intake quickly since he was having so much difficulty extracting milk from the breast. Lisa shared that it took Joe a very long time – 40 minutes or more – to take even a few ounces from a bottle. Had he been weaned completely – and prematurely – from the breast rather than undergoing frenotomy, Joe would have continued to be a poor bottle-feeder with all of its attendant risks.

Tongue-tied babies may be placed on bottle teats that do not demand or cultivate as efficient a sucking performance as the baby can muster. Some suffer the consequences and demonstrate feeding behaviors that indicate they are stressed, disorganized, and possibly experiencing oxygen saturation compromise. Tongue-tied babies on a bottle may have difficulty protecting their airways and will tongue-thrust (causing dribbling), hump their tongues (collapsing the teat and causing dribbling), swallow lots of air, and/or fuss throughout the feed, showing multiple stress signs, such as sitting on air, gaze aversion, hand and foot clench, and arm and leg cycling. The bottle-fed infant most likely will experience good weight gain, and the mother will mercifully not suffer nipple problems, but long-term consequences stemming from poor suck-swallow-breathe coordination may develop. Among those consequences are airway compromise, poor tongue coordination due to muscular weakness, a deviate swallow, malocclusion, and aversive feeding.

Clinicians merely *assume* that tongue-tied babies do better on a bottle. No research supports bottle-feeding for tongue-tied infants. In fact, a recent study examining the impact of frenotomy on infant feeding included a subcohort of bottle-feeders. The bottle-feeders and breastfeeders experienced similar difficulties with feeding (Hogan et al., 2005). The study details feeding compromises as a result of tongue-tie in their bottle-fed cohort: Seventy-six percent were slow feeders; 71 percent dribbled, indicating poor tongue seal around the teat and possible tongue-thrusting; and 24 percent had excess wind. All but one of these babies experienced improved feeding after frenotomy. More research on the impact of tongue-tie on bottle-feeding would be welcome – perhaps finally putting to rest the notion that the solution to tongue-tie is bottle-feeding.

IMPACT ON CHEWING AND DIGESTION

In normal chewing, the tongue shifts food from one side of the mouth to the other and back again. The teeth macerate the food. The movement of the tongue initiates and perpetuates the release of saliva, which then mixes with the food with the help of the tongue. Eventually, these combined efforts prepare the food to the correct consistency. Next, the tongue-tip moves to the posterior aspect of the superior alveolar ridge, as it grooves to help center the bolus, or "food packet," on the tongue-blade and form the gutter along which the bolus will travel to the back of the mouth for swallowing. If the tongue action follows the appropriate sequence, a minimum of air and energy is consumed. The bolus of food drops into the pharynx, while the airway is protected, for the remainder of its journey down the esophagus.

The progressive contraction of the tongue sets the stage for the swallowing sequence, which uses reflex progressive contractions all along the length of the "food tube." This peristalsis continues into the lower gastrointestinal tract. The reflex action initiated by the tongue-tip makes the eating sequence part of the overall digestive and nutrition absorption sequence. Tongue-tied individuals do not have tongue-tip-to-anus progressive contractions. As a result, sluggish digestion develops, which leads, in turn, to gastrointestinal tract inflammation, reflux, excess gas and bloating, poor nutrient absorption, and poor elimination. Infants may be colicky, experience reflux, and/or have secondary lactose intolerance if breastfed (Coryllos et al., 2004; Griffiths, 2004).

Older children and adults may experience gas, bloating, reflux, constipation, poor nutrient uptake, or leaky gut syndrome, and may have difficulty burping or passing gas (Fernando, 1998; Furer, 2008).

Elijah, one of these "colicky" babies, had difficulty burping and experienced prolonged periods of fussiness due to the discomfort of excess gas and bloating. He had green, bloody, and mucousy stools, and eczema all over his body from leaky gut. After having his posterior tie surgically corrected, his tongue motion returned to normal, and his stools changed dramatically. They turned mustardy yellow; the blood and mucous disappeared. His fussiness gradually diminished, he started to burp easily, and his eczema resolved.

My gassiness and bloating was one of the first things to resolve after I had my frenulum clipped. For 42 years, I suffered after nearly every meal. What a relief to be able to eat a meal, truly relax while I did so, and then feel satisfied and comfortable after I finished! Evi, a lactation consultant colleague, describes the increase in her digestive efficiency after having her tongue-tie surgically corrected. Gone were the bloating and gas she often experienced for no apparent reason even when she properly minded her diet. Her dentist, Roee Furer (2008), notes that symptoms of constipation, bloating, and gas appear commonly in his tongue-tied patients. Many of them experience relief after surgical correction.

A bolus of food can be poorly prepared, leaving food too lumpy, pasty or thick for swallowing without setting off dribbling, coughing, sputtering and/or gagging. The lack of coordinated tongue movements requires a tongue-tied individual to use compensatory movements to protect his or her airway, which increases air-swallowing. The loss of efficiency in airway protection creates a ratchety sequence: Tongue-tied people may have to hold their breath during chewing, then gasp for air just before the swallow. Or they may breathe intermittently through the mouth or nose during chewing, and then hold their breath during the swallow, gasping for air after the swallow occurs. Many tongue-tied people chew with their mouths open for this reason. They need to take in as much air as they can because of their difficulty breathing during the chewing-swallowing process.

Fernando (1998) describes a common compensatory eating pattern that includes preferring foods that are easy to chew or already are finely processed, such as applesauce. The children and adults with whom she works often consume large quantities of liquids to wash down food, especially if they choose to swallow large lumps, avoiding mastication because it poses too much challenge. Often these individuals spit particles of food while they chew or have food dribble out of their mouths. She describes the emotional consequences of criticized messy or "inappropriate" eating habits:

> Although his [child patient] surgery was successful, he needed play therapy and counseling before he could relinquish his irritating passive-aggressive eating habits. Unfortunately, his very real symptoms had given him a chance of enjoying individual attention and although this was negative attention, he was unwilling to forfeit it by conforming. Symptom formation is always a possibility when children have to cope with physical difficulties that have socially unacceptable consequences. (p. 15–16)

I recall trying desperately to chew with my mouth closed, finding it difficult to breathe through my nose while I tried to move the food around my mouth. I always resorted to open-mouthed chewing despite my mother's admonishments. Keeping my mouth closed left me feeling panicky and stressed out. I took to eating very small bits – and finishing after everyone else was done – or taking too-large bites, chewing just a little, and then attempting to get the food down in one big lump. The latter often left my throat feeling sore.

Either way, after each meal I always had gas that did not resolve with burping. As you might imagine, I hated to eat – an emotion that remains even after being free of my tie for nearly a decade, and despite learning new chewing habits. I also felt ashamed when I ate, especially when my mother corrected me at the table. Eventually, I avoided eating in front of people I did not know. Fortunately, that shame-based shyness went away after my frenotomy and subsequent tongue-retraining therapy.

The morphofunction established during early infancy, whether bad or good, spawns function in later stages of development (Defabianis, 2000; Fernando, 1998). A baby who cannot move its tongue around its mouth as part of the sucking sequence also will not be able to move the tongue around the mouth for appropriate chewing activity (whether bottle-fed or breastfed). Chewing requires a full range of motion to prepare the bolus of food – masticating it into the appropriate consistency, mixing it with saliva, and forming a glob of food that is the right-sized package for an efficient, non-threatening swallow.

Fernando (1998) comments about the inability of some toddlers to handle solid foods, no matter how the food is prepared. Their mothers continued to breastfeed them exclusively for more than two years to avoid the coughing, choking, and sputtering that accompanied attempts to feed them otherwise. Correcting the tie during infancy can prevent or minimize the development of mastication deficits.

CHAPTER FOUR TAKEAWAY

1. Tongue-tie generates multiple feeding compromises that are not specific to feeding method.

2. Tongue-tie often causes ineffective milk removal that, in turn, leads to milk stasis. Mothers may experience engorgement, plugged ducts, or other forms of breast inflammation associated with milk back-up. Babies may experience compromised weight gain, slow feeding, or frustration during feeding; they may refuse to feed altogether.

3. Sore nipples may or may not be present in the breastfeeding mother. If positioning and deep attachment alone do not correct a sore nipple problem within 24 hours, another explanation for the soreness must be considered. Soreness from tongue-tie may be mild to severe. If a mother experiences gnawing, biting, rasping, numb, tingling, burning, sharp, bruised, or achy sensations in the nipple, areola, and/or breast during or after a feed, consider tongue-tie as a possible explanation.

4. No mother should be left untreated for any length of time when nipple and breast soreness is present. Sore nipples should never occur when good management is employed and in the absence of other breastfeeding problems. Do not accept the notion that sore nipples are normal in the first two weeks. They are not, can be prevented, and should be treated immediately.

5. Breast pain may result from tongue-tie. Breast neuralgia may occur due to compromised sucking. Breast pain may also be due to milk stasis.

6. Babies who are bottle-fed may also experience feeding difficulties. Little research on the subject has been done, but studies looking at bottle-feeding compromise indicate that tongue-tied bottle-fed babies can experience problems similar to those of their breastfed counterparts. Therefore, bottle-feeding does not constitute an effective alternative feeding strategy for tongue-tied babies.

PHOTO GALLERY

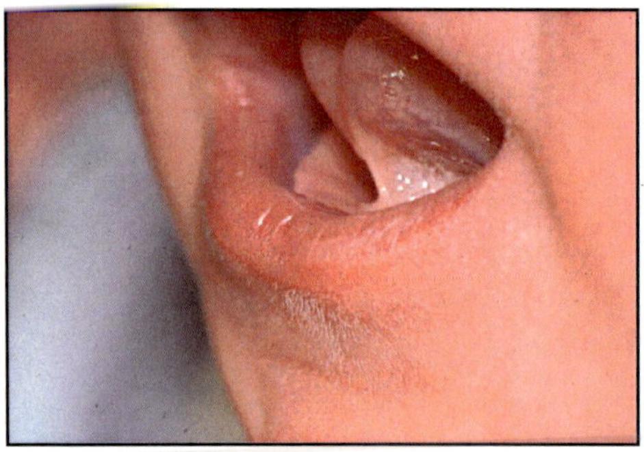

Photo 1. Heart-shaped tongue; short, tight frenulum. Classic. © Greg Notestine

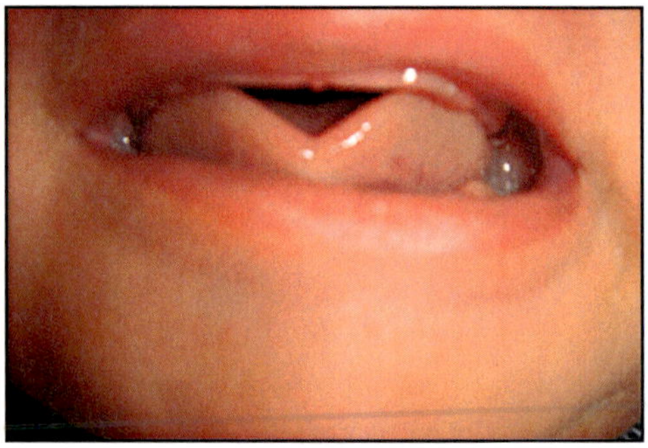

Photo 2. Heart-shaped, no lift without mouth closure. © Lisa Marasco

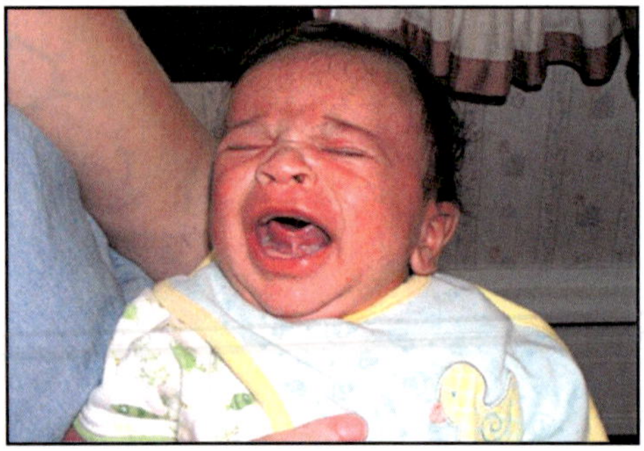

Photo 3. Impaired lift. © Jan Barger

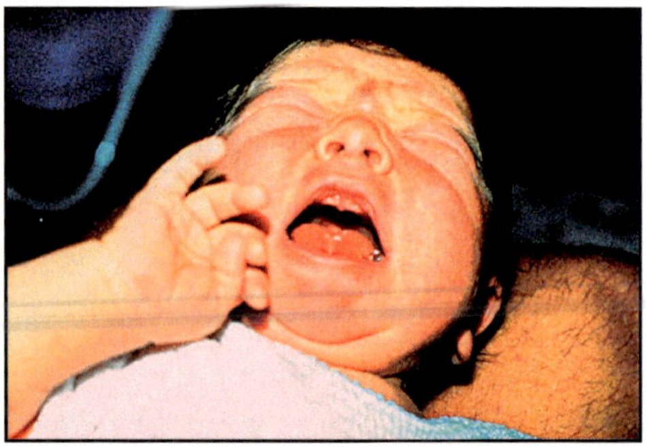

Photo 4. Author's first son just prior to frenotomy. Classic heart-shaped tongue. Thick frenulum attached at ridge and tongue-tip.© Alison Hazelbaker

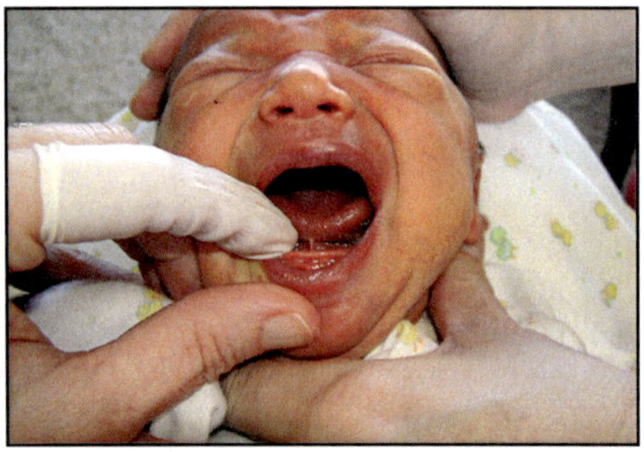

Photo 5. Very short, mid-tongue humps. © Lisa Marasco

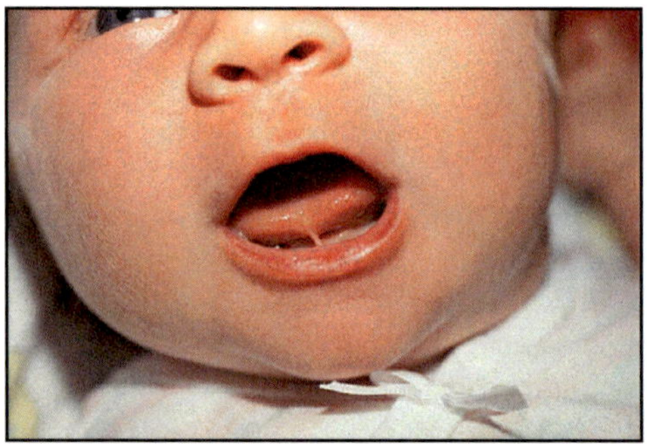

Photo 6. Thin, relatively elastic, short, at tip and ridge. © Barbara Wilson-Clay and Kay Hoover. *The Breastfeeding Atlas, 4th Edition*, 2008. Used with Permission.

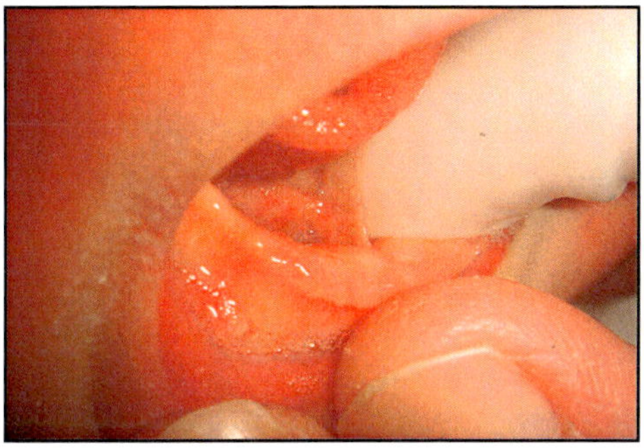

Photo 7. Tied at tip and ridge, very thin.
© Lisa Marasco

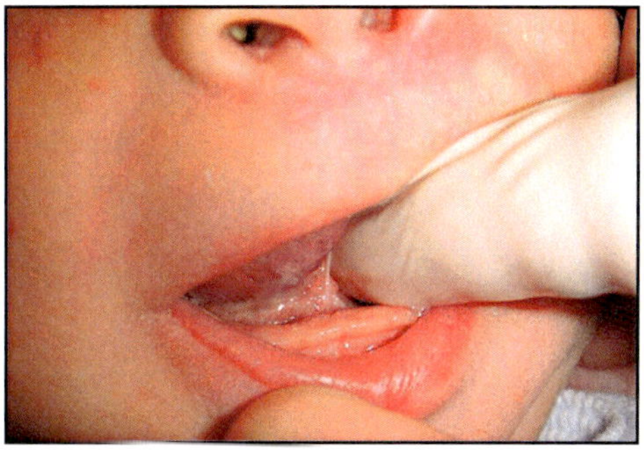

Photo 8. Short, tight, well behind ridge.
© Lisa Marasco

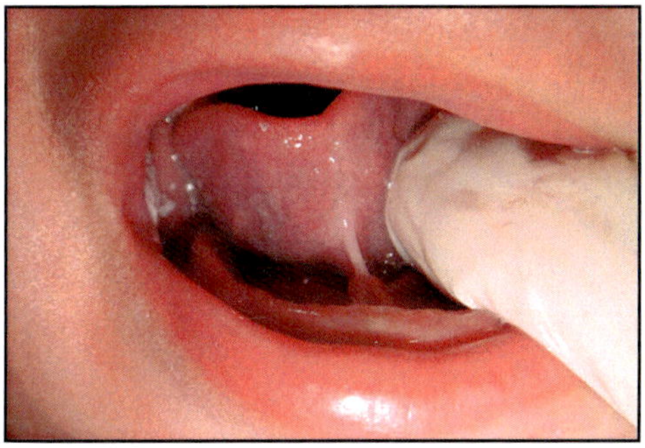

Photo 9. Posterior, short, medium thick.
© Lisa Marasco

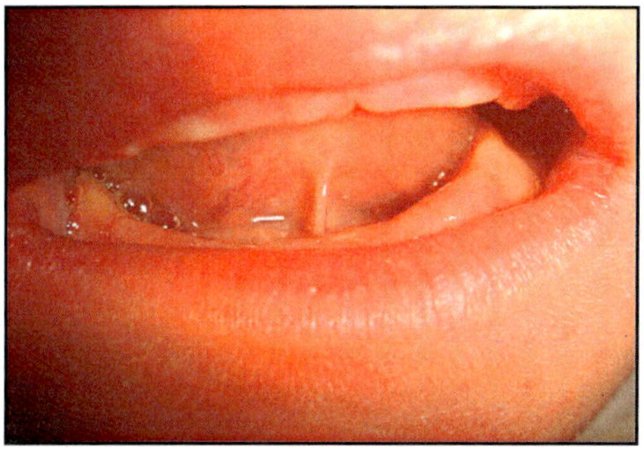

Photo 10. Thick, short, tied at ridge and behind tip.
© Lisa Marasco

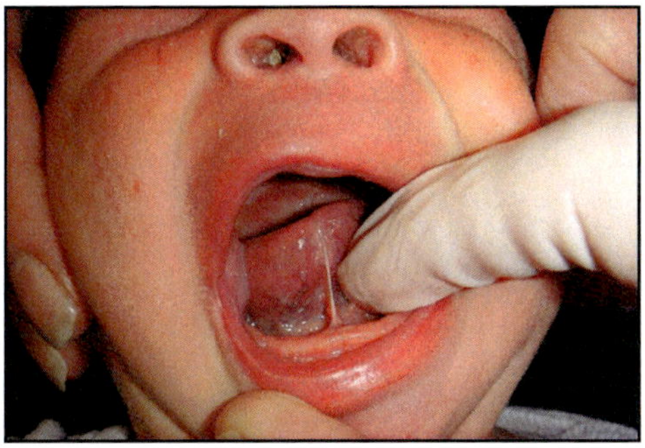

Photo 11. Thin, high on ridge, behind tip.
© Lisa Marasco

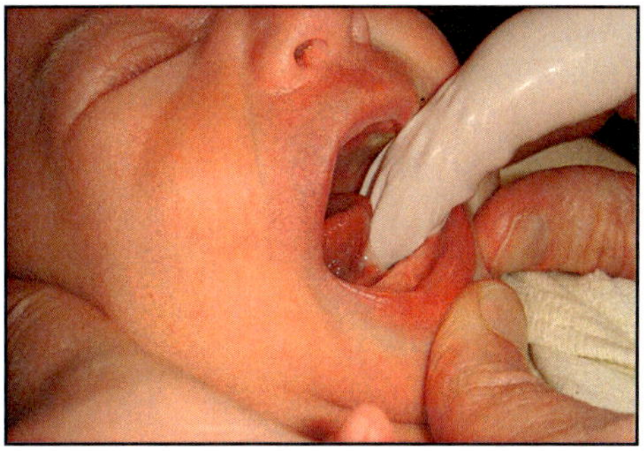

Photo 12. Diaphanous, barely visible.
© Lisa Marasco

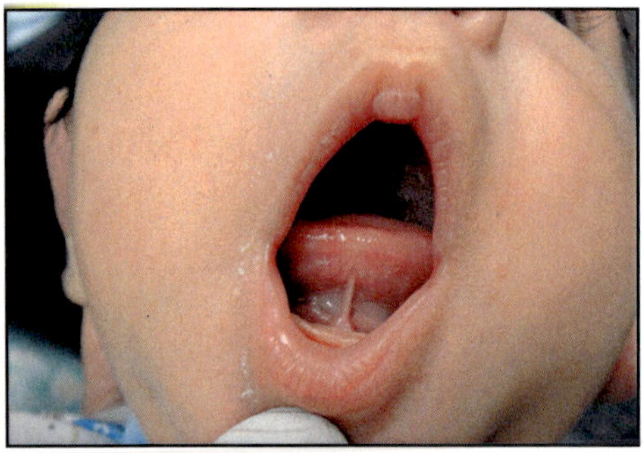

Photo 13. Moderate tie, behind tip, high arched palate. © Lisa Marasco

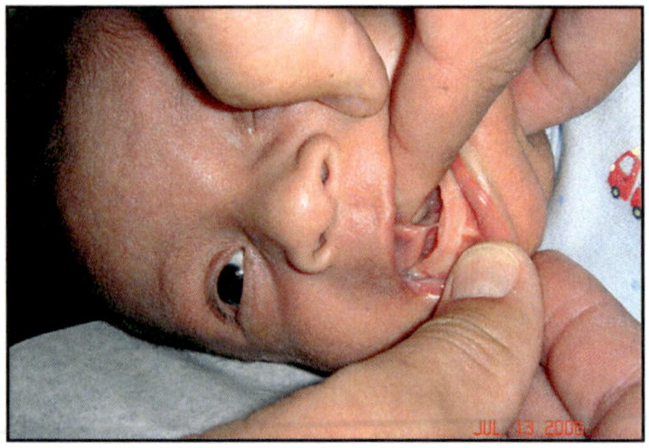

Photo 14. Extremely short, tied at ridge and tongue-tip. © Lisa Marasco

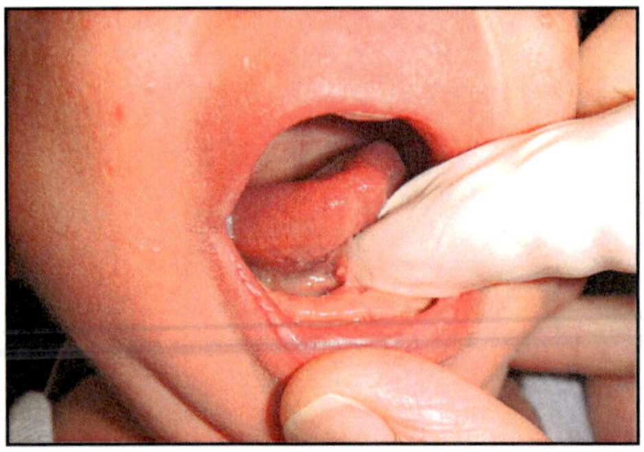

Photo 15. Short, thick and tight. © Lisa Marasco

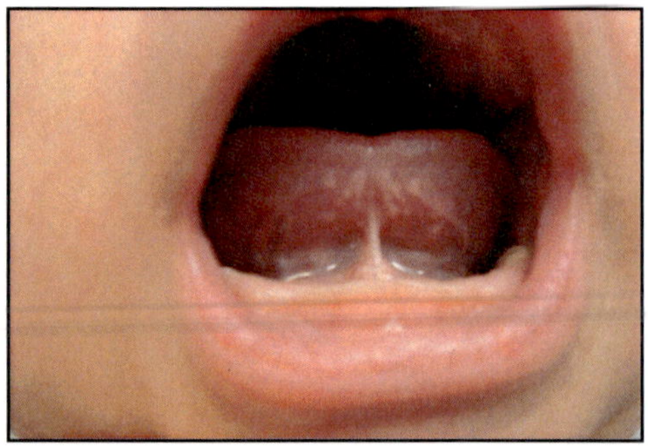

Photo 16. Short, moderately thick, behind tip, at ridge. © Lisa Marasco

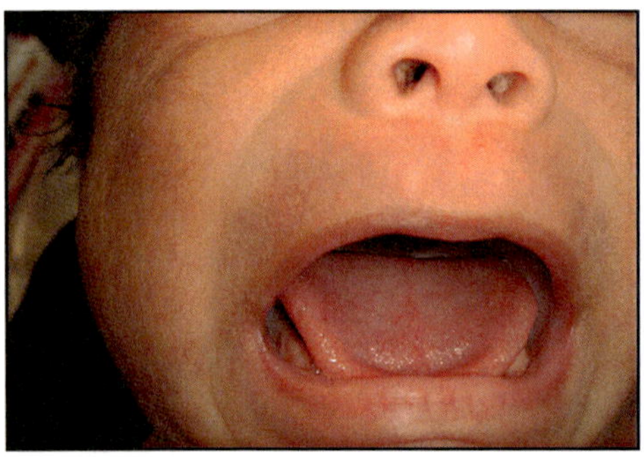

Photo 17. Back of tongue humping , anterior tongue dimple. © Lisa Marasco

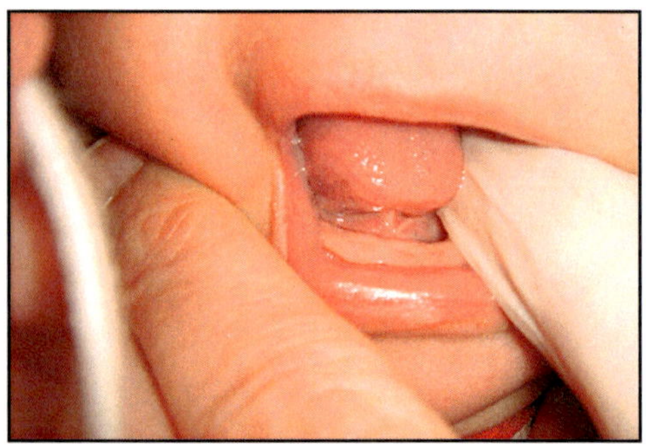

Photo 18. Checking for lateralization. © Lisa Marasco

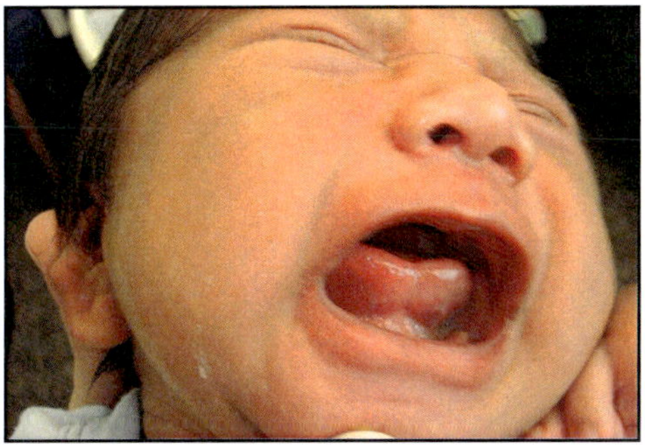

Photo 19. Non-obvious tie. Notice slight notch at tip of tongue. © Lisa Marasco

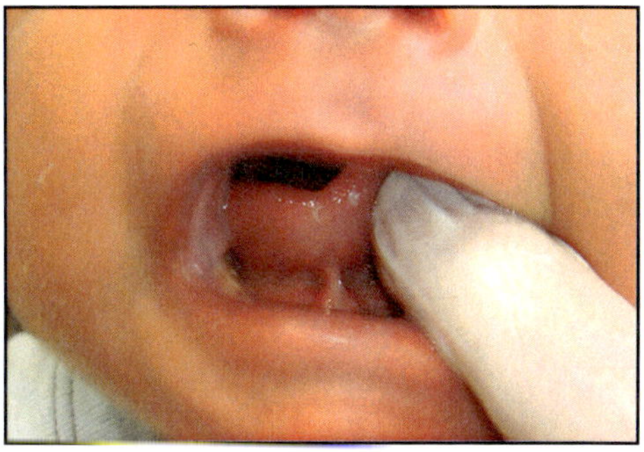

Photo 20. Non obvious tie becomes obvious when examined thoroughly. © Lisa Marasco

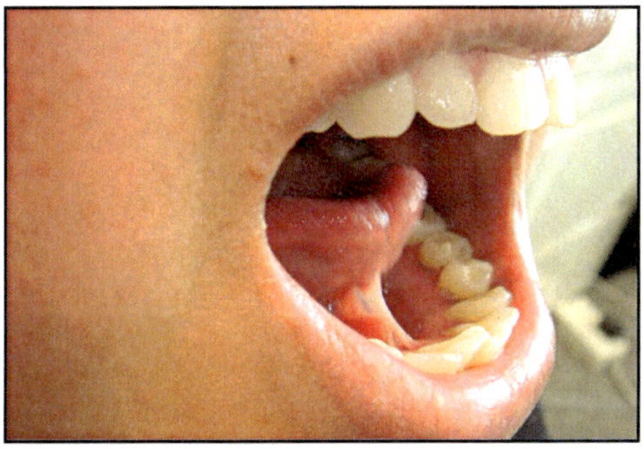

Photo 21. Tongue-tied mother of the baby with the non-obvious tie. © Lisa Marasco

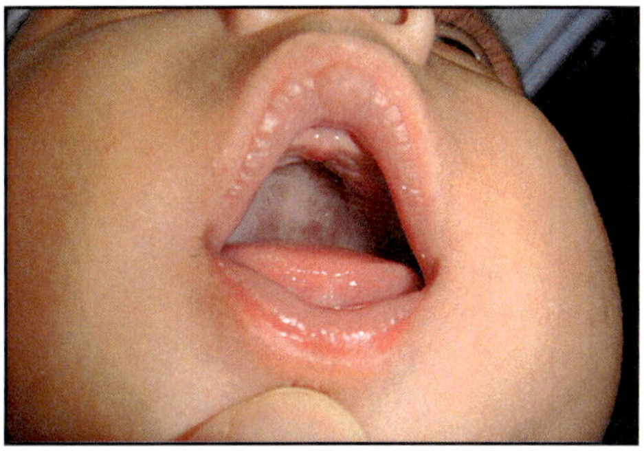

Photo 22. High arched palate.
© Lisa Marasco

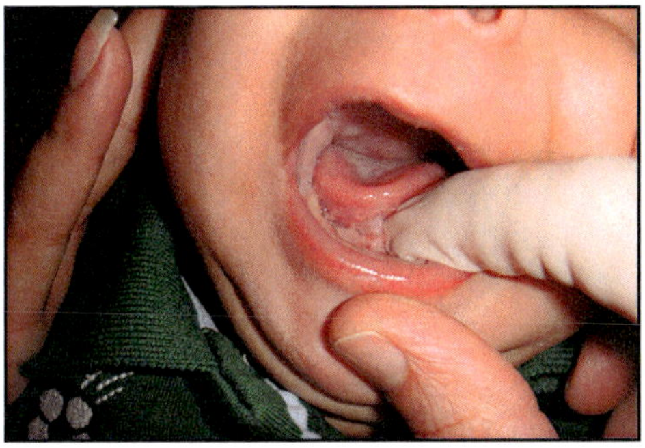

Photo 23. Anterior tongue dimple.
© Lisa Marasco

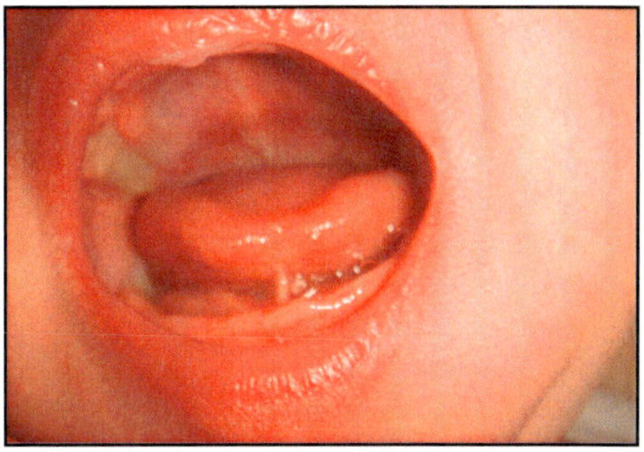

Photo 24. No thinning at tip, poor lift, backward tongue posture. © Lisa Marasco

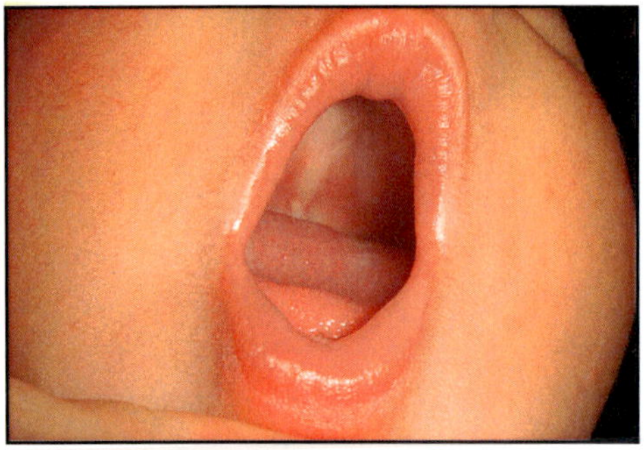

Photo 25. Mid-tongue humping.
© Lisa Marasco

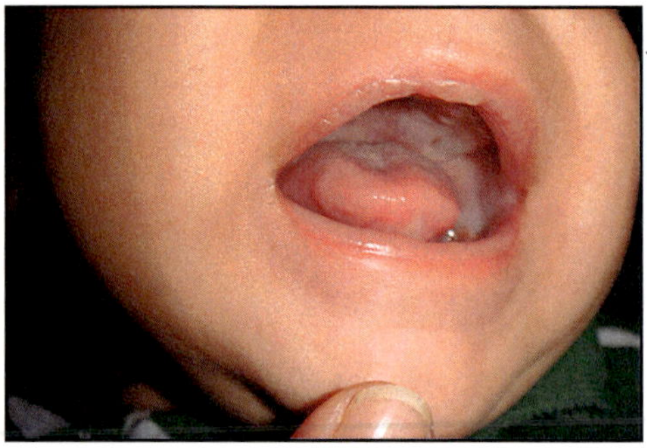

Photo 26. Bunched tongue, near square tongue edge. © Lisa Marasco

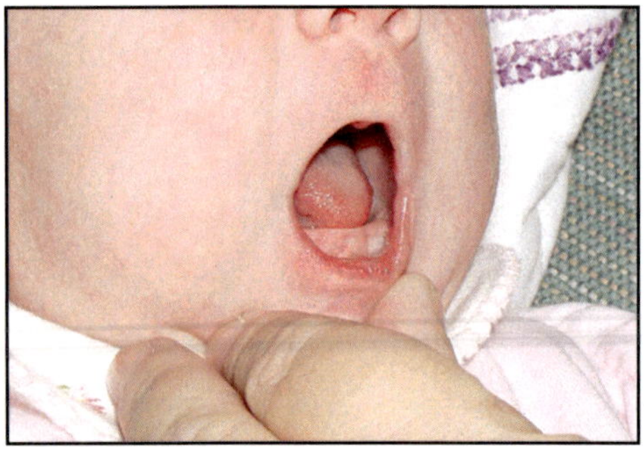

Photo 27. Bunched tongue in newborn.
© Lisa Marasco

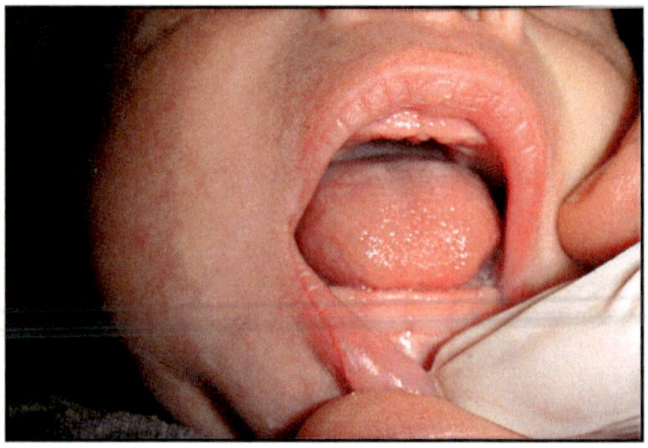

Photo 28. Tongue humping on extrusion.
© Lisa Marasco

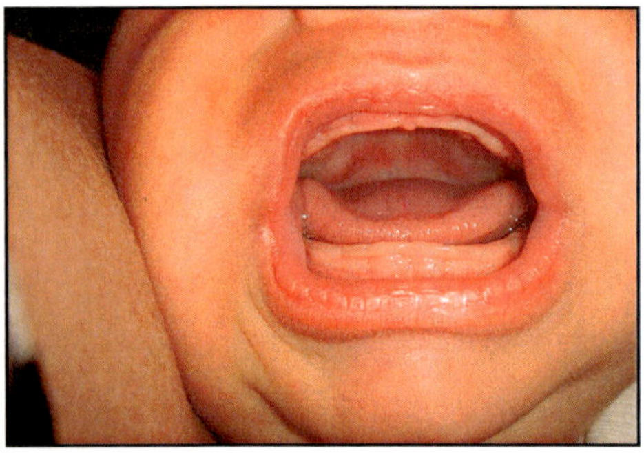

Photo 29. Side edges attempting to cup.
© Lisa Marasco

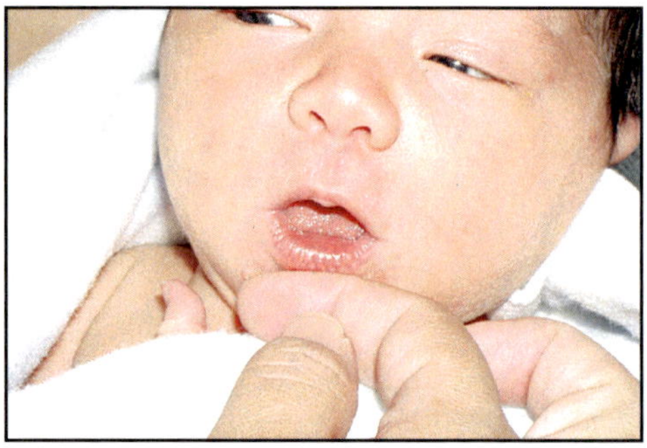

Photo 30. Poor tongue extension.
© Lisa Marasco

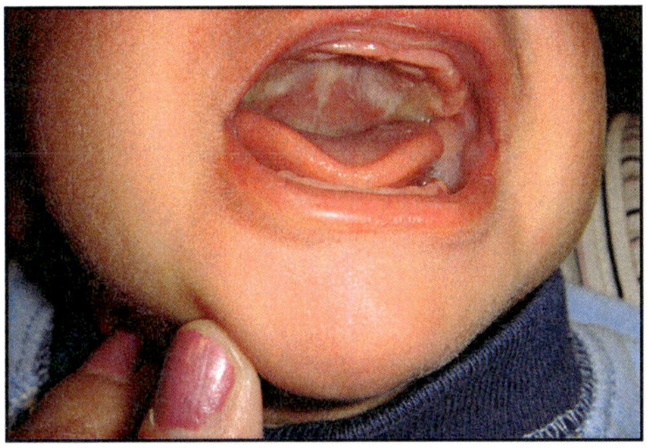

Photo 31. Good anterior spread, not able to cup. © Lisa Marasco

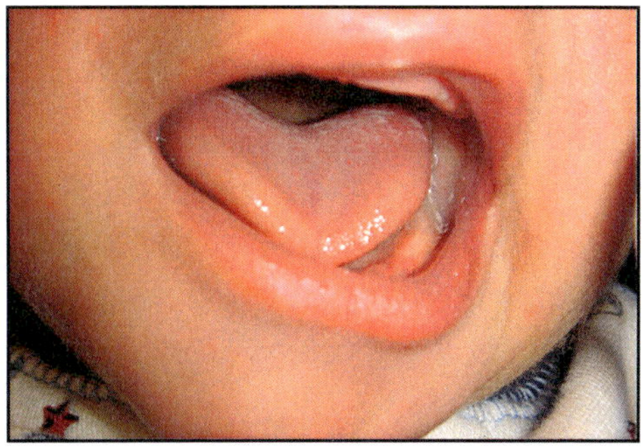

Photo 32. Anterior tongue dimple. © Lisa Marasco

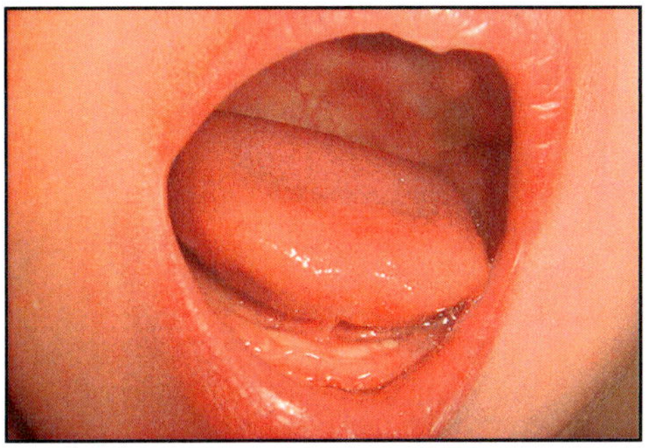

Photo 33. Absent thinning and spread for good cupping. © Lisa Marasco

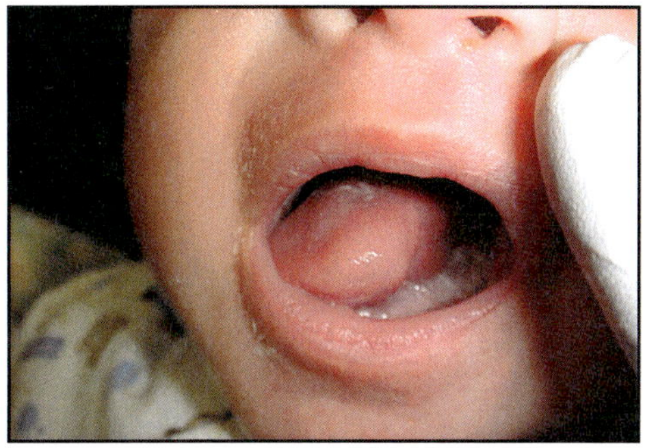

Photo 34. Good lateralization in spite of tongue-tie. © Lisa Marasco

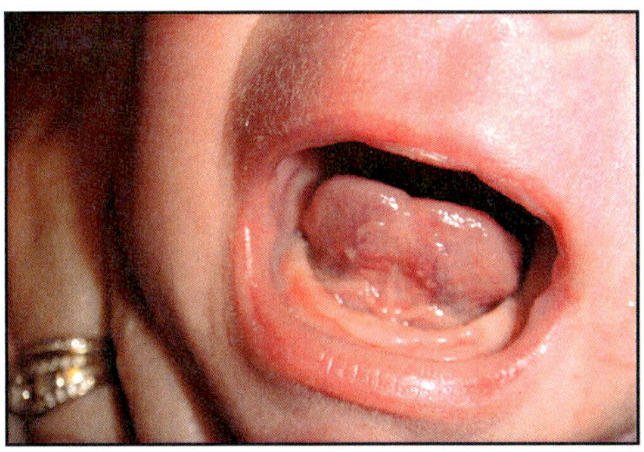

Photo 35. Good tongue lift. © Lisa Marasco

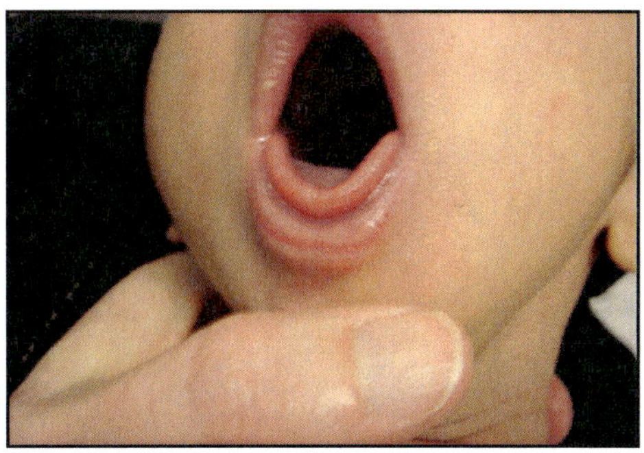

Photo 36. Excellent anterior tongue spread and cup with tongue tip and edges involved. © Lisa Marasco

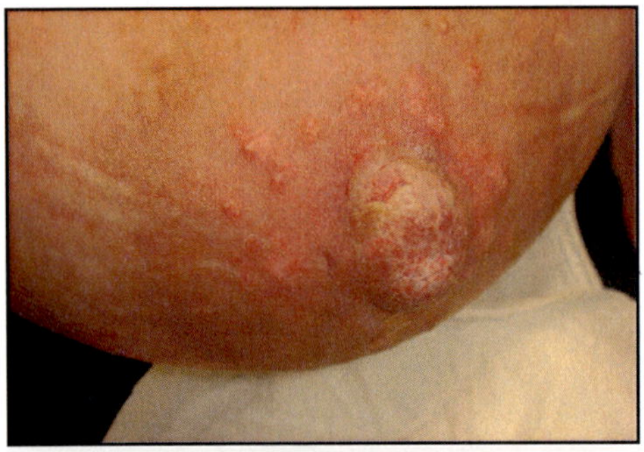

Photo 37. Nipple damage from tongue-tied baby. Notice the crust forming over wound.
© Lisa Marasco

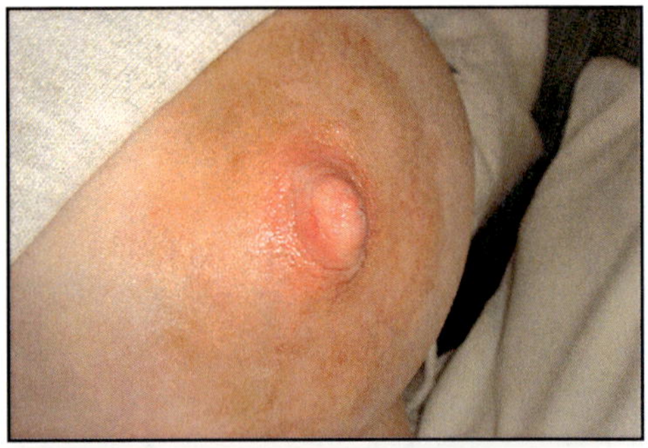

Photo 38. Nipple compression. Damaged tip tissue. © Lisa Marasco

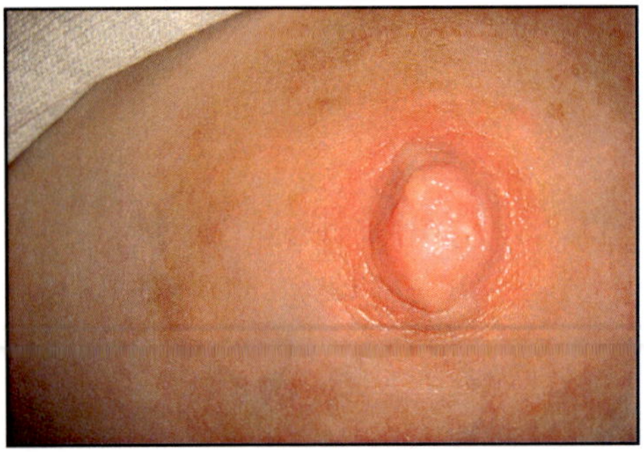

Photo 39. Nipple tip damage and inflammation. © Lisa Marasco

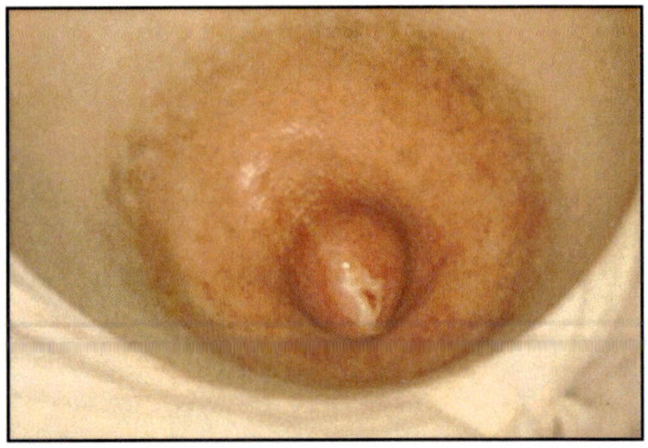

Photo 40. Nipple compression stripe.
© Barbara Wilson-Clay and Kay Hoover. *The Breastfeeding Atlas, 4th Edition*, 2008. Used with Permission.

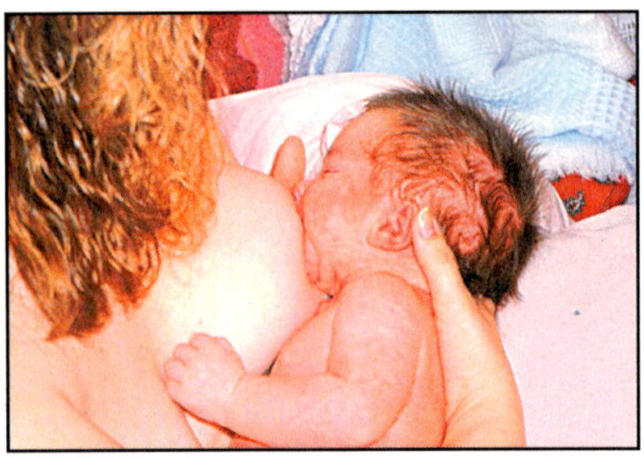

Photo 41. Pre-frenotomy. Poor latch-on.
©Alison Hazelbaker

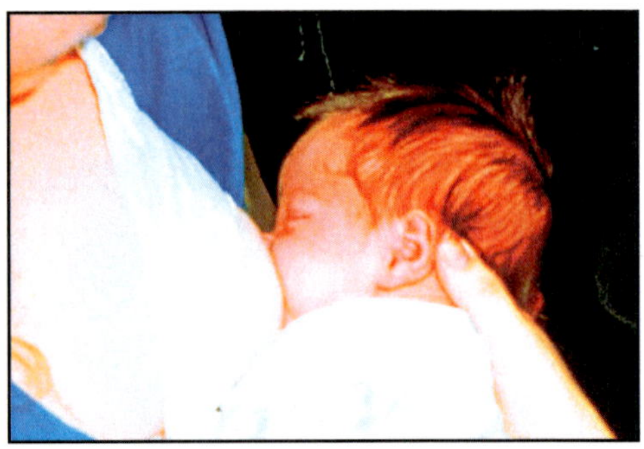

Photo 42. Post frenotomy. Improved latch-on.
©Alison Hazelbaker

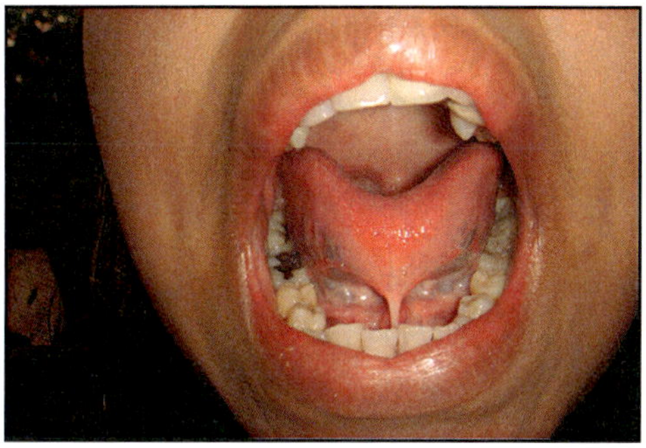

Photo 43. Severely tongue-tied mother. © Lisa Marasco

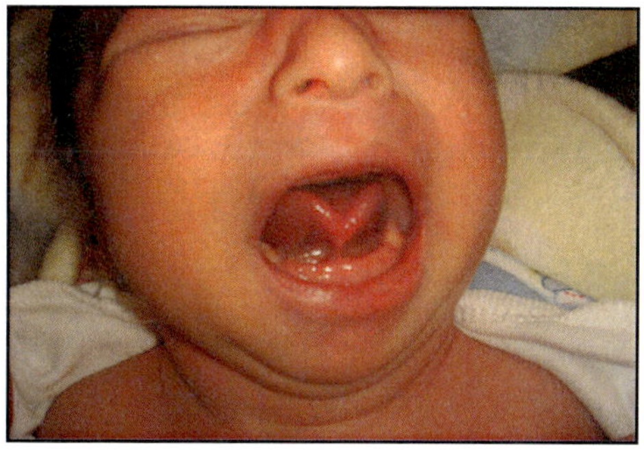

Photo 44. Baby of the severely tongue-tied mother. Notice the similarities in the presentation of their ties. © Lisa Marasco

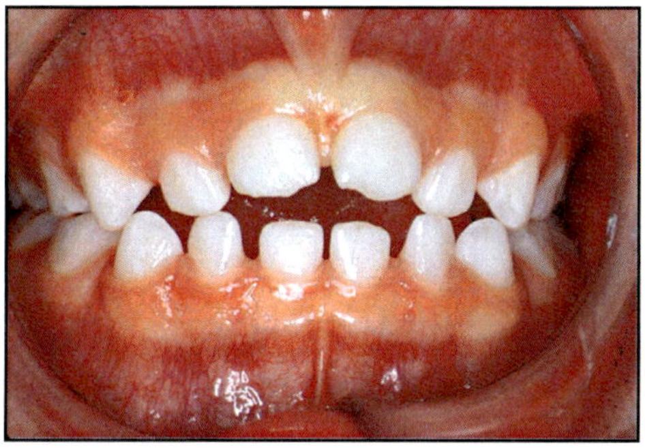

Photo 45. Open bite malocclusion from tongue thrust habit. © Brian Palmer

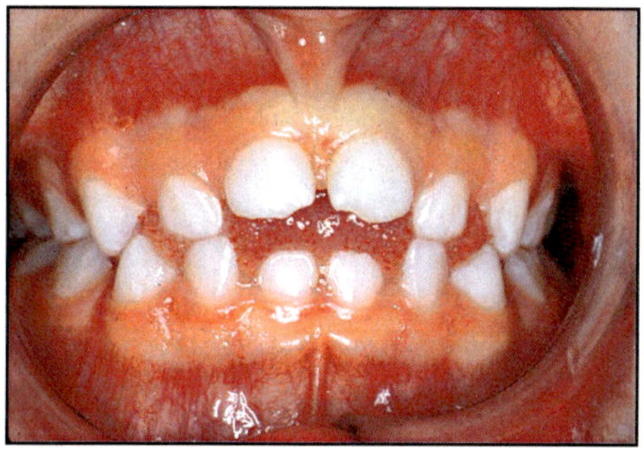

Photo 46. Same child. Notice the thrusting tongue. © Brian Palmer

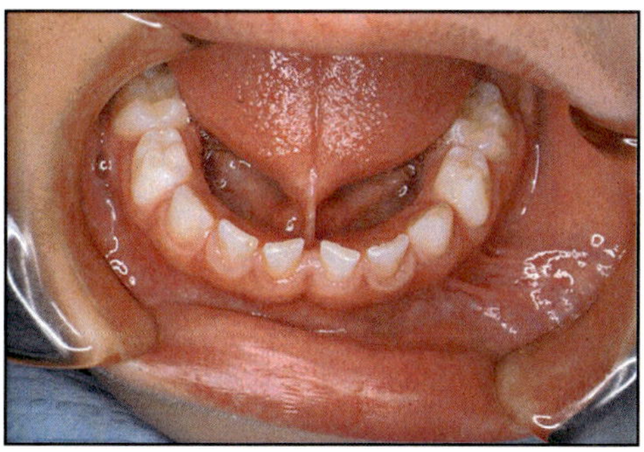

Photo 47. Tongue-tied child. Notice the pull of the tie at the lower alveolar ridge and the resulting diastema of the central incisors. © Brian Palmer

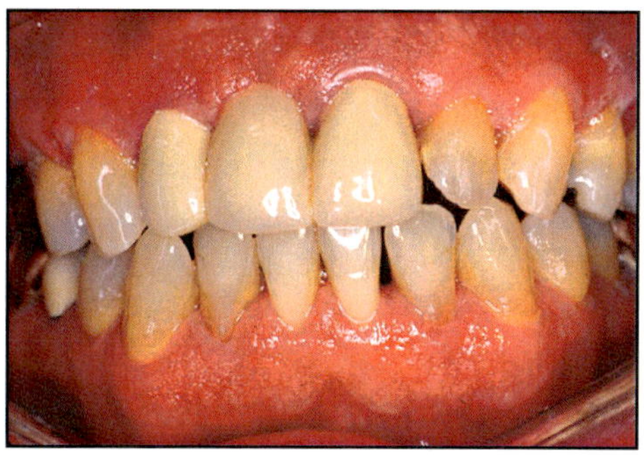

Photo 48. Open bite malocclusion from tongue thrust in an adult. © Brian Palmer

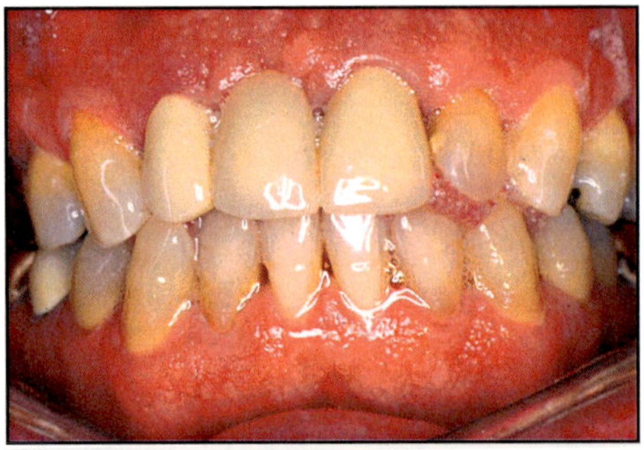

Photo 49. Same adult. Notice the tongue thrust. © Brian Palmer

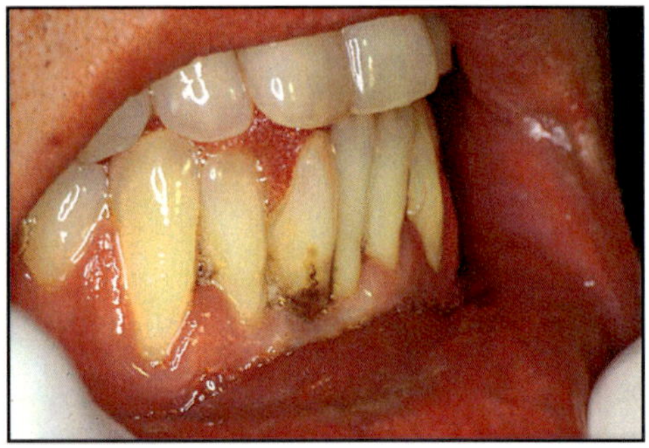

Photo 50. Loose tooth from tongue thrusting. The tooth was so damaged it had to be removed. © Brian Palmer

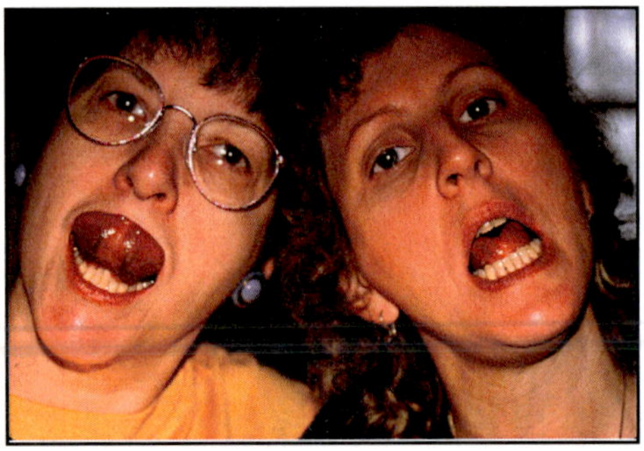

Photo 51. The author when tongue-tied as compared to her normal friend. Both are lifting their tongues. © Kay Hoover

Photo 52. Both are sticking out their tongues. © Kay Hoover

Photo 53. Both are attempting to touch their noses. © Kay Hoover

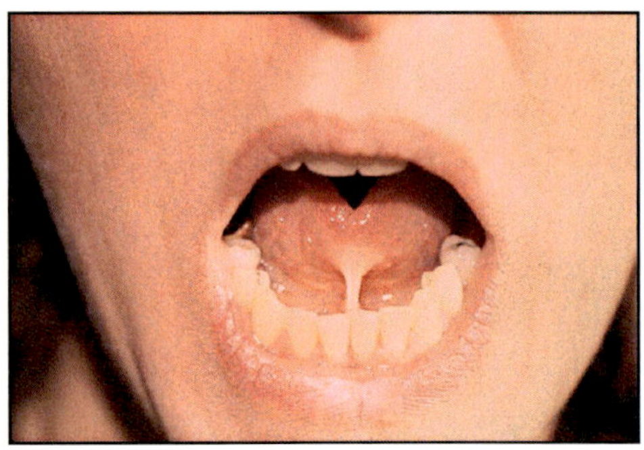

Photo 54. The author lifting her tongue pre-frenotomy. Notice the strain during the lift and the pull at the lower central incisors from the tight frenulum.
© Barbara Wilson-Clay and Kay Hoover. *The Breastfeeding Atlas, 4th Edition*, 2008. Used with Permission.

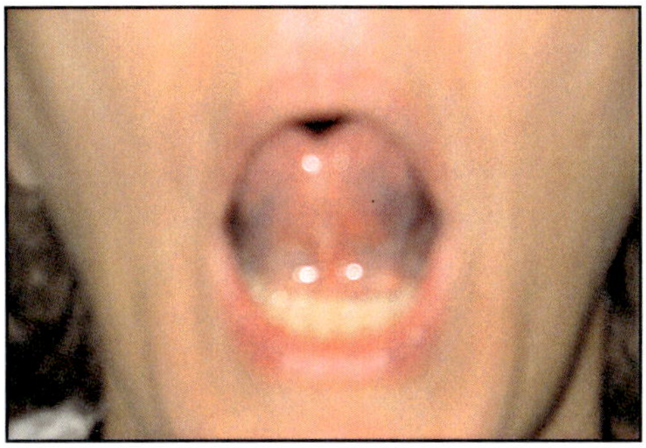

Photo 55. The author lifting her tongue post-frenotomy. Notice that she no longer strains. Also, the lower central incisors have returned to a more normal position.
© Alison Hazelbaker

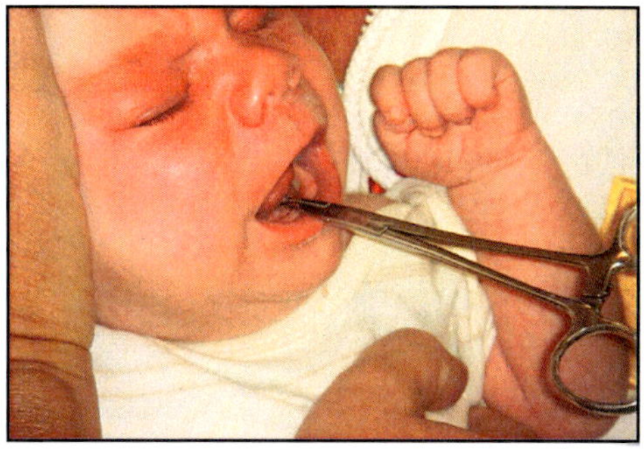

Photo 56. Hemostat placement to reduce blood loss during the frenotomy. © Lisa Marasco

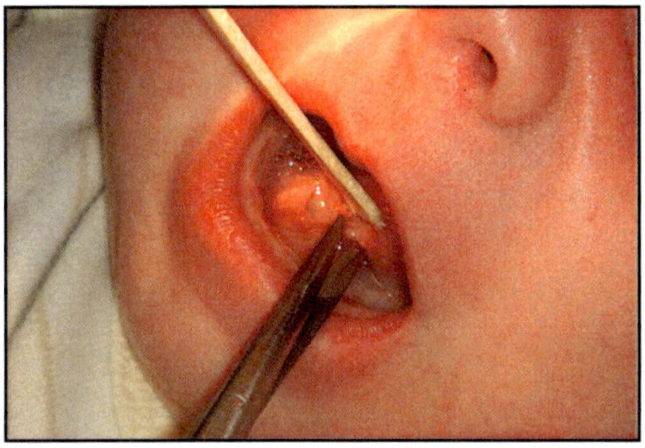

Photo 57. Same baby as prior photo. Frenotomy with a sterile scissors. © Lisa Marasco

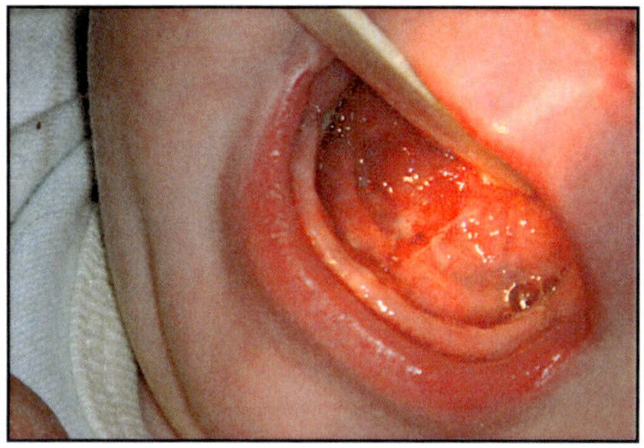

Photo 58. Same baby as prior photo. A drop of blood.
© Lisa Marasco

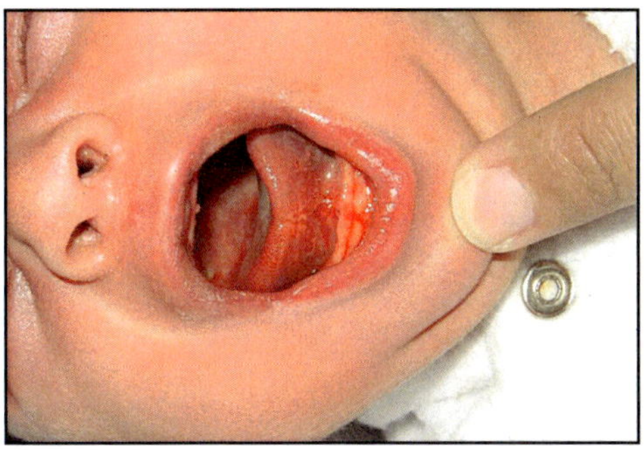

Photo 59. Different baby post-frenotomy.
A drop of blood mixing with saliva.
© Lisa Marasco

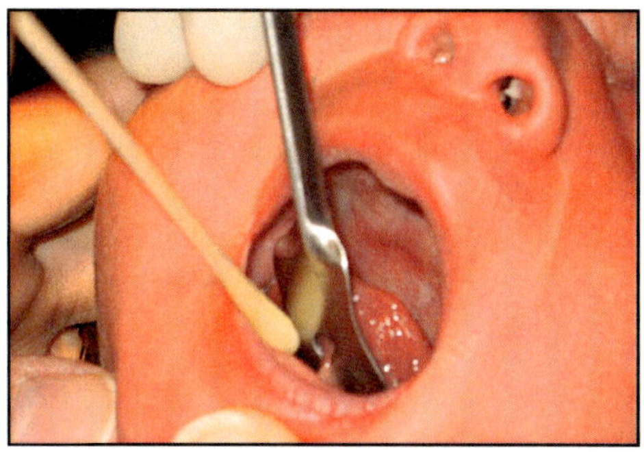

Photo 60. Using a grooved director and topical anesthetic for the frenotomy.
© Lisa Marasco

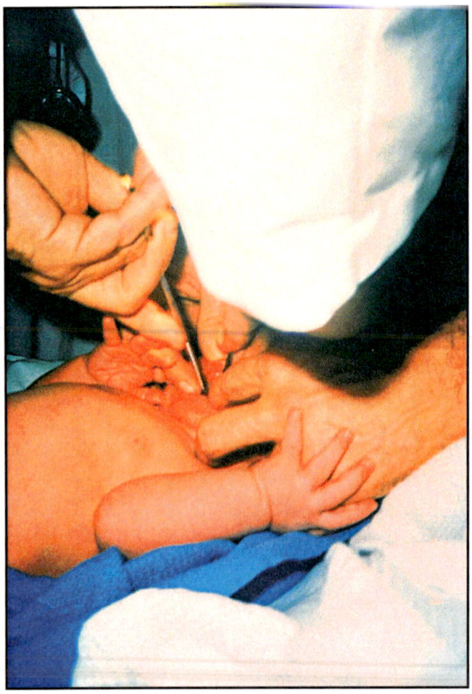

Photo 61. The author's son undergoing frenotomy at home. The pediatrician stopped by after office hours. Notice the hands stabilizing the baby's head for the procedure. © Alison Hazelbaker

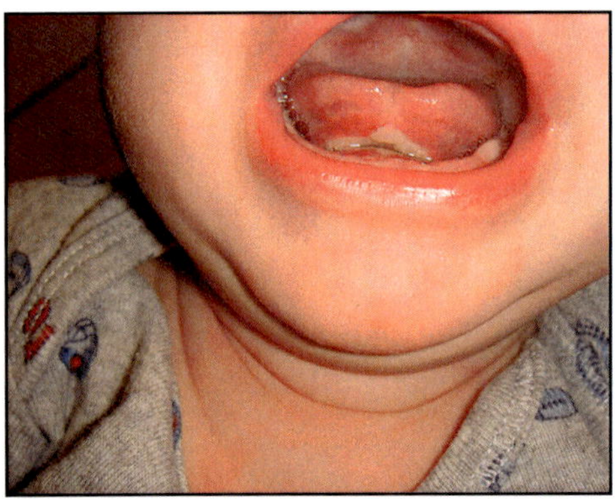

Photo 62. Reaction to electrocautery treatment. © Lisa Marasco

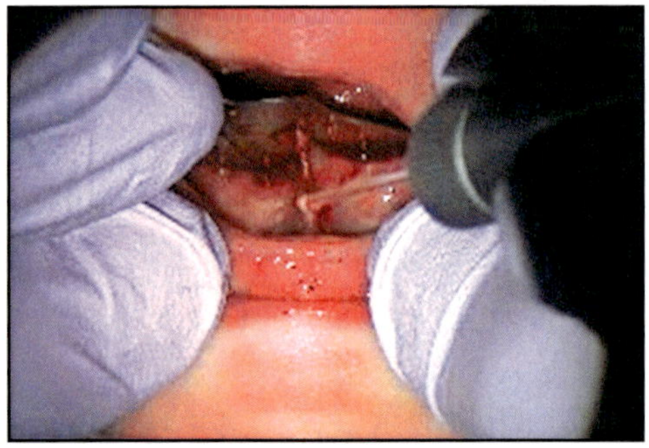

Photo 63. Frenotomy using an erbium: YAG laser and grooved director. © Larry Kotlow

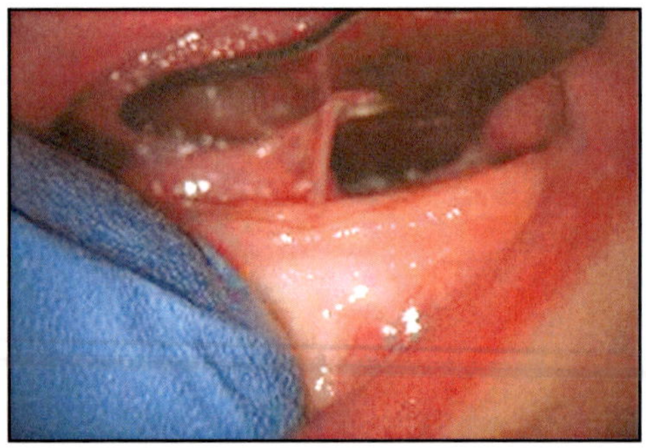

Photo 64. Commonplace tongue-tie. Notice the grooved director holding up the tongue. © Larry Kotlow

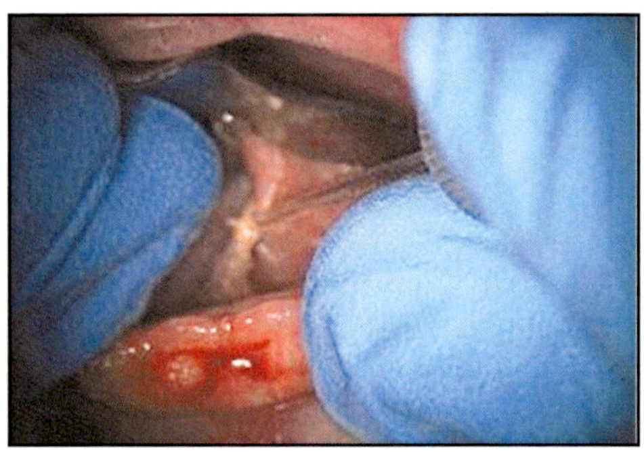

Photo 65. Frenotomy (revision) using the erbium: YAG laser. © Larry Kotlow

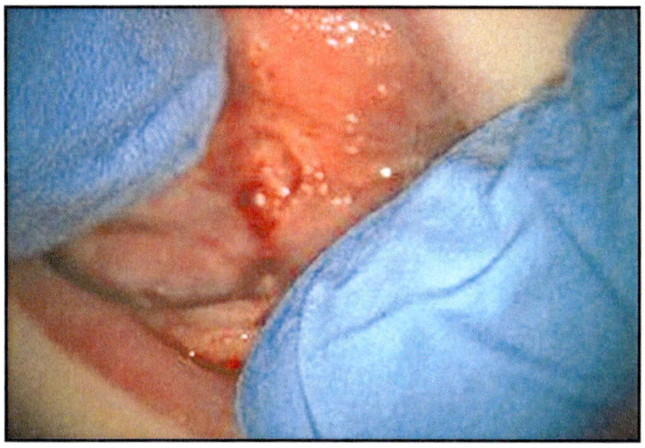

Photo 66. Diamond-shaped wound immediately post-frenotomy. © Larry Kotlow

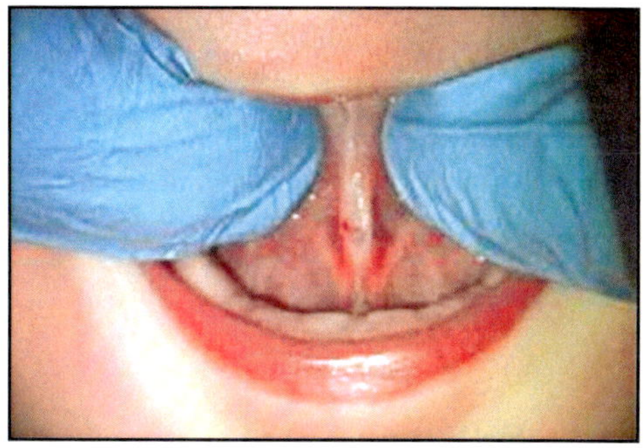

Photo 67. Excellent healing on the 4th day post-frenotomy. © Larry Kotlow

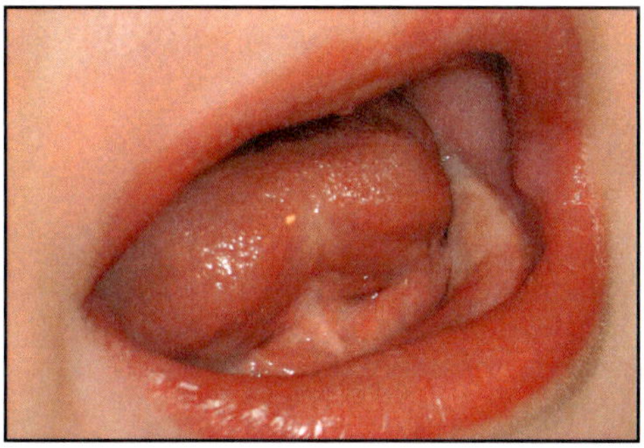

Photo 68. Posterior sub-mucousal tie prior to treatment. A "type 4" in Coryllos, Watson Genna and Salloum's typing schema. © Cathy Watson Genna

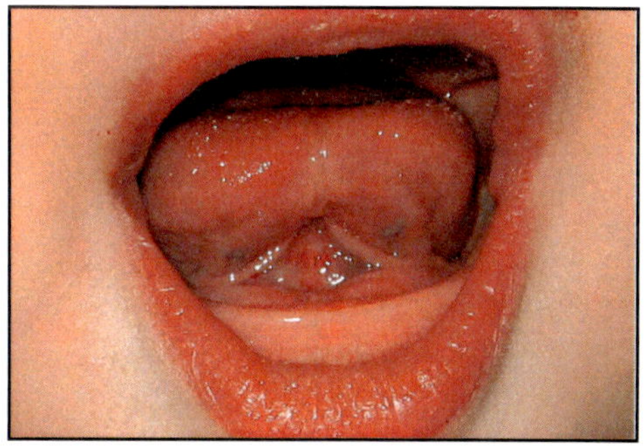

Photo 69. Same posterior tie immediately post frenotomy. Dr. Coryllos' minimal treatment did not resolve all of the tie but the treatment was sufficient to rescue breastfeeding in this 3 month old infant. © Cathy Watson Genna

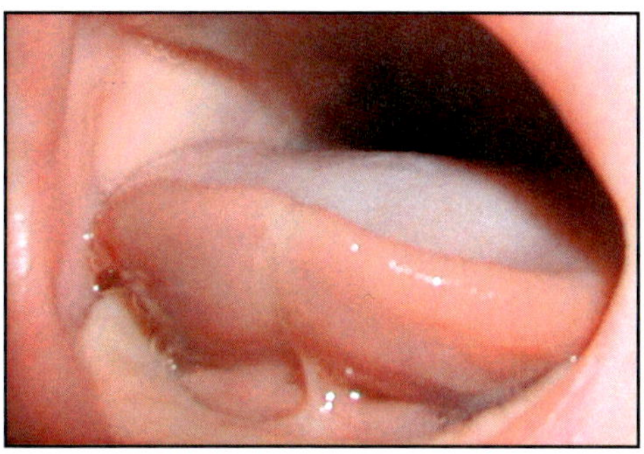

Photo 70. Posterior tongue tie. Notice the restriction of tongue lift. This is a "type 3" in the Coryllos, Watson Genna, Salloum typing schema.
© Cathy Watson Genna

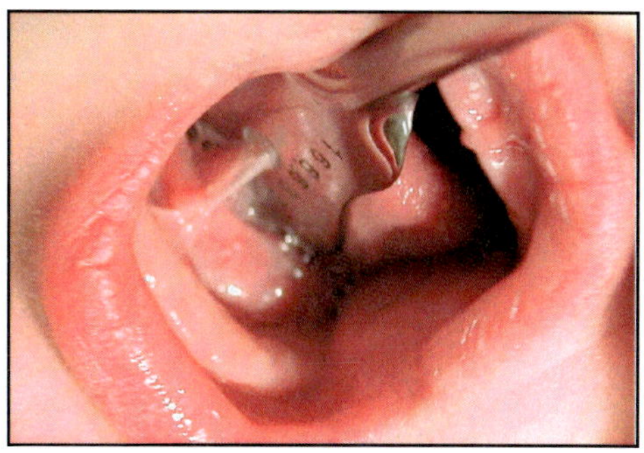

Photo 71. Same infant. Notice the change in the appearance of the lingual frenulum as it is stretched using the grooved director. © Cathy Watson Genna

CHAPTER FIVE

IMPACT: SPEECH AND OROFACIAL CONSIDERATIONS

PALMER (PERSONAL COMMUNICATION, JAN 2010) shares a story about a mother whose child had not developed speech by the age of 26 months. He couldn't protrude his tongue, but the specialists involved in his care kept telling the mother that his inability to protrude his tongue had nothing to do with his inability to speak; rather, as one speech therapist informed her, he was autistic and needed the services of a neurologist! The mother, fed up with the lack of result, went on a fact-finding mission. She uncovered information that empowered her to challenge these "experts," finally getting her ENT to relent and perform a frenotomy. Six weeks later, despite the ongoing concerns of the professionals, this young boy started talking and hasn't stopped since, much to the delight (and sometimes chagrin) of his parents.

Tongue-tie compromises the ability to make oneself properly heard, a unique and valued trait of humans. For those whose speech is adversely affected by tongue-tie, a feeling of isolation, either chosen or imposed, results. Along with tongue mobility comes freedom of expression. However, as the reader will soon see, this is not a view shared by all.

TONGUE-TIE AND SPEECH

THE PRIOR VIEW

During the mid-1900s, the research discussion focused on tongue-tie's impact on speech. Most writers of this time were not concerned at all about infant suck. In 1968, Fletcher and Meldrum conducted a study that employed a system of measuring the lingual frenulum and speech articulation testing. Their findings showed a significant relationship between anterior tongue restriction and speech articulation errors. The more restricted the tongue movement, the more articulation errors were made. These researchers were the first to develop a systematic approach for determining the impact of a short and/or tight lingual frenulum on speech. Fletcher and Daly (1974) repeated these measurements on younger children and again were able to find a significant relationship.

Prior to and concurrent with the Fletcher studies, controversy existed regarding the impact of tongue-tie on speech. MacCarthy (1964) claimed that a short frenulum was never a cause of late speech or an impairment to speaking. Hooley (1967) believed that a short frenulum only rarely interfered with tongue function and stated that speech therapists do not believe tongue-tie is the sole cause of articulation problems. He admitted, however, that a heavy, fibrous lingual frenulum that extends to the tip of the tongue can interfere with the free protrusion of the tongue. Wallace and Lond (1963) said that tongue-tie does not delay the start of normal speech. They believed that a spontaneous cure for a tight frenulum (rupture) may occur as the tongue is used in articulation efforts, but that a tight frenulum can interfere with pronunciation and the playing of wind instruments.

Oldfield, in a 1955 article, stated that "a congenitally short frenulum linguae is relatively common and, though it does not prevent a child from acquiring speech at the normal age, it does sometimes cause minor difficulties, e.g., in the pronunciation of certain consonants" (p. 528). Browne (1959, p. 952) said that the effect of a tongue-tie in older children is "a curious muffled voice," and that in one case, the child experienced "an immediate and very marked" improvement in speech articulation after his tongue-tie was treated.

Douglas and Kresberg (1954) agreed that the length and place of attachment of the lingual frenulum are factors that determine the degree of tongue-tip movement during speech and mastication, and that speech is affected when tongue-tip movement, extension, and elevation are limited. Less committed were Green and Richmond (1962), who stated "functional or neurological impairment of tongue movements may interfere with normal feeding and speech processes" (p. 64).

In 1968, Jolly, an Australian, wrote that marked ankyloglossia usually produces speech defects. Greene (1937), however, believed that the tongue plays only a relatively minor role in speech articulation and was adamant that the absence of the tongue altogether would not much matter. Greene somewhat agreed with Makuen. In 1897, Makuen remarked:

> The tongue, on account of the prominent part it plays in articulation, has ever been regarded as a synonym for speech, and yet it is not absolutely necessary, as is shown by the fact that several people are on record as having acquired very fair speech after its removal. The fact is that no tongue at all is better for speech than a diseased tongue or one that is faulty in its action. (p. 325)

Gardner (1949) and Goldberger (1973) clearly were convinced of tongue-tie's impact on speech. Gardner said:

> In applying therapy to children with speech defects, the main problem consists in the child learning to compensate for the deformity and thus produce normal speech. ... In the case of a child with tongue-tie ... the tongue is held down in the floor of the mouth on a few sounds such as the l and r. (p. 746)

Goldberger (1973, p. 670) said, "Tongue-tie restricts the action of the tongue and, therefore, can be a contributing factor to a tongue thrust habit. ... The tongue-thrust habit may cause not only a speech defect, but also an orthodontic problem. (p. 670)

Tuerk and Lubit (1959, p. 271) said, "The effect of this [ankyloglossia] on speech is so well known that the lisping type of speech produced is referred to by the layman as 'tongue-tied.'"

Despite the fact that many studies have shown a definite link between tongue-tie and articulation errors, the controversy still appeared to remain strong to the end of the century. The many authors who write about tongue-tie after 1974 seem to be adamant about their positions. Equal numbers of debaters cling to each side of the issue.

On the side that claims tongue-tie has little or no impact on speech, we find Block (1968), who defines the issue as one related to the ability of a child to compensate for limited tongue mobility. If he or she can produce the necessary sounds at all, despite the tongue-tie, then the tongue-tie is not a problem. He claims that it is the exception that a short frenulum affects speech sound production. Arena (1969) claims that tongue-tie is normal and disappears with growth of the tongue. He states that frenotomy (surgical incision) does not help speech problems.

Jones (1983) says that speech problems that may be the result of tongue-tie are resolved with time. Mangelsdorf, in her 1986 article on effective sucking, cites this same argument, using the words of popular author Penelope Leach to make the point:

> Now we know that a true 'tongue-tie' – one which will not right itself with growth – is exceedingly rare. Most of the growth of the baby's tongue during the first year of life is in the tip so that by the first birthday the tongue is fully mobile. In the meantime, its close anchorage has no effect on suckling, eating, or speech. (p. 28)

Hoekelman's 1987 textbook, Primary Pediatric Care, states that protrusion of the tongue can be limited by a thick, short lingual frenulum, but rarely does it interfere with speech. Hingley's 1990 case history of two siblings, both diagnosed with tongue-tie, did not receive treatment. Neither experienced speech problems later. Kaban (1990) says that speech problems are uncommon in the presence of tongue-tie.

In another textbook, Summitt (1990) says, "When the frenulum is attached far forward, protrusion of the tongue causes a concavity at the tip. This does not interfere with nursing nor does it produce a speech defect later in childhood." (p. 313)

Warden (1991), in agreement with Summitt, softens his statement about serious speech impediments rarely being caused by tongue-tie with, "However, even a slight impediment may cause a psychological problem." (p.252)

Of those authors who believe tongue-tie affects speech, Ketty and Sciullo (1974) note a strong connection between tongue mobility and speech. They present a case of a tongue-tied boy who was having speech articulation problems. These problems disappeared after treatment of the tie, combined with speech therapy. In *A Textbook of Oral Pathology*, Shafer, Hine, and Levy (1974) explain that tongue-tie restricts tongue function, thereby causing speech difficulties, especially with pronunciation of certain consonants and diphthongs. They claim that some cases are self-correcting, but the majority require treatment.

Ayers and Hilton (1977) report a case of a tongue-tied boy who was diagnosed with speech problems and used compensatory tongue movements to articulate certain sounds. The boy underwent a lingual frenectomy (excision of the lingual frenulum), and his speech problems resolved after the surgery and subsequent speech therapy.

Lomcali (1987) states that tongue-tie "has negatory affects on chewing, speaking, and in pronunciation of some voices" (p. 124). Fifteen of 24 tongue-tied patients who were referred to Young and Sacks, as described in their 1979 article "Examining for Tongue-Tie," had defective speech related to their tongue-ties. Both *Taber's Cyclopedic Medical Dictionary* (Thomas, Ed., 1985) and *Dorland's Illustrated Medical Dictionary* (1988) list speech difficulty as a symptom of tongue-tie. Horton et al. (1969) declare their belief that tongue-tie affects speech in this strong and succinct statement: "Does tongue-tie contribute to difficulty in rate and range of articulation? An affirmative answer must be given" (p. 16).

THE CURRENT VIEW

Despite the clinical controversy regarding speech problems generated by tongue-tie, most researchers agree that speech problems do exist as a result of an untreated tie. Their research focuses on quantifying the impact and nature of the speech problems, and cites the efficacy rate for surgical treatment.

Brinkman et al. (2004) wanted to determine consistency of opinion regarding surgical treatment of tongue-tie among modern health professionals of various fields practicing in Australia. Of 323 respondents, 80.5 percent thought reduced tongue mobility was the most legitimate reason for surgically treating tongue-tie; 65.3 percent also regarded poor speech/articulation as an indication for surgical release. Although this study does not establish the incidence of speech problems among tongue-tied individuals, the fact that so many practitioners (75 percent) reported positive results from surgical release, with or without subsequent speech therapy, indicates that these surgeons commonly observed speech problems associated with this anomaly.

Messner and Lalakea (2000a) found an even split among speech pathologists in the United States regarding the association of speech problems with tongue-tie. This survey respondent group also were equally divided on the efficacy of speech therapy for tongue-tie-related speech problems, but the majority agree that tongue-tie is effectively treated by surgical release. The authors do not cite any reason for this curious split among a group whose main clinical focus is to treat speech disorders.

In this same study (Messner and Lalakea, 2000a) otolaryngologists "are at least twice as likely as pediatricians to believe that tongue-tie is associated with a speech disorder" (p. 130). The vast majority of otolaryngologists report surgical intervention to be a successful way to alleviate speech problems. The authors suggest that pediatricians are far less likely to see patients for speech problems, and therefore are less knowledgeable about the issue as it pertains to speech.

Fernando (1998) notes that children under 3 who undergo surgical correction typically are able to self-correct through Activities of Daily Living. After this age, the impact of tongue-tie on speech and other oromotor functions increases, and so does the length of time needed to rectify the problems once the frenulum is released. The worst problem, she reports, is the deficit of the "oral kinesthetic sense" (p. 34). The ability to be aware of the geography of the mouth "results in poverty of lingual, sensory, and locomotor experiences; contributes to feeding and speech problems; and produces oral movements which are poorly controlled and limited in range and variety" (p. 35). Fernando further states:

> It is impossible to predict accurately how much disability will result from any particular untreated tongue-tie. The vast range of movements possible to healthy lingual musculature gives the individual the capability for much variation in the field of communication. (p. 2)

Agarwal and Raina (2003) note speech articulation deficits during pronunciation of "lingua-alveolar and lingua-dental consonants such as *t, d, l, n, r,* and *Th*" (p. 404). Bowen (2000) reports that tongue-tie doesn't necessarily impair speech, but that restricted tongue-movements increase the risk of speech problems. She notes that some individuals may have "imprecise articulation, especially at speed" (p. 2). Cinar and Onat (2005) conducted a retrospective study of 940 children. Of the 19 tongue-tied children, 63.1 percent experienced speech articulation problems. Of those children who had speech problems, the mothers of only three noticed their speech issues. This lack of attention may indicate that speech problems are under-reported due to failure to recognize that a problem exists.

Furer (2008) notes speech delay, stuttering, and difficulty articulating *z, sh, r, ts, d, t, l,* and *n* in his study population. He further reports that individuals may jut out their lower jaws to properly articulate labial and dental letters *d, tl'n, z,* and *s'sh*. His article underscores the notion that speech articulation errors may be more or less severe, depending on the language spoken – in this case, Hebrew.

Garcia Pola and Gonzalez Garcia et al. (2002) identify lingual dysglossia in their study cohort.

They define the dysglossia as an inability to pronounce the rolling Spanish *r*; rather the sound comes out as a soft *r*. The presence of dysglossia was an indication for surgical treatment.

Klockars (2007) determined the tongue-tie "pedigree" in a Finnish family. Thirteen members of 26 from three generations were tongue-tied. Several were examined by the study author. All but one experienced speech articulation errors (*d*, *l*, alveolar *r*). Several more not examined by the author were reported also to have articulation errors. Heller, Gabbay, O'Hara, Heller, and Bradley (2005) noted persistent articulation errors in their study population. They evaluated the nature and severity of the speech problems using a four-grade scale. Post-treatment, depending on the type of frenectomy performed, 91 percent of their cohort demonstrated one to four orders of improvement in speech.

In a literature review, Lalakea and Messner (2002) found multiple studies showing that some, but not all, tongue-tied individuals have difficulty with the rate and range of articulation, therefore decreasing their intelligibility. In another study designed to measure speech articulation changes after surgical intervention, these same authors found a significant improvement in speech intelligibility. They adamantly point out that tongue-tie does not cause speech delays – a sentiment mirrored by several other authors (Klockars, 2007; Kupietzky and Botzer, 2005; Wright, 1995).

Marchesan (2004) looked specifically at incidence of speech disorders in a tongue-tied population. Of 1,402 patients seen at her clinic for speech problems, 9 percent were classified as tongue-tied, and 48.81 percent had speech problems. These problems included omissions and substitutions of phonemes; frontal and lateral lisps; distortions and imprecise pronunciation; closer approximation of the maxilla and mandible; excessive lateral and anterior mandibular movements; and excessive production of saliva. Parida (2008) suggests that severity of tongue-tie is positively correlated with speech articulation problems: The worse the tie, the greater the impact on speech.

Kummer (2005) instructs her American Speech-Language-Hearing Association (ASHA) readers that most lingual-alveolar sounds can be made without much effort from the tongue. She indicates that the sounds most likely to be affected by tongue-tie are the lingual alveolar */l/* and the interdental */th/*, albeit rarely. She suggests that tongue-tie and speech problems are coincidental occurrences rather than cause–effect events. She proposes that the tongue-tied individual learn to make the sounds clearly by using his or her tongue in a compensatory manner. She cautions that leading parents and affected individuals to believe that speech will improve post-frenotomy may disappoint them.

In stark contrast, Fernando (1998), also a speech-language pathologist, emphasizes that speech symptoms due to tongue-tie may manifest in a variety of ways: articulation; voice; fluency; and/or development of language. She stresses the importance of thorough evaluation of speech because tongue-tied individuals and their parents often do not know that a speech disorder exists and will not report symptoms accurately. Often patients develop "masking" or compensatory strategies to hide a symptom or distract the listener. Perhaps this same tendency to compensate showed up in Kummer's above-noted population?

Compensation strategies often seen in Fernando's 1998 study cohort were "talking slowly, quietly, in a monotone, in short sentences or with the mouth nearly shut," permitting the individual to enunciate "clearly enough" (p. 25). She remarks that nonverbal aspects of communication, such as pitch, rhythm, volume, and variations of facial expression also can be negatively affected by tongue-tie. She asserts:

> Sifting of the information received will show that speech only appeared to be normal because of the small demands made on the patient at earlier developmental levels. Speech assessment must include testing the ability of the patient to speak clearly in connected speech; with lengthy utterances; and with changes of speed, pitch, and volume. Voice quality must also be checked, since these patients often show a tendency to become dysphonic or excessively nasal under stress. A striking finding in the study was that, contrary to popular opinion, the lingual sounds were not the only, or even the primary, sounds to be defective in the speech of patients with tongue-tie. Very often, sounds that were quite clear in isolation or even in single words were produced incorrectly in sentences, or 'connected' speech. Where specific sounds are consistently defective, lingual sounds are as likely to be affected as any other. Tongue thrusting on sibilants is often present – which was an unexpected finding of the study. In fact, such thrusting is highly consistent with the disability. (p. 26)

Personally, I had difficulty with articulation that continually declined the longer, louder, or faster I had to speak. Very commonly, people asked me to repeat what I said. I slowed down my speaking to be sure the consonants were understandable. I especially had difficulty with *s*, *l* and *Th*. Since my frenotomy, I have had articulation issues only rarely, but I still stumble if I am speaking quickly or feel fatigued. Until I saw a speech-language pathologist who was also an expert on the post-surgical treatment of tongue-tie-related speech disorders, I did not realize I had a classifiable speech problem; nor did my parents. I just knew I had to work harder than others to speak clearly. I was accused of mumbling more times than I care to admit, which only served to make me more self-conscious and less likely to speak up.

The psychological consequences of speech disorders have yet to be fully quantified and appreciated. The Cinar and Onat (2005) study indicates that the children with tongue-tie-related articulation problems were no more shy than their non-tied peers. Shyness, however, was the only social factor investigated. Fernando (1998) assesses emotional disturbances related to an individual's tongue-tied condition. She sees behavioral disturbances often enough to consider them an important indication for surgical treatment.

Lalakea and Messner (2003a) performed a study with adolescents and adults. The most common finding among the participants was speech difficulty. Nearly half indicated that they felt embarrassed by their tongue-tie; just over 25 percent were teased by "childhood peers," and 60 percent wished they had received surgical treatment when they were children (p. 748).

OROFACIAL/DENTAL DEVELOPMENT AND THE DEVIATE SWALLOW

Writers often overlook the impact tongue-tie has on orofacial development. Aside from the potential harm to proper orofacial development from bottle-feeding (Picard, as cited in Garliner, 1976) and tongue-tie's indirect role in that negative impact (premature weaning from the breast resulting from untreated tongue-tie), tongue-tie has a direct influence on orofacial development and proper swallowing. It seems logical and obvious that restricted movement of the tongue would have a negative impact on orofacial muscular balance and deglutition, depending on how severe the restriction. As the lead set of muscles in the orofacial muscular complex, the tongue has a unique and essential role in deglutition and subsequent orofacial development.

THE DEVIATE SWALLOW

Garliner, the creator of myofunctional therapy, has written extensively on the factors that contribute to what he calls the deviate swallow. During proper swallowing, the tongue-tip is supposed to rise to a point on the hard palate just behind the maxillary incisors as the forward-to-back progressively contractile motion of the tongue begins. This progressive contractility propels food back into the pharynx for swallowing.

In a deviate swallow, the tongue does not rise to this point, and the proper wavelike action of the tongue is impeded. Instead, the tongue-tip may move elsewhere in the mouth, putting substantial pressure against oral structures that are not capable of withstanding such pressures. This, in turn, causes other orofacial muscles to be used incorrectly, more than necessary, or not at all. When the tongue applies pressure against the dentition, the masseter muscles are inactive, the mentalis is active, and the orbicularis oris has little or no movement against the dentition or moves with too much force against the upper central teeth. Garliner (1968, p. 301) reminds us that "maintenance of a satisfactory occlusal relationship depends on concomitant balance of the oral musculature."

Researchers report that the average individual swallows 2,000 times every 24 hours (Straub, as cited in Garliner, 1974). The force of this intermittent swallowing applies 3,000 to 12,000 pounds of accumulated pressure somewhere in the oral orifice. Garliner (1974) explains:

> The muscles of the oro-facial complex in conjunction with the anterior or posterior movement of the lead muscle, the tongue, create an environment in which they, the muscles, can operate. If the dentition is in the way, the lead muscle, the tongue, asserts its dominance over the dentition and pushes it out of the way. ... It is not difficult, therefore, to visualize that the erroneous placement of this pressure against the dentition, rather than against the hard palate, could create significant problems in occlusion.... Abnormal oro-facial muscle function will not permit an existence of a normal and stable occlusal relationship. (p. 11)

Similarly, Goldberger (1973) has this to say about tongue-tie and tongue-thrust:

> Tongue-thrust, or reverse swallowing, is evidenced by the incorrect placement of the tongue between the upper and lower teeth in swallowing and at rest. There are four types of tongue-thrusts. ... All four types of tongue-thrusting affect the formation of the teeth. ... Tongue-tie restricts the action of the tongue and, therefore, can be a contributing factor to a tongue-thrust habit. (p. 667)

She goes on to say that tongue-thrust can not only cause speech defects, but also orthodontic problems. She recommends eliminating the causes of tongue-thrust so that the teeth can move back into a normal occlusal relationship.

Garliner (1974) specifies that the short lingual frenulum can cause the tongue to move outward between the teeth, forward and downward toward the teeth, or downward toward the lower teeth – all of which produce a tongue thrust and deviate swallow. Fernando (1998) refers to this tongue thrusting as a persistent infantile swallow. She found an infantile swallow repeatedly in her study cohort. Very often, the infantile swallow generated open-bite malocclusions and lisping. She notes that some cases of speech problems due to tongue thrusting do not correct until the infantile swallow disappears with the increased control resulting from post-surgical speech therapy exercises.

OROFACIAL DEVELOPMENT

Watson Genna (2008, p. 183) discusses compromise in orofacial development in utero. The tongue plays a major role in creating and spreading the palatal shelves during gestation. Restriction of normal in utero tongue-movements, as in the case of tongue-tie, may result in a narrow, high-arched palate. Not every tongue-tied person presents with this type of palate at birth, and the incidence of such a morphofunctional finding is unknown. However, this palatal presentation occurs often enough to be reported over and over in anecdotal accounts.

One of my tongue-tied sons was born with a high-arched and narrow palate, and the other was not. The former had a more severe tie with severe tongue mobility restriction due to a thick, short, and inelastic frenulum that inserted at the very tongue tip. The latter son had a thin, relatively elastic frenulum that was attached behind his tongue-tip. Each had his frenulum clipped at less than 24 hours post-birth. Would one have had dental and swallowing issues and the other not? Based on my personal experience in regard to these issues, I wasn't willing to take the risk of either son developing these problems.

Early in the discussion of tongue-tie, Horton and Crawford et al. (1969) referred to the role it plays in open-bite malocclusion and prognathism:

> The growing tongue of the infant can be raised to the roof of the palate with the mouth open. Any band or condition restricting freedom of motion of the tip of the tongue and preventing it from touching the anterior palate may interfere with the development of

> the adult swallow and perpetuate the infantile swallow, resulting in an open bite deformity. Here the plastic release of the ankylosis of the tongue is an important adjunct to orthodontia. Bone growth and molding are markedly influenced by function and by the stress and strain applied. The forces responsible for the molding of bones include function, gravity, and those applied by soft tissues. ... The jaws, which grow in utero along a mostly hereditary pattern, develop after birth under the influence of their function. As growth proceeds, well-proportioned tongue thrust [tongue thrust here refers to the forward pressure of the tongue during proper deglutition], repetitive during deglutition against both maxillary and mandibular arches, helps control their harmonious forward and lateral growth so that normal facial proportions are maintained. ... any limitation of the upward motion of the tongue, which directs tongue-thrust forward only, will result in excessive growth of the anterior portion of the mandible. (p. 13)

Tuerk and Lubit (1959) remind us, as do Horton and Crawford et al. (1969), that bone is plastic and yields to pressure, abnormal swallowing contributes to jaw malformations and facial deformities, and that tongue-tie causes improper development of the swallow, which leads to open bite and prognathism of the mandible. Whitman and Rankow (1961) claim that abnormal anatomy, such as tongue-tie, influences tongue function, which in turn influences tooth position. Lomcali (1987) comments, as well, on the role the lingual frenulum plays in facial development:

> For the reason the tongue is a muscular organ, which serves us to taste, swallow, masticate, and speak, it is known that it has some affects upon dental arches and jaws during its physiologic functions. The damage or disorder of the functions which the tongue participates, will cause some differentiations in adjacent tissues. ... Ankyloglossia...is a dental defect. (p. 124)

Defabianis discusses "mesial drift" in her 2000 case report (p. 28). The soft tissue pressure caused by the tongue and cheek contacts against the dentition caused shifts in tooth position over time. She also talks about how low tongue posture and "large, thick tongues are associated with maxillary hypodevelopment, mandibular hyperdevelopment and tongue-related problems" because the tongue is a "morphogenetic organ," and its posture and the subsequent placement of its pressures during swallowing lead to negative consequences in orofacial development. She further states:

> Intrinsic genetic factors play only an initial role in determining size, shape and growth of a bone; extrinsic functional or environmental factors become the predominant determinator of bone form. Since the environment is constantly changing, bones never attain a final morphology and their shape is continuously changing. ... The 'environmental' soft tissues of the tongue must be evaluated very carefully too. The floor of the mouth can be palpated and one can imagine that a soft, depressible floor of

> the mouth can help adapt a large tongue to a small tongue box. On the contrary, a very strong, tense floor of the mouth does not leave much freedom for soft tissue compensation ... Sometimes, such confinement of a normal tongue to a "tongue box" restricted by the environmental musculature – without much freedom for soft tissue compensation – may trigger pathogenetic morphogenetic action on both the upper and the lower jaws. (pp. 31–32)

Ruffoli et al. (2005) correlated degree of tongue-tie (as measured by interincisal distance) with morphofunction. Nearly half of their cohort exhibited a persistent infantile swallow, which contributed to bite deformations. The more severe the tie, the greater the compromises seen.

Indirect contribution of tongue-tie to malocclusion also occurs via premature weaning from the breast. Although the number of breastfeeding mothers who switch to bottle-feeding because of tongue-tie is not known, based on anecdotal reports and research articles such as one of the written by Griffiths (2004), it is logical to assume that premature weaning from the breast occurs often enough to be of concern.

Labbok and Hendershot (1987) found an inverse correlation between duration of breastfeeding and malocclusion: The longer the duration of breastfeeding, the lower the rate of malocclusion. They report that bottle-feeding leads to a habit of forward tongue thrusting and a weakened development of the orbicularis muscle. Palmer (2005) asserts that bottle-feeding contributes significantly to the formation of a narrow, high-arched palate and to tongue-thrusting habits. Tongue-thrusting, as noted previously, causes open-bite malocclusions.

Furer (2008) makes one of the most adamant statements about the role of the tongue in orofacial morphofunction:

> The tongue is a powerful tool. It drains the ears, nose and sinuses. It scrubs the palate and the tonsils [during normal] movement. It shapes the skull bones, the palate, the nostrils and the respiratory tract, and it is the main factor responsible for the activity of the digestive system and the quality of the digestive process. (p. 2)

DENTAL ISSUES

In *Surgery of the Mouth and Jaws*, Moore (1985) claims that a tight lingual frenulum interferes with the normal cleansing action of the tongue, which can lead to a high incidence of dental caries. Lomcali (1987) mentions the inhibition of the normal cleaning movements of the tongue as an effect of tongue-tie. Fernando (1998) also discusses the role of tongue-tie in formation of dental caries. She saw a reduced ability to locate food in the mouth – a problem she attributes to poor oral kinesthesia. Most of the tongue-tied children in her study over the age of 7 had numerous carious lesions despite good and consistent brushing.

In Fernando's 1998 study cohort, parents had to investigate the mouths of their tongue-tied children for food particles unreachable by the tongue. The tied tongue cannot perform its normal sweeping motions that clear away food debris from teeth surfaces – especially on the lateral and posterior aspects. The concern, then is the decay of food leading to plaque formation, caries, and gingivitis. Fernando also describes a common habit among her patients: using the fingers to clean the lateral teeth surfaces. This socially unacceptable and unappealing habit is often performed in public which leads to criticism and moralization about the "manners" of tongue-tied people.

My inability to clean my teeth well with my tongue led to abcesses in three adult molars, requiring extensive dental treatment. I have had major gum recession, an often-cited consequence of untreated tongue-tie in older adults, and extensive tooth reconstruction to save several of my remaining molars. My dental saga continues despite meticulous preventive dental care – perhaps the result of 42 years of insufficient tongue-related oral toilet. Palmer presents case after case (many like mine) in his 2001 presentation illustrating the dental consequences of tongue-tie. Substantial dental intervention became necessary in each case to address the gingival recession, extreme decay, and malocclusions.

Hasan (1973) addresses the role of tongue-tie in the formation of a diastema of the lower central incisors. Diastema, a separation of the superior or inferior central incisors, results from a prominent labial frenum, and a short and/or tight lingual frenulum, respectively. The positioning of the frenum in the midline of the alveolar ridge either creates tension on the soft tissues, causing the teeth to rotate as they come in, or serves as a rigid tissue wall between the teeth. Constant pulling on the gumline during the swallow can generate gingival recession, susceptibility to decay, and loosening of the teeth. Palmer (2001) presents the case of an adult with tongue-tie related diastema, whose four front inferior teeth eventually had to be pulled from the combination of looseness and poor hygiene. Although tooth separation can be hereditary, tongue-tie significantly contributes to the formation of diastema.

Ketty and Sciullo (1974) mention the rotation toward the tongue of the mandibular central incisors resulting from tongue-tie. Of 24 tongue-tie cases, they found six that "displayed periodontal pockets and gingival recession in the region of the mandibular incisors" (p. 43). These dental issues, of primary concern to dentists and oral surgeons, seem to elude other clinical practitioners despite the fact that only one author (Paradise, 1990, p. 2371) declines to commit to the dental effects of tongue-tie: "Debate continues about the possibility of dental or related effects of tongue-tie, but such effects apparently are not common either." And yet, these risks are often cited in the cross-field research literature (Brinkman and Reilly et al., 2004; Messner and Lalakea, 2000a; Segal et al., 2007).

Dental issues related to tongue-tie appear to be incontrovertible fact – yet many clinicians rarely consider dental issues when making assessments and recommendations about treatment options.

ET CETERA

UNCONTROLLED SALIVATION

Fanibunda and Adams (1998) report on a case of a 16-year-old boy who spurted saliva every time he spoke. The saliva forcefully ejected from the sub-mandibular ducts each time he raised his tongue even a little. His tie was so tight that the floor of his mouth rose easily with even slight tongue elevation. Neither duct showed signs of abnormal development or function when imaged by sialogram. After surgical release of the tie under local anesthesia, the problem resolved completely with no recurrence. There were no postoperative complications.

Fernando (1998, p. 10) cites uncontrolled salivation as a common manifestation of tongue-tie in her study cohort. "Dribbling and splashing" occurred often during speech, resulting in a "very wet, messy facial appearance". As a result of poor tongue control of saliva produced during normal speaking, these individuals would often keep their lips more closely approximated; consequently, their speech was less intelligible. Any effort to clarify for the mystified listener would result in saliva spilling over the labial margins. The faster the speaker needed to speak, the worse the problem became. This symptom of tongue-tie is often misinterpreted as sloppiness or laziness, rather than as a structural problem interfering with normal control.

Palmer (2001) notes the accumulation of saliva in the anterior mouth or buccal vestibules. The tongue-tied individual cannot move accumulating saliva to the back of the mouth for swallowing. Before my frenotomy, I often choked on accumulated saliva, sometimes when I was in the midst of a speaking engagement. Embarrassing? Yes. Recuperating from the oxygen deprivation was even worse.

AIRWAY INTEGRITY AND APNEA

Tongue placement during infant feeding plays a key role in airway protection for the rest of a person's life. Correct tongue placement develops proper muscular habits for the swallow. Where the tongue goes during the swallow determines what happens to the alignment of the bony structures as the baby develops into an adult. Muscle always wins out over bone in morphogenesis. As previously stated, the restricting lingual frenulum in tongue-tied infants compromises tongue placement, but because the structures of the throat are so closely apposed during early infancy, a certain level of compensation is possible even if tongue placement is suboptimal.

As the neck and throat lengthen during normal development, the structures in the throat become less apposed. This separation of previously apposed structures increases airway vulnerability, demanding more compensation from the airway protective mechanisms: the gag reflex, the cough reflex, and movements and positioning of the tongue to control the swallow. Infants who had no difficulty with airway protection earlier may develop problems at this point (Wolf and Glass, 1992).

When airway protection is compromised by tongue-tie, the infant may exhibit apnea of varying lengths during the feeding process. The apnea may be so marked that the baby becomes cyanotic.

Even in less severe cases, the infant may be an inefficient feeder; be fussy during feeding, stopping and starting frequently; and exhibit the stress signs mentioned in Chapter 4.

Ongoing apneic events may decrease oxygen saturation so dramatically that an affected baby's welfare is seriously compromised. Mukai et al. (1991) suggest that some cases of sudden infant death can be attributed to the apnea spells experienced by babies who present with tongue-tie, along with deviations of the epiglottis and larynx. Surprisingly, they commonly found these companion deviations in their study cohort. Although the incidence of these throat abnormalities in tongue-tied babies has yet to be quantified, the risk factors associated with them, as discovered by these researchers, clearly must be taken seriously.

The greatest increase in craniofacial development occurs in the first four years of life. It is nearly complete (90 percent) by about age 12, with only minor changes occurring thereafter (Shepard et al., 1991). Tongue-tie left untreated for this long can generate malocclusive relationships, high-arched palate, and tongue-thrusting habits that set the stage for later airway problems. How, exactly, does this happen? Changes in throat tone, palatal shape, and craniofacial misalignment generate poor tongue posture and mouth breathing, which in turn contribute to weakness of the throat musculature. Over time, muscular weakness can cause airway collapse and the formation of obstructive sleep apnea (OSA).

Lowered tongue posture itself can also obstruct the throat. Furer (2008) reports an increased incidence of heavy snoring and sleep apnea in his tongue-tied patients because of poor tongue posture. He recommends surgical intervention in infancy as a prevention strategy. In the 2005 study by Ruffoli et al., those patients having the worst occlusive relationships also exhibited a low tongue posture. Poor tongue posture in its various forms can also be the result of premature weaning which is a risk of untreated tongue-tie (Labbok and Hendershot, 1987).

Bottle-feeding contributes in its own way to airway compromise. Palmer (2005) states:

> Bottle-feeding, pacifier use, excessive oral habits and tongue-thrusting can actually have a negative impact on the shape of the oral cavity by placing abnormal forces on bone and teeth within the oral cavity. The malocclusions formed rarely go away by themselves. Orthodontics and retraining the tongue to swallow properly usually are needed. These [abnormal] forces create the high palates, narrow dental arches and retruded chins that put individuals at risk for snoring and sleep apnea. ... The reason these characteristics are risk factors for OSA is that they infringe on tongue space and force the tongue back into the throat area due to a lack in space. (pp. 2–3)

Each facet of the orofacial complex influences the others. The craniofacial, oral, and pharyngeal structures are so complex and physiologically linked, one compromised factor can disturb all the others. Tongue-tie comprises the first "domino." As Palmer (2001) states so pointedly,

"There is NO MEDICAL BENEFIT to having a tight lingual ... frenum. There are many major medical and dental consequences that result from tight frena" (p. 1).

Having a brother who suffers from complications of sleep apnea, Palmer has dedicated much of his career identifying and educating others about the factors that influence airway collapse. Tongue-tie figures prominently on his list of contributing factors.

CHAPTER FIVE TAKEAWAY

1. Tongue-tie contributes to the formation of speech articulation errors, other speech disorders, oral cleanliness compromises, and suboptimal formation of the jaw and mouth. Compromised orofacial development may possibly lead to long-term dental and airway integrity issues.

2. Potentially, social issues may arise from tongue-tie: embarrassment; self-esteem compromise; social sensitivity; sexual performance deficits related to the use of the tongue; and difficulty engaging in the Activities of Daily Living such as playing certain musical instruments, and licking the lips, lollipops, and ice cream cones. Little research quantifies these issues. Despite the lack of research evidence, anecdotal reports show that these issues can have a profound impact on the individual, and should be seriously considered when making treatment decisions.

3. Although more research needs to be done to confirm this hypothesis, infancy still appears to be the ideal time to treat tongue-tie. Early treatment may prevent the development of problems later in life, when treatment is much more complex and invasive. Treating tongue-tie in early childhood, for example, may require a more extensive surgical procedure known as frenectomy, extensive speech therapy, psychological counseling, and orthodontia.

CHAPTER SIX
ASSESSMENT

"THIRTY YEARS AGO, WHEN I had my first baby," writes Pam, "my father came to visit. While holding the baby, he began looking in his mouth. I laughed and asked if he was checking to see if the baby had a black palate as my dad swore that dogs who had dark-roofed mouths were more easily trained. He said 'No, I'm checking to see if the baby is tongue-tied because all my mama's kids were, and he is, so you need to have the doctor clip his tongue so he will be able to get enough breast milk.' So, my pediatrician did just that and I noticed an immediate improvement in the baby's ability to maintain a latch. I had five children, all of whom were tongue-tied and clipped very soon after delivery. Tongue-tie is the first thing I look for when I evaluate a mother and baby. I fondly think of my sweet daddy who taught me this lesson 30 years ago."

Pam's thorough routine assessment, a rarity these days among non-IBCLC medical professionals, serves her mother/baby population well. The shift away from routine assessment has no evidence-based foundation. As well, none of the writings from earlier times provide descriptions of assessments. After reading hundreds of articles on tongue-tie and its assessment and treatment, I am left with the impression that prior to 1993, assessment of tongue-tie was largely a matter of eyeballing the situation and guessing whether the baby required treatment. While the guess might have been educated, it was nonetheless highly subjective.

This visual approach seems to persist to this day, albeit with the additional consideration of the secondary manifestations of tongue-tie, and the impact it has on feeding, speech, breathing, dental development, orofacial development, and oral toilet. Lack of an objective assessment focused on tongue function and movement hampers the clinician's ability to securely and soundly identify and recommend treatment approaches.

ASSESSMENT ISSUES

Because tongue-tie has been defined as an anatomical anomaly that adversely impacts tongue function, assessment ought to include evaluation of tongue function as a primary goal. Unfortunately, clinicians and researchers often still first look at the frenulum and then determine if this visual inspection warrants further functional evaluation. This approach leads to an incomplete evaluation, sometimes to the child's detriment; some ties will be missed by such a cursory exam. And if the substantial clinical experience of Coryllos et al. (2004) tells us anything, it is that visual inspection may completely miss the most severe presentation of tongue-tie – the hidden submucosal posterior tie.

Recently, attempts have been made to quantify the impact tongue-tie has on feeding. It appears this trend largely has taken hold because Lactation Consultants embrace tongue-tie as a probable cause of breastfeeding problems. As a result, much of what was written about tongue-tie in the latter-20th century and in the early-21st century appears in the lactation literature. Although feeding is the primary Activity of Daily Living for the infant, speech, oral toilet, chewing, swallowing, and effective breathing all must be taken into consideration in older age groups.

This complex web of skills presents a challenge for the clinician and researcher who must evaluate tongue-tie in older children, adolescents, and adults. Both clinicians and researchers can get lost in the maze. Activities of Daily Living adversely affected by tongue-tie are secondary criteria to the primary concern: tongue movement. Assessment of tongue-tie really should be an evaluation of tongue range of motion and deficits, along with an assessment of its impact.

The assessor needs to answer three fundamental questions:

1. Can the tongue move freely in all the ways it normally should?

2. If not, to what degree is it restricted?

3. What impact do the restrictions have on the individual?

This simplification of the assessment goal makes the assessment process straightforward and easy to implement. That is not to say that the assessment process lacks thoroughness. Each tongue-movement criterion requires quantification. Additionally, the clinician or team involved in assessment also must know what strategies to implement so they can address the secondary issues, which become more complex and substantial the longer the tongue-tie is present.

Standardizing the assessment process remains a troubling and complex issue. Age differences, variations in presentation of functional deficits, and differences in perspective all stand in the way of developing a standardized assessment process.

At one time, negative attitudes about breastfeeding kept clinicians from taking tongue-tie seriously as a contributor to breastfeeding problems. Therefore, assessment for tongue-tie as a cause of breastfeeding problems went undone. In some circles, these attitudes still may be a barrier. Some believe that if the baby can feed on a bottle, the mother should switch to bottle-feeding since there are no particular advantages to breastfeeding. This position was then, and remains, untenable and indefensible.

In older groups, the focus on speech articulation disorders kept clinicians from eagerly embracing tongue-tie as a possible cause of other speech and various morphofunctional problems. A lack of good research in this domain undermined the ability of clinicians to justify surgical treatment. The new research on morphofunction is slowly changing these negative attitudes. An inability to lick an ice-cream cone, once thought a minor concern, also means that the child may develop sleep apnea over time or already may suffer from it. At worst, sleep apnea kills. At best, it has an adverse impact on a child's ability to learn in school. Seen from this perspective, the ability to freely move the tongue in the oral space takes on a new and more important dimension warranting the development of thorough assessment protocols.

No matter what the impact of tongue-tie, its assessment must consider every possible reason for tongue-movement deficit. Only when it does will the appropriate criteria be employed for making the surgical intervention decision.

FAVORED CRITERIA

In the past, many authors seemed to have had one or two favorite criteria they used during their assessments. For example, Huggins (1986), Meintz-Maher (1988), Mohrbacher and Stock (1991), all mention a heart-shaped appearance and the inability of the tongue to reach over the lower lip as their main assessment criteria. Boo-Chai (1963) suggested that if a baby could protrude its tongue to the mucocutaneous junction of the lip, treatment was not necessary. Avery and First (Eds. 1989) recommended treatment if the tongue appeared to lack normal mobility.

Block (1968) said, "If tongue-tip sounds are produced incorrectly, but the individual can be stimulated to produce these sounds, a frenulotomy [frenotomy] would not be indicated on the basis of speech production." Browne (1959) mentioned the inability of a child to touch the tip of his tongue to the hard palate as the lone criterion. Oldfield (1955), one of the most often-quoted authors, mentions only tightness of the frenulum. Nezu (1987), who, by her own admission, overtreated for the condition because no assessment criteria were employed other than the fact that the tongue appeared to be tied, subsequently employed the criterion of heart-shaped tongue or the frenulum's being attached to at least two-thirds of the bottom of the tongue to justify frenotomy in infants. As a result, her rate of surgical intervention declined dramatically.

Brinkman et al. (2004) and Messner and Lalakea (2000a) found that different professions favor different criteria. In the Messner and Lalakea study, lactation consultants were more likely than pediatricians and otolaryngologists to think that tongue-tie causes feeding difficulties. Otolaryngologists were far more likely than pediatricians and speech pathologists to believe that tongue-tie causes speech problems, the latter group being equally divided on the issue. This study clearly indicates that clinical specialty determines a practitioner's assessment focus.

Brinkman et al. (2004, p. 602) found that 94 percent of Australian surgeons surveyed use tongue protrusion as their main assessment criterion. Of those respondents, only 54 percent also "palpated the tongue and frenulum to assess the extent of a tongue-tie." Although 80.5 percent of the total cohort in this study indicated that reduced tongue mobility warranted surgical release, pediatric surgeons were more likely to perform surgical release for cosmetic reasons than for poor oral hygiene, whereas this tendency was reversed in the oral-maxillofacial surgeon group. Plastic surgeons were less likely to perform surgical release for cosmetic reasons and were more likely to treat surgically for speech articulation than the pediatric general surgery group. No group used a formal standardized assessment tool or process.

FORMAL ASSESSMENT

Recent studies about tongue-tie concentrate on treatment and its outcome rather than on assessment criteria. Of the more than 60 studies published after 1993 that I reviewed for this book, fewer than 10 used some formal assessment process. Hearkening back to the Rogers and Douglas study from 1952, some recent studies use tongue protrusion and/or elevation as a tongue mobility test (Cinar & Onat, 2005; Dollberg et al., 2006; Garcia Pola et al., 2002; Hillan, 2008; and Klockars, 2007). Although this tendency reflects the consensus in definition that has emerged over the centuries (restricted tongue mobility caused by a short and tight lingual frenulum), using one or two criteria hardly comprises a valid or reliable assessment. For example, Cinar and Onat (2005) measured tongue-tip protrusion past the lower teeth. Their average measurements for their two groups (one with speech articulation problems; one without) were 11.09mm and 11.4mm respectively – an insignificant difference. This may tell us that degree of tongue protrusion has little effect on speech articulation. It, therefore would be the wrong standalone measure to determine the presence of tongue-tie.

Six breastfeeding studies (Amir et al., 2005; Ballard et al., 2002; Griffiths, 2004; Hogan et al., 2005; Ricke et al., 2005b; and Srinivasan et al., 2006) attempted a more rigorous assessment approach. The Ballard, Amir, and Ricke studies sought to determine inter-rater reliability of the Hazelbaker Assessment Tool for Lingual Frenulum Function (ATLFF) as one of their study goals. Unfortunately, all of them used the ATLFF as a secondary assessment after using an initial informal assessment that visualized the frenulum. The ATLFF was employed not as a screening tool, which is its purpose, but as a tool to validate or quantify the tongue mobility issues the infants were experiencing. The Ricke study used the ATLFF so inappropriately as to completely invalidate the results relative to its use (Hazelbaker, 2005; Ricke et al., 2005b).

Griffiths (2004) used a combination of criteria in his assessment: percentage of the tongue underside occupied by the frenulum; thickness of the frenulum; and the appearance of the anterior edge of the tongue. Hogan et al. (2005) used multiple assessment criteria based on the training criteria they developed for the U. K. National Health Service. Their examination included palpating and visualizing the frenulum, the tongue underside, and mouth floor. One specific criterion was percentage of the tongue underside occupied by the frenulum (a range of 25 to 100 percent).

Three studies used the Kotlow classification system (Kotlow, 1999; Kupietzky and Botzer, 2005 and Naimer, Biton, Vardy, and Zyulunov, 2003). Similar to Coryllos (2004), Kotlow classifies the frenular attachment first, and then uses functional criteria to buttress the initial observations for justifying treatment decisions. Naimer et al. slightly modified the Kotlow criteria for their study, rewording the functional criteria for clarity and ease of use (p. CR434). The Kupietzky study cites the Kotlow classification system and the ATLFF as two assessment approaches. They further recommend a thorough intra-oral exam, including an inspection of the tongue and floor of the mouth. Along with these oral assessments, they suggest that dentists also should interview the mother about an infant patient's feeding (pp. 12-13).

There is no substitute for formal assessment, as illustrated by Mindy and Elijah's story. Mindy, who was introduced in Chapter Four, brought her son, Elijah, to me for persistent sucking issues that were causing her severe nipple pain and damage. Elijah had had his tongue assessed by another lactation consultant; he subsequently was treated with a simple frenotomy. No follow-up management was provided by the initial assessor or the ENT physician. Elijah did not show significant improvement after the simple frenotomy. Since he already had been screened and treated for tie, I focused on assessing his suck from a different perspective. He had been vacuum-extracted at birth and showed dramatic structural and soft-tissue-related issues that were impairing his sucking coordination.

I scored him on the Neonatal Oral-Motor Assessment Scale (NOMAS), which verified a dysfunctional suck. He underwent a series of craniosacral therapy (CST) treatments to correct the remaining issues. Although he experienced significant improvement, Mindy's nipple pain still did not improve to her satisfaction, even though her nipple wounds had healed. Elijah's failure to respond fully to the CST treatments indicated another factor was affecting the situation.

Because of Mindy's persistent nipple soreness, I re-evaluated Elijah for tongue-tie – looking for tight, short, or fibrous tissue at the base of his tongue. Sure enough, he had a band of fibrous tissue anchoring his tongue base, keeping him from placing his tongue-tip over his lower gumline. Mindy traveled to see Dr. Coryllos, who performed a frenotomy at the tongue base. At first, there was little improvement, but with a combination of continued CST treatment, tongue exercises and impeccable management, Elijah started to show dramatic improvement, and Mindy's nipple pain decreased.

SCREENING

Determining who is and is not tongue-tied remains one of the persistent controversies in tongue-tie management. Routine screening, rather than post-problem development assessment, allows clinicians and parents to make timely and appropriate decisions. Early intervention comprises an excellent and cost-effective prevention strategy. Even if a particular infant does not have feeding problems, knowing that an infant has a tie alerts parents and professionals to monitor the infant's development more closely and intervene if necessary. Screening also provides an opportunity for tracking those infants who do not receive early treatment to ascertain which children develop problems as time passes. Screening, however, must be done with an appropriate tool whose development is based on the performance of normal infants.

The Assessment Tool for Lingual Frenulum Function (ATLFF), for example, was developed after observing a substantial number of normal infants over a 3-year period. Each item was revised multiple times to reflect the various compromised performance of affected babies vs. performance of normal babies. This rigorous development process increased the tool's potential for validity and reliability. Its level of specificity also is high, making it a very sensitive instrument for screening.

Some authors state that we cannot make clear and solid claims about impact if we can't standardize our assessment philosophy and process (Hall and Renfew, 2006; Segal et al., 2007). Moving away from appearance criteria only and focusing on tongue mobility issues moves us toward that standardization. Using primary tongue function criteria such as tongue elevation and lateralization, as opposed to secondary criteria, such as nipple pain in breastfeeding mothers or inability of the individual to lick an ice-cream cone, strengthens the assessment process because secondary criteria are not universal manifestations of the tongue-tie phenomenon.

I am not suggesting, however, that appearance criteria or secondary criteria be ignored. Ballard et al. (2002) found that mean function scores and mean appearance scores on the ATLFF showed significant correlation. The degree to which these two general criterion categories correlate should be a subject for future study. If it is discovered that certain appearance items correlate strongly with the functional criteria that indicate tongue-tie, we can then use those appearance criteria as a determinant for the presence of tongue-tie. Until then, it seems best to continue to assess both along with secondary criteria for the purpose of further quantifying the phenomenon.

To address the issue of standardization, a few systematic methods of assessment were developed in the 20th century (Fernando, 1998; Fletcher & Daly, 1974; Fletcher & Meldrum, 1968; Hazelbaker, 1993). Several others have taken shape in this century. Most use a blend of appearance and function criteria; some tack on secondary criteria to augment the assessment process. Unfortunately, of these various systems, only the ATLFF and the Tongue-tie Assessment Protocol (TAPP) are rigorously designed. The ATLFF has been found to possess content validity and inter-rater reliability, (Amir et al., 2005; Ballard et al., 2002; Hazelbaker, 1993), and Fernando's TAPP has content validity.

Using a set of calipers, Fletcher and Meldrum (1968) measured the distance from the mandible to the sub-lingual gland, the length of the lingual frenulum, and the length of the free portion of the tongue. Results of these measurements were correlated with speech articulation disorders.

Those children with the most limited lingual freedom made the greatest number of articulation errors. Fletcher and Daly (1974) elaborated on these findings by suggesting other criteria for making a treatment decision:

> The following 'rule-of-thumb' guidelines are suggested to help identify those who would be candidates for the more careful, quantitative evaluation: inability of a child to raise his tongue-tip to contact the alveolar ridge, to move a protruded tongue from one corner of the mouth to the other, or to achieve contact for the lingua-dental and lingua-alveolar consonants as evidence of an abnormally restricted tongue; a 'notching' of the tongue-tip when the tongue is protruded, or sublingual restriction that prevents the tongue from being protruded beyond the lower gum. (p. 296)

Young and Sacks, in their 1979 (p. 298) article "Examining for Tongue tic," emphasize what they consider to be key elements in assessing the impact of a short lingual frenulum on tongue function. They are:

- History, including questions related to poor sucking in infancy, inability to chew certain foods, biting the tongue, inability to clean food off the teeth and gums, and the inability to lick the lips.

- Oral examination, including examining the anterior dentition for open bite or prognathism, and for a tongue-thrust during swallowing. The mouth should be examined for incidence of poor oral hygiene and for periodontal disease, especially in the area of the lingual frenulum.

- Speech assessment, including investigation of the production of tongue-tip sounds that require the greatest vertical range of motion: */t/ /d/ /n/ /l/* should be assessed in syllables and words, e.g., *ta*, *te*, *time*, *water*, *cat*. Overall intelligibility of speech also should be observed by engaging the patient in conversation.

Marmet et al., (1990, p. 118): in their work with breastfeeding babies, developed assessment criteria based on their experience assessing infant sucking over time, saying:

> When the frenulum is extremely tight, a visual evaluation may be all that is needed to prompt the recommendation of a frenotomy, especially when the tongue-tip is heart-shaped at rest or with slight extension. More often, however, a digital suck examination may be necessary to evaluate function. In less obvious cases, the ability to function, rather than appearance, is the key to determining if a frenotomy needs to be performed. The frenulum may look short but have sufficient elasticity to function.

CLASSIFICATION OF ANKYLOGLOSSIA			
Type	**Superior Attachment**	**Inferior Attachment**	**Characteristics of Frenulum**
1	Tip of tongue	Alveolar ridge	Often thin, may be elastic
2	2 to 4 mm behind tongue tip	On or just behind alveolar ridge	Often thin, may be elastic
3	Mid-tongue	Middle of floor of mouth	Usually thicker, more fibrous, inelastic
4	Submucosal	Floor of mouth at base of tongue	Usually thick, fibrous, shiny, and inelastic

Table 6-1. Coryllos-Watson Genna-Salloum Typing System. Note. From "Congenital tongue-tie and its impact on breastfeeding," by E. Coryllos, C. Watson Genna, and A.C. Salloum, 2004, *Breastfeeding: Best for Mother and Baby Newsletter,* Summer, pp.1-2. © 2004 by American Pediatric Association. Reprinted with permission.

These clinicians clearly believe there is more to lingual frenulum assessment than just what meets the eye. Despite an emerging consensus relative to function criteria, several authors still maintain that the heart-shaped tongue remains the definitive sign indicating the presence of tongue-tie (Fiorotti et al., 2004; Kummer, 2005; and Hillan, 2008). In reality, fewer than half of tongue-tied babies have a heart-shaped tongue upon extension or elevation (Hazelbaker, 1993; Griffiths, 2004). The last author found that those babies presenting with what others would classify as mild ties based on appearance still experienced major feeding problems. Appearance can be deceiving.

PERSISTENT CONTROVERSY

The myriad ways in which tongue-tie presents visually and functionally accounts for the persistent controversy regarding tongue-tie assessment. No two tongue-tied people are exactly alike. The degree to which tongue-tied individuals are affected also presents as a continuum. This issue might be easier to resolve if we were to classify tongue-tie as a syndrome. Such a classification would allow for the substantial variability in presentation and impact.

It is certain that persistent use of a single criterion, such as the heart shape, forces clinicians to miss those tongue-ties that do not present with that lone criterion. Many tongue-ties present visually as more or less severe than the "classic" heart-shaped manifestation; they also may lack certain functional qualities but possess other functional qualities. As a potent example, Coryllos et al. (2004) describe the "posterior" tie, which is a tie at the base of the tongue rather than at the tip. The posterior tie often eludes visual inspection and presents different functional qualities than those ties that possess more obvious visual characteristics.

In the United Kingdom, Westcott (C. Westcott, personal communication, February 2, 2009) describes the posterior tie as a "broad band running from side to side at the base of the tongue."

Westcott trains practitioners to assess and treat tongue-tie in infants. She reports that she insists practitioners feel under the tongue as part of the assessment process to avoid missing these dramatic yet less-visible ties.

Clearly, the discussion about tongue-tie has expanded and deepened. As new evidence continues to emerge, "quick and dirty" assessments aren't enough. Assessments that consider only one or two favorite criteria do not possess the validity and reliability necessary for evidence-based clinical decisions, nor will they hold up for research purposes.

It is a fact that tongue-ties defy simple classification. To continue to try to classify them using one, two or a few categories does not serve. Discussion must now be oriented toward standardizing an assessment process. A standardized assessment tool and/or process possessing the necessary validity and reliability makes such research easier to conduct, research results more definitive, and moves us in the right clinical direction sooner rather than later.

Below are the most recent classification and assessment systems that appear in the literature, ranging from the simplest to the most sensitive. From this presentation, a pattern should emerge that identifies the common and foundational elements that can form the basis for a standardized assessment tool or process.

INFANT ASSESSMENT SYSTEMS

THE CORYLLOS–WATSON GENNA–SALLOUM TYPING SYSTEM

Coryllos et al. developed their Typing System from clinical observation. Several years ago, Watson Genna's client, Baby R, presented with typical functional tongue-tie signs and symptoms; however, he did not have an anterior tie. Rather, he had a short, tight, white band at the tongue base. Puzzled, Watson Genna asked Dr. Coryllos to examine the child. After assessing the situation and seeing the white fibrous strip of tissue near the tongue base, Coryllos remained doubtful and hesitant to treat, despite the mother's desire to have the "frenulum" clipped. After a few days of careful observation and application of appropriate management with no appreciable resolution of the breastfeeding problems, Baby R's mom requested Coryllos perform a frenotomy. Coryllos incised the fibrous band at the tongue base; afterward, Baby R went to breast and sucked properly for the first time. From that time forward, Watson Genna and Coryllos assessed babies for this atypical tongue-tie presentation. Over time, they saw a pattern that enabled them to classify these unusual posterior ties into their Type 3 and 4 categories (B. Coryllos, personal communication, February 28, 2009).

During a conversation with me, Watson Genna shared that the purpose of the typing system was to "increase appreciation that the lingual frenulum does not have to extend along much of the length of the tongue to restrict its function" (personal communication, January 28, 2009). Watson Genna states in her book Supporting Sucking Skills in Infants that "tongue-tie can be classified according to the sites of attachment of the lingual frenulum on the tongue and floor of the mouth," but that

TONGUE RANGE OF MOTION CRITERIA			
Degree of tongue extension beyond the lower dental ridge and lip	Elevation of the tongue to the palate with the mouth wide open	Transverse tongue movement from one corner of the lips to the other without tongue twisting	
BREASTFEEDING CRITERIA			
Effectiveness of milk transfer determined by test weights	Adequacy of latch	Efficiency of bolus handling as evidenced by coordination of suck, swallow, and breathe coordination	Feeding fatigue as evidenced by jaw or tongue tremor, fussiness and arching away at breast, or feeding again and again after short periods of rest

Table 6-2. Coryllos et al. Functional Criteria. From "Congenital tongue-tie and its impact on breastfeeding," by E. Coryllos, C. Watson Genna, and A.C. Salloum, 2004, *Breastfeeding: Best for Mother and Baby Newsletter*, Summer, pp. 2-3. © 2004 by American Pediatric Association. Reprinted with permission.

"tongue range of motion is the most important factor in the infant ability to breastfeed with ankyloglossia" (2008, p. 188).

In the original article on the subject, Coryllos et al. (2004) clearly describe their distinguishing criteria that allow for easy classification. They buttress these visual criteria with several functionally oriented diagnostic criteria inspired by the Kotlow and Hazelbaker assessments: degree of tongue extension; tongue elevation when the infant's mouth is open; and lateralization of the tongue. Additionally, they advocate assessing the infant at breast, the infant's ability to coordinate sucking with breathing, milk transfer using test weighing, and nipple and breast tissue integrity. The advocacy of these further assessments concurs with recommendations made by other researchers (Geddes and Langton et al., 2008; Griffiths, 2004; Hazelbaker, 1993; Hogan et al., 2005; Marmet et al., 1990).

Watson Genna thoroughly discusses functional criteria in her 2008 book. Her criteria of inadequate cupping, grooving, and lateralization; tongue-sliding; tongue-humping; and excessive jaw excursions match previous reports of deficits cited in the literature (Hazelbaker, 1993; Marmet et al., 1990).

My concern about this classification system includes the risk of false positives and the possibility that using it for assessment shifts the focus from function to appearance . For example, a Type 1 in this system may describe a certain subset of tongue-tie presentations. But if a baby crosses categories, e.g., shows a visual characteristic from the Type 1 category and another from the Type 2 category, an assessor might then determine that the baby is not tongue-tied.

In my experience (Hazelbaker, 2003), ties can be visually confused with other phenomena. I have seen tongue restrictions that look like tongue-tie but aren't: Connective tissue restrictions can occur

TONGUE-TIE PARAMETERS	
Thickness [of lingual frenulum]	Diaphanous
	Medium
	Thick
Shape [of tongue tip]	Dimple
	Heart
	Pointed
Percentage of tongue anchored by tissue	100%
	75%
	50%
	25%
Treatment criteria	Baby has difficulty latching on to the breast
	Mother has painful, sore, and/or bleeding nipples
	Baby has a continuous feeding cycle (is inefficiently feeding)

Table 6-3. The Griffiths Classification System. From "Do tongue ties affect breastfeeding?" by D.M Griffiths, 2004, *Journal of Human Lactation*, 20, 411. © 2004 by SAGE Publications. Reprinted with permission by SAGE Publications.

as a result of intrauterine lie and childbirth issues, (e.g., a cord wrapped around the neck, asynclitic presentation, rapid descent, and aggressive use of suctioning equipment.)

Each one of these issues can restrict the soft tissues of the head and neck in ways that affect the positioning of the tongue and cause tightness in the tongue's connective tissue, including the lingual frenulum (Hazelbaker, 2003; Wall and Glass, 2006). Also, a congenital short tongue can look remarkably similar to a tied tongue. Therapies other than surgical intervention, such as craniosacral therapy, would be indicated to treat these problems.

In a personal communication, Watson Genna reports that this typing system was not intended to be carved in stone or for grading tongue-tie. It therefore should be used more as a visual guide than as a diagnostic tool.

The strength of this classification system lies in its ability to get assessors to be thorough – looking and palpating under the tongue and at its base for a non-obvious or hidden tie. These authors contribute significantly to the discussion on tongue-tie by naming and describing the posterior tie, which had gone unnoticed by other researchers and clinicians.

THE GRIFFITHS CLASSIFICATION SYSTEM

In his 2004 study in the *Journal of Human Lactation*, (p. 411) Griffiths presents a classification system that utilizes three criteria to describe the presence of tongue-tie: thickness of the lingual frenulum, shape of the tongue-tip, and the percentage of the tongue underside anchored by tissue. Under each of these three criteria headings, he uses descriptors that evaluate qualities suggesting mild to severe presentation.

Tongue-tied infants in his study presented with various combinations of these factors. Presumably, infants who are not tongue-tied do not present with these combinations of factors, although Griffiths does not indicate that he also examined normal babies prior to developing his assessment criteria.

Griffiths also used other feeding data to make a decision regarding surgical division of the tie. Some of these secondary criteria also appear as a Frenotomy Decision Rule for Breastfeeding Infants in the Srinivasan et al (2006) article, "Ankyloglossia in breastfeeding infants: The effect of frenotomy on maternal nipple pain and latch."

Griffiths' classification system employs appearance criteria only. His buttressing symptoms related to feeding issues suggest tongue-function deficits, but he does not specify those deficits. In his study, only the most severe impact on breastfeeding constitutes justification for surgical intervention. With these limited tongue-tie presentation and intervention criteria, it is possible that this system would miss some cases of tongue-tie. A subsequent study for which he was an investigator (Hogan et al., 2005) found that the length of tongue-underside occupied by the frenulum correlated poorly with degree of impact. It therefore seems that appearance of the lingual frenulum helps little in determining the degree of impact on function. His system would benefit by including greater specificity in all criteria and by adding functional factors to the assessment process.

THE HAZELBAKER ASSESSMENT TOOL FOR LINGUAL FRENULUM FUNCTION

The Assessment Tool for Lingual Frenulum Function (ATLFF), developed in the early 1990s, screens for tongue-tie in the total population of infants from newborn to 6 months. Three years of observation of breastfeeding babies formed the basis for the items scored on the tool. Multiple revisions refined the tool until it was capable of screening normal babies from those who were functionally impaired due to tongue-tie (for more information see Appendix C.)

Based on the recommendations of experts using the tool in their clinical practices, adjustments have been made to the ATLFF to improve its performance. Most recently, descriptive language was added to the assessment items to enable the practitioner to better determine the presence of a posterior tie. The 2009 version appears in Table 6-4.

SCREENING AND ASSESSMENT USING THE ATLFF

I designed the ATLFF to screen for tongue-tied infants in the total population of babies. The scoring design and assessment procedure were developed to make the distinction between affected and non-affected infants. A short and/or tight lingual frenulum will affect different babies differently and to varying degrees; not every tongue-tied baby scores low on the same items. And there are other causes of tongue function impairment that this screening process distinguishes from tongue-tie.

Table 6-4. Hazelbaker Assessment Tool for Lingual Frenulum Function Chart Note. © 2009 Alison K. Hazelbaker, PhD, IBCLC. Reprinted with permission.

Mothers name: ______________________ Baby's age: ______________________

Baby's name: ______________________ Date of assessment: ______________________

FUNCTION ITEMS	
LATERALIZATION	**CUPPING OF TONGUE**
2 Complete **1** Body of tongue but not tongue-tip **0** None	**2** Entire edge, firm cup **1** Side edges only, moderate cup **0** Poor OR no cup
LIFT OF TONGUE	**PERISTALSIS (PROGRESSIVE CONTRACTION)**
2 Tip to mid-mouth **1** Only edges to mid mouth **0** Tip stays at alveolar ridge OR tip rises only to mid-mouth with jaw closure AND/OR mid-tongue dimples	**2** Complete anterior to posterior (originates at tip) **1** Partial: originating posterior to tip **0** None OR Anterior thrusting
EXTENSION OF TONGUE	**SNAP BACK**
2 Tip over lower lip **1** Tip over lower gum only **0** Neither of the above OR anterior or mid-tongue humps AND/OR dimples	**2** None **1** Periodic **0** Frequent OR with each suck
SPREAD OF ANTERIOR TONGUE	
2 Complete **1** Moderate OR partial **0** Little OR none	

APPEARANCE ITEMS	
APPEARANCE OF TONGUE WHEN LIFTED	**ELASTICITY OF LINGUAL FRENULUM**
2 Round OR square **1** Slight cleft in tip apparent **0** Heart shaped	**2** Very elastic (excellent) **1** Moderately elastic **0** Little OR no elasticity
LENGTH OF LINGUAL FRENULUM WHEN TONGUE LIFTED	**ATTACHMENT OF LINGUAL FRENULUM TO TONGUE**
2 More than 1 cm OR absent frenulum **1** 1 cm **0** Less than 1 cm	**2** Posterior to tip **1** At tip **0** Notched OR under the mucosa at the tongue base
ATTACHMENT OF LINGUAL FRENULUM TO INFERIOR ALVEOLAR RIDGE	
2 Attached to floor of mouth OR well below ridge **1** Attached just below ridge **0** Attached to ridge	

SCORING	
Function Item score: ____________ Appearance Item score: ____________	Combined Score: ____ / ____

TREATMENT RECOMMENDATIONS BASED ON SCORING

14 Perfect Function score regardless of Appearance Item score. Surgical treatment not recommended.

11 Acceptable Function score only if Appearance Item score is **10**.

< 11 Function Score indicates function impaired. Frenotomy should be considered if management fails. Frenotomy necessary if Appearance Item score is **< 8**.

Since the pattern of impact for individual babies is so variable, the ATLFF assesses every aspect of tongue function and appearance that possibly could be affected negatively by tongue-tie. The inclusion of a 0 to 2 Apgar-like scale, in addition to high specificity in descriptors, allows for an accurate differential diagnosis in the face of this variability.

The type of scoring employed by the ATLFF accurately identifies those babies who are functionally impaired and will need treatment. Babies who are unaffected by tongue-tie and who have no sucking deficits from other causes typically receive perfect scores. Those who may be mildly affected will receive moderate scores, and those who are affected enough to be treated immediately will receive low scores. Some babies who have moderate Function Scores have an atypical sucking pattern or some tongue function impairment not associated with tongue-tie; these babies usually score high or perfectly on the Appearance items. This tendency to score high on the Appearance items indicates the role that the Appearance items play in helping to distinguish tongue-tie from other infant sucking deficits; one of finer distinction.

Some babies will appear to have a short and/or tight lingual frenulum, but will score high on the Function items. These babies typically will not need to have their lingual frenula "clipped." However, they may require careful management or therapy to correct their particular types of sucking problems.

I cannot stress enough the importance of screening all babies with this tool. It requires about ten assessments on normal babies to understand the normal range of motion of the tongue. Another ten assessments will allow the practitioner to feel comfortable with the sensitivity of the instrument in distinguishing sucking deficits not related to tongue-tie. When the occasional tongue-tied baby appears, the clinician will have no difficulty picking up tongue-tie's unique impact on tongue function.

The ATLFF has been criticized for being too difficult to use in a busy practice (Segal et al., 2007). In fact, once the practitioner learns the process, the assessment actually takes only a minute or two. Any new skill presents one with a learning curve. And when it comes to infant sucking issues, the clinician should spend time performing a thorough assessment as a matter of course, especially when a feeding problem occurs. Incorporating the ATLFF into the overall assessment regimen poses no burden; the clinician assesses the components of the tool when he or she assesses the infant's general sucking ability. Any surgical intervention such as tongue-tie division can be justified only by thorough assessment.

Clinicians should not, on the one hand, demand thoroughness to justify treatment and, on the other hand, complain about the time it takes to be thorough. Thoroughness prevents overtreatment and supports accurate differential diagnoses. Cavalier overtreatment led to the knee-jerk reaction of undertreatment in the mid-20th century – a response from which we have yet to recover. "Quickie" assessments may throw us right back into those murky waters.

Watson Genna brought up a specific concern about the ATLFF (Watson Genna, personal communication, January 27, 2009). She used it for years and then found it did not pick up on the more severe but non-obvious ties that her research team now has classified as Type 3 and 4. Adjustments have been made to alleviate these concerns, and adjustments will continue until the instrument is sensitive enough to pick up on these ties.

Some clinicians criticize intra-oral assessment. In my view, when a baby has a breastfeeding problem, such intervention is warranted as long as the baby receives optimal respect during the process. There is no research that shows babies are less inclined to suck properly or to feel unsafe or uncomfortable during breastfeeding just because a practitioner has assessed his or her suck by putting a finger into his or her mouth, as long as that assessment has been performed after the first breastfeed.

Oral-digital examination, as taught by the Lactation Institute (Marmet et al., 1990), is an excellent vehicle for performing the ATLFF. One can, however, use one's own method of oral assessment as long as it renders the necessary information needed to score a baby correctly.

All assessments of infants who have feeding problems should include watching the baby feed, observing the mother-infant interaction, evaluating the infant's growth and overall well-being and observing the response to management changes designed to optimize the feeding experience. If a practitioner also has been trained to administer the Neonatal Oral-Motor Assessment Scale (NOMAS), I encourage him or her to do so. The NOMAS adds an extra dimension to the sucking assessment process to guide the clinician's hand when making intervention decisions.

If the mother experiences pain during feeding or has damaged breasts and nipples, the clinician should take these issues seriously and treat them immediately. These clinical strategies represent fundamental management that should be carried out, no matter what the cause of the feeding problem.

To make a differential diagnosis of tongue-tie, scoring the baby with the ATLFF will determine the presence or absence of the anomaly. The other assessments simply determine what deficits in the feeding relationship as a whole exist as a result of the tongue-tie, enabling the clinician to further identify the intervention regimen and better measure postoperative outcomes.

THE SRINIVASAN FRENOTOMY DECISION RULE FOR BREASTFEEDING INFANTS

Srinivasan and colleagues endeavored to determine the effectiveness of frenotomy for resolving latch changes and maternal nipple pain during breastfeeding. Using standardized assessment tools and a newly developed instrument, the Frenotomy Decision Rule for Breastfeeding Infants (FDRBI), they identified infants for frenotomy from a cohort seen at the Goldfarb Breastfeeding Program in Montreal, Canada. Although this as-yet unvalidated tool may have assisted the research process for this study, it has yet to undergo testing for validity and reliability as an assessment tool for the presence of tongue-tie requiring surgical intervention in a general population of babies.

BREASTFEEDING PARAMETERS		LINGUAL FRENULUM	TONGUE FUNCTION PARAMETERS
Maternal nipple pain/trauma AND/OR inability to maintain latch AND/OR poor weight gain in infant (less than 15g/d)	AND	A visible membrane anterior to the tongue base that restricts tongue movement, leading to ➔	An inability to touch the roof of the mouth OR an inability to cup an examining finger OR an inability to protrude the tongue past the gumline

Table 6-5 Srinivasan Frenotomy Decision Rule for Breastfed Infants. Note. From "Ankyloglossia in breastfeeding infants: the effect of frenotomy on maternal nipple pain and latch," by A. Srinivasan, C. Dobrich, H. Mitnick, and P. Feldman, 2006, Breastfeeding Medicine, 1, 216-224

The strength of this tool lies in its brevity and its ability to quickly identify certain candidates for surgical intervention. It addresses some common secondary manifestations of suck dysfunction in breastfed babies, but fails to take into account that babies can be tongue-tied and gain adequately, transfer milk relatively well, and not cause nipple damage or pain in the process.

The gains made from brevity naturally generate a sacrifice of specificity and sensitivity. For example, does the item related to touching the tongue to the roof of the mouth mean with the mouth open or closed? This fine point matters because many tongue-tied babies can touch the roof of the mouth when the mouth is closed. It is the effort required to touch the roof of the mouth and the degree to which the lingual frenulum restricts this motion with the mouth open that, in part, determines the severity of the tie (Hazelbaker, 1993).

The visible membrane item completely rules out the presence of posterior ties hidden under the oral mucosa. In addition, these factors do not allow this tool to be used on bottle-fed babies. Of course, the test name clearly states it is a decision rule for breastfed babies, but a standardized tool for infants would include criteria for assessing tongue-tie no matter what the feeding method – thereby identifying all manifestations of tongue-tie in the infant population.

Although the notion of brevity is tempting, the way the items combine to create the decision rule must truly represent the way in which tongue-tie adversely affects tongue function (rather than just tongue function related to breastfeeding) to make it useful both for research and in the clinical setting in the broader population of babies. Perhaps the authors simply wanted to create a decision rule for those breastfed babies seen in clinical settings, or for the purposes of research. If so, their tool seems to have helped them accomplish the limited goal of ascertaining the effectiveness of frenotomy in their cohort of breastfed babies experiencing breastfeeding problems. If the authors continue to research their tool and validate it as an appropriate measure for deficits characteristic of all tongue-ties in babies, then they have a useful instrument for assessment and for making surgical treatment decisions.

IN SUMMARY

The assessment systems presented in this section share a level of formality that strengthens the assessment process. Each notes the appearance of tongue-tie, and each either suggests or directly addresses the functional deficits that accompany tongue-tie. Coryllos, Griffiths, and Srinivasan strive for brevity by isolating what they think are key characteristics of tongue-tie and its impact. The ATLFF strives to be sensitive and specific so that tongue-tied babies can be identified from the larger population of babies. All desire to achieve the goal of tongue-tie identification so that appropriate treatment recommendations can be made. The success of each assessment in achieving that fundamental goal should be the subject of future research.

It is as unethical to overtreat as it is to undertreat. One must ask if any of the assessment processes noted in this chapter have the level of sensitivity and specificity in its classifications to strike the correct balance. A thorough assessment that accurately screens those who are significantly affected from those who are not reduces the number of babies who are treated when they should not be and, hopefully, increases the number of babies who will be treated when necessary. Tania's story points to this notion.

Tania's son, Jackson, was born at home and went to breast well within 30 to 45 minutes after birth. The midwife noted he had a heart-shaped tongue. Tania had an abundant milk supply, and a fast milk ejection reflex (let-down), one that caused Jackson to gulp and sometimes vomit post feed. Tania never experienced sore nipples, nor did Jackson have difficulty gaining weight. When Tania expressed some interest about the heart shape of Jackson's tongue, the doctor had the nurse hold the baby down while he quickly snipped Jackson's frenulum. Tania was mortified. She merely had wanted to have a discussion about the possibility of clipping the frenulum. She reported that after the clipping, Jackson took less time to feed but that his latch and suck felt the same to her. She feels uncertain that the clipping was responsible for the shorter feeds; Jackson then was 8 weeks old and simply might have gotten stronger and bigger. Was he tongue-tied or not?

Treatment without thorough assessment creates this kind of confusion. Parents should be adequately educated so they can make informed decisions about their child's care. Just because the treatment for tongue-tie is most often a simple snip with the scissors does not warrant the abandonment of careful assessment, thoughtful conversation, and informed consent.

ASSESSMENT SYSTEMS FOR CHILDREN AND ADULTS

THE FERNANDO TONGUE TIE ASSESSMENT PROTOCOL

Fernando developed the Tongue Tie Assessment Protocol (TAPP) using normal ranges of tongue motion as a basis for determining degree of deficit in tongue-tied individuals, which provides a screening tool for children and adults. Fernando chose the seven criteria of the protocol "because they were consistently found to be affected in the majority of subjects with tongue-tie and, in my experience, are generally found to be within normal limits in patients without tongue-tie." Her seven criteria include cosmetic appearance, oral hygiene and dental health, feeding skills, lingual movement, oral kinaesthesia, speech, and emotional status. She remains the only researcher-clinician who espouses assessment of the emotional impact of tongue-tie.

These seven categories are broken down into five descriptors that classify a range of impact. She assigns a 0 to 4 point value, with each point value corresponding to a specific degree of impact. A 4 assigned to a certain descriptor means the individual performs at an above-average level; a 3 means within normal limits; a 2 means a mild problem; a 1 means a moderately severe problem; and a 0 means a severe problem. The clinician assigns a point value for each category and then adds them to get the total score. The lower the number of points, the more affected the individual (as in the ATLFF scoring system). For example, under Cosmetic Appearance, if the individual's tongue has a normal appearance, a pointed tip, and an intact lingual margin, he or she receives 4 points. If he or she has a frenum and tongue that are conspicuously different at rest and during movement, he or she receives 0 points. Fernando recommends surgery for individuals who receive a total score of 15 or less.

This more complex scoring system, based on a thorough assessment process, allows the assessor to pick up on the variable presentations of tongue-tie and enables the clinician to target therapeutic strategies for optimal postoperative support. This well-thought-through assessment possesses content validity, but has not undergone any reliability studies. The entire TAPP appears in Table 6-6.

Fernando (1998) presents her complete assessment process in her book Tongue Tie: From Confusion to Clarity. She discusses the nuances of the assessment, provides tips on specific aspects of the process, and makes recommendations to the clinician on how to assess certain items in different age groups. Her charting document appears on page 71 of the book, a useful adjunct to the assessment and documentation process. Surgical options appear in the Appendix.

THE GARCIA POLA LINGUAL MOBILITY CLASSIFICATION SYSTEM

Garcia Pola et al. (2002, p. 60) created a classification system designed to distinguish tongue-tie in two groups of children: 6-year-olds and 14-year-olds. Using a caliper micrometer, they took two measurements in each group. In the group of 6-year-olds, they first measured "the distance between the cuspid of an upper canine tooth and a lower homolateral canine tooth in maximum opening."

COSMETIC APPEARANCE		ORAL HYGIENE AND DENTAL HEALTH	
FINDING	**SCORE**	**FINDING**	**SCORE**
The frenum and tongue are conspicuously different at rest and during movement	0	There are dental caries, food debris, a bitten tongue, a rash and frequent dribble	0
The frenum is tight, and there is obvious abnormal movement	1	There are dental caries, food debris, rash and dribbling	1
The frenum is visible during speech and is tight on palpation	2	There are dental caries or dribbling and rash around the lips	2
The frenum is visible during speech but is not tight	3	There is hypersalivation during rapid speech and occasional dribble	3
The tongue has normal appearance	4	There are no current problems or history of excessive dribbling	4

FEEDING SKILLS		LINGUAL MOVEMENT	
FINDING	**SCORE**	**FINDING**	**SCORE**
Current breastfeeding problems, or other severe persistent feeding problems still apparent	0	1 task achieved	0
Slow, fussy feeding, poor chewing and licking, drinking during meals to facilitate swallowing	1	2 tasks achieved	1
Slow eating all foods, and inability to lick	2	3 tasks achieved	2
Problems in infancy but none now	3	4 tasks achieved	3
No problems at any stage	4	5 tasks achieved	4

Note. Lingual movement tasks include protrusion with downward pointing; horizontal protrusion; protrusion with upward pointing; circumlocution; lateral movement; and retraction of the tongue.

ORAL KINAESTHESIA: PART 1		ORAL KINAESTHESIA: PART 2	
FINDING	**SCORE**	**FINDING**	**SCORE**
Able to coordinate 1 consonant only in 10 slow repetitions	0	1 task achieved	0
Able to coordinate 1 consonant in 10 fast repetitions	1	2 tasks achieved	1
Able to coordinate 2 consonants together in 10 slow repetitions	2	3 tasks achieved	2
Able to coordinate 2 consonants together in 15 fast repetitions	3	4 tasks achieved	3
Able to coordinate 3 consonants together in 15 fast repetitions	4	5 tasks achieved	4

Note. Kinaesthesia tasks include: Hold air in the cheeks and pop; protrude the tongue in the midline, withdraw and protrude to the right, withdraw then protrude to the left; protrude and make a cross on the lips with the tongue; protrude and make a cross (x) on the lips; poke tongue into left cheek, out at middle of lips, and into right cheek.

SPEECH		EMOTIONAL STATUS	
FINDING	**SCORE**	**FINDING**	**SCORE**
Severely defective, or disorders in 3 modes (articulation, voice, resonance, fluency, or rhythm) or more	0	Difficult to manage and has more than one symptom of behavioral disturbance	0
Moderate speech disorder in 2 modes	1	Upset by failures during testing and has one symptom of behavioral disturbance	1
Mildly defective in the articulatory mode only	2	Upset by failures in testing, speech or lingual difficulties	2
Within normal limits with a few inconsistencies	3	Confident in all areas, but sensitive about lingual difficulties	3
Normal speech at all times	4	Confident and stable with no emotional or behavioral problems	4

Table 6-6. The Fernando Tongue tie Assessment Protocol. Note. From Tongue-tie: From Confusion to Clarity by C. Fernando, Concord, New South Wales: Tandem Publications.

The second measurement recorded "the distance between the same points of reference when the tip of the tongue reaches the palatal papilla." In the 14-year-olds, they first measured the distance between the upper central incisor border and the lower homolateral central incisor border; and the second, as with the 6-year-olds, measured "the distance between the same points of reference when the tip of the tongue reaches the palatal papilla." From these measurements, the authors developed a classification system for lingual mobility. Three levels were established for each group: LI, LII, and LIII (p. 60):

- LI = Lingual mobility between 51 and 100 percent of the measurement for maximum opening
- LII = Lingual mobility between 31 and 50 percent of the measurement for maximum opening
- LIII = Lingual mobility less than 30 percent of the measurement for maximum opening

The researchers then paired an individual's lingual mobility classification with his or her ability to pronounce a rolling r. If the person could not, he or she was classified as dysglossic (rhotacism). Individuals who were classified as LII or LIII and who were dysglossic were considered candidates for surgery.

Several problems using this classification system seem obvious. The authors measured only 6-year-olds and 14-year-olds. To be generalizeable, an assessment process should establish normal ranges of motion for children in multiple age groups. In addition, the performance of a rolling r may or may not be an indicator of dyglossia in all cultures. Many English-speaking people who have normal tongue motion cannot perform a rolling r.

The authors assessed only tongue lift. Although there was a positive correlation between dysglossia and LII and LIII classification, the inclusion of tongue extrusion, lateralization, bolus handling, and other tongue motions probably would generate more specificity in the screening process. It is possible that these authors missed some tongue-ties as a result of these limitations of their assessment tool. More research should be conducted to establish the validity and reliability of this system.

THE KOTLOW ANKYLOGLOSSIA CLASSIFICATION SYSTEM AND DIVISION CRITERIA

Kotlow presented a system of ankyloglossia classification (1999) to help others determine the presence of tongue-tie in the general population of children. He used a Boley gauge to measure the distance of attachment of the lingual frenulum from the tongue base to its tip in a group of 322 children who ranged in age from 18 months to 14 years. He then used nine criteria of tongue motion to determine which frenula required surgical treatment. In his system, Class III and Class IV were most likely to present with the greatest tongue mobility deficits. He advised that these frenula always be divided. His classification appears in Table 6-7 and the division criteria in Table 6-8.

CATEGORY	CLASS	LABEL	MEASUREMENT OF FREE TONGUE
1	Clinically acceptable	Normal range of free tongue	> than 16 mm
2	Class I	Mild ankyloglossia	12-16 mm
3	Class II	Moderate ankyloglossia	8-11 mm
4	Class III	Severe ankyloglossia	3-7 mm
5	Class IV	Complete ankyloglossia	< than 3 mm

Table 6-7. Kotlow Ankyloglossia Classification System. Note. From "Ankyloglossia (tongue-tie): a diagnostic and treatment quandary," by L.A. Kotlow, 1999, *Pediatric Dentistry*, 30, 259-260.

	CRITERIA FOR DIVISION
1	The tip of the tongue cannot protrude outside the mouth without clefting
2	The tip of the tongue strains when sweeping the upper and lower lips
3	The retruded tongue causes blanching of the tissue near the lingual anterior teeth
4	The tongue places excessive force on the mandibular anterior teeth
5	The lingual frenulum does not allow a normal swallowing pattern
6	The lingual frenulum causes a diastema between the mandibular central incisors
7	The underside of the infant tongue exhibits abrasion
8	The frenulum prevents the breastfed infant from correctly attaching to the mother's nipple
9	Children exhibit speech difficulties

Table 6-8. Kotlow Ankyloglossia Classification System. Note. From "Ankyloglossia (tongue-tie): a diagnostic and treatment quandary," by L.A. Kotlow, 1999, *Pediatric Dentistry*, 30, 259-260.

Kotlow's criteria suggest the worst possible presentation of tongue-tie. He lists only symptoms that occur in the worst ankyloglossia situations as noted by other researchers. His criteria also are vague in spots, lacking the necessary specificity to generate an objective evaluation. His classification system seems to lack correlation with his criteria. Although he states that Class III and IV were most likely to correlate with the worst symptoms, he does not indicate which of the symptoms serving as criteria for surgical treatment correlate with Class I and II. Two studies – one by Naimer et al. (2003) and another by Kupietzky and Botzer (2005) – used Kotlow's system as the assessment basis for their studies. Neither of these studies addresses validity or reliability of this classification system.

Kotlow makes a valiant attempt to formally assess tongue-tie criteria as a way to more accurately define the condition and identify cases in which surgical treatment is necessary. This system gives dental clinicians a better guide for assessing tongue movements and orofacial development than they had previously. Perhaps his presentation of this system has influenced dentists to be more cognizant and thorough in their routine oral assessments. The system could benefit from substantial further refinement.

RUFFOLI INTERINCISAL DISTANCE

Ruffoli et al. undertook a study (2005) to compare measurements of interincisal distance and lingual frenulum length against morpohofunctional tongue factors. They generated a mean for both measurement methods by evaluating 200 Italian children aged 6 to 12. To obtain the frenular length mean, they measured the length of the lingual frenulum from mouth floor to tongue insertion when the subject opened his or her mouth to its fullest extent while keeping the tip of the tongue touching the palatal papilla. They obtained the interincisal distance mean by performing a measurement of distance between the incisal margins of the upper central and the lower homolateral central incisor. All measurements were taken with a Boley gauge.

Once the researchers established a mean (a measure of less than 2.3 cm indicates the presence of tongue-tie), they compared it against several morphofunctional criteria previously identified as deficits associated with tongue-tie. This study found that interincisal distance compromise accurately correlates with these other deficits. They suggest that the interincisal distance measure is an easy and efficient way to determine the presence of tongue-tie in this population of children, and can easily and confidently be substituted for other assessments.

In an earlier study, Lalakea and Messner (2002) concluded that interincisal distance was a more accurate gauge of tongue-tie than tongue protrusion. The Ruffoli et al. (2005) study certainly confirms this premise. However, using only this single criterion may potentially miss mild ties that can adversely affect aspects of morphofunction, such as tongue lateralization and position of the tongue-tip during swallowing. If further study confirms the substitutability of interincisal distance for other movement parameters, then this simple single-criterion assessment could be adopted as a standard for this age group.

THE MARCHESAN CLASSIFICATION SYSTEM

Over a 23-year period, Marchesan evauated 1,402 patients for tongue-tie. Patients ranged in age from 8 months to 62 years. Using a caliper to measure maximal distance, she first measured the distance between the upper right incisal edge and the lower right incisal edge. The second measure was taken with these same oral markers but with the tongue sucked up onto the palate. If the difference between these two values was one-half or more, the lingual frenulum was classified as normal. In addition to these measurements, Marchesan identified eight other criteria that refined her assessment of an "altered" frenulum (pp. 32, 35):

1. The frenulum did not allow adequate movement of the tongue.

2. The frenulum had an insertion in or beneath the inferior alveolar ridge.

3. The frenulum did not allow tongue suction on the palate even if there was an insertion in the middle of the tongue.

4. When the tongue was raised, the shape of the tip was more square than round.

5. When the tip of the tongue was raised toward the palate, only the edges could raise.

6. For the tongue to reach the palate, the patient had to nearly close the mouth.

7. When the tongue was sucked up on the palate, the distance between the incisal edges was less than 13mm.

8. The frenulum inserted anteriorly, from the middle of the tongue underside to the tongue tip.

Marchesan's system (Marchesan, 2004) shows a level of specificity missing in other assessment schemas. Her breakdown of factors looks similar to those of the ATLFF. She bases her criteria on the comparative performance of normal vs. abnormal frenula. This system represents a jumping-off place for a standardized assessment process. I wonder, however, if she found variations from patient to patient in the degree of presentation of these various criteria? For example, were there degrees of ability to maintain tongue suction for a certain time limit, rather than the subject's ability to perform the task at all? Did some patients show an ability to raise the tongue toward the palate but an inability to perform other tongue movements adequately? In her article "Lingual Frenulum: Classification and Speech Interference," she does not indicate the possible variations of presentation or how to assess them

The strength of this assessment schema lies in its sensitivity. Although it needs further development to become more objective and consistent, it has the potential to be an excellent standardized assessment and/or screening tool for children and adults.

IN SUMMARY

There is no question which of these systems stands the chance of garnering a detailed and accurate assessment for the presence of tongue-tie while determining the degree to which it affects Activities of Daily Living. Although Fernando's TAPP assessment process involves assessing multiple complex factors and requires an assessor possessing a high level of skill and knowledge, it ensures that clinicians correctly identify tongue-tied individuals who need surgical intervention. Although the system may be too complex for some specialists to grasp, the process appears appropriate for use by speech- language pathologists and orofacial myologists – most of whom have the skills needed to perform the assessment. A shorter, less complex version may be needed for use in other professions.

Several of these systems for older individuals use interincisal distance as a marker for the presence and severity of tongue-tie. This factor represents only one indicator of tongue function and has yet to be validated for use as a singular marker for identifying tongue-tied individuals. Srinivasan and colleagues attempted to create an algorithm for making the decision to perform frenotomy, and several of these later researchers may be contemplating a similar approach. They simply want a justification assessment for intervening surgically rather than a formula for an overall treatment plan based on thorough clinical assessment of the types and degrees of deficits.

If the briefer form is used, surgery can be justified, but such a decision rule may miss certain types of tongue-tie presentation, leaving the individual without appropriate and timely treatment. If a longer and more specific assessment process is used, practitioners will have to learn new skills to accommodate that assessment process, but also will be able to formulate a more thorough treatment plan.

Is it realistic and/or practical for practitioners across various professions to learn the same assessment skills? Should certain practitioners in certain fields be the sole discriminators of the presence of tongue-tie? Or should practitioners work in teams to properly assess and determine appropriate courses of action? Is there a way to be both thorough and brief? If so, what are the requirements that will allow for both, and still identify all tongue-tied individuals? Is classification different from assessment, and if so, how? Does classification serve to provide a common language for clinicians, but fail to provide appropriate markers for intervention decisions? Are assessment processes, by nature, too complex to provide that universal set of standards that enables clinicians and researchers to share language when discussing tongue-tie? These represent fundamental questions that require answers.

Consensus is building. Already there is a move to thoughtfully consider standardization. Researchers and clinicians must continually engage in dialogue until all the issues receive their just attention. This discussion process will continue to uncover new questions and answer old ones until a solid groundwork is laid – a foundation for building a solid structure that will truly meet the needs of those individuals afflicted with tongue-tie.

METHODOLOGICAL CONSIDERATIONS

Reviewers rightly have pointed out the flaws in the design, execution, and conclusions drawn by tongue-tie researchers. We still must resolve some fundamental issues relative to the impact, assessment, and treatment of tongue-tie. The lack of recognition of a universally standardized definition, coupled with the lack of a universally accepted assessment tool for tongue-tie, keeps us from accumulating the kinds of data about which all researchers and clinicians feel confident. Some of the criticism launched at current systems of measurement arises from methodological considerations. Any assessment or measuring tool must satisfy two general methodological principles: validity and reliability. When an assessment process is able to achieve both, researchers and clinicians can feel confident in the assessment tool and/or process.

VALIDITY

Validity concerns the degree to which a measure accurately assesses a concept or manifestation – in this case, the presence of tongue-tie. **Face validity** refers to the degree to which a measure seems to be an accurate means to gain the information it is designed to gain. Does it seem accurate? Does it seem well-designed? **Content validity** refers to the degree to which a measure reflects the specific content domain. For instance, when assessing for tongue-tie, an assessment of tongue elevation inside the mouth would be considered more valid than assessing the ability of the individual to touch the tip of the tongue to the eyebrow. Observations clearly show that many people with normal tongues cannot touch their eyebrows with their tongues, but that tongue elevation inside the mouth may be dramatically impaired when a lingual frenulum is shorter and/or tighter. **Construct validity** refers to the degree of agreement between a theoretical concept and a specific measuring device or procedure. Theoretically, a tongue-tied individual will experience decreased tongue mobility relative to non-tongue-tied individuals. Does the measuring tool address decreased tongue mobility, and how and to what degree does it do so?

RELIABILITY

Reliability refers to *consistency*. Does a measuring tool consistently measure what it is designed to measure? Does the tongue-tie screening tool consistently measure the presence of tongue-tie, or does it result in false positives that are actually other types of structurally related sucking problems? The first important aspect of assessment tool reliability is its stability. On repeated trials, does the tool consistently yield the same result? On a second and third assessment using the same measures, will the subject assessed as having tongue-tie still be assessed as having tongue-tie?

A second important aspect of reliability is internal consistency. To what extent does the assessment tool assess a characteristic or quality? This is a measure of precision. Since tongue-tie causes tongue extrusion deficits (poor tongue extrusion has been found to negatively impact breastfeeding), does the assessment tool or process contain a measure for the degree of tongue-extrusion deficit in the breastfed baby using precise markers? The third important aspect of reliability is interrater reliability which refers to the extent to which two or more raters agree. It reflects the consistency of the *implementation* of a measuring tool. When two assessors assess the same individual's ability to lateralize their tongue, do their results agree?

CRITIQUING RESEARCH

When performing or interpreting research, the researcher or clinician must consider how the study was designed. Was the study as a whole valid? (Are its results generalizeable and/or transferable, and was it rigorous?) Was the study reliable, i.e., can it be replicated? Were the measurement or assessment tools valid and reliable? The degree to which validity and reliability can be asserted determines the degree to which one can consider the results to be robust and applicable.

The reader must always read and interpret a study, assessment process, or procedure with a critical eye, looking especially for favored criteria. Although clinical experience and anecdotal evidence are important, ultimately a shift in clinical practice must be grounded in strong empirical evidence. The move in the mid-20th century to stop clipping lingual frenula was a poor clinical decision based on a lack of empirical evidence. Studies examining the issue should have been undertaken before determining that clipping frenula was never necessary. The resistance to reinstating a screening process and treatment protocol for tongue-tie also is based on a lack of empirical evidence.

Fortunately, we are moving toward a much stronger base of evidence that will ultimately support early screening and intervention for tongue-tie. We still need more research that moves us toward universal standards: a universally accepted definition; valid and reliable assessment tools; and rigorous studies that help us determine best treatment practices and identify long-term consequences of various strategies. The exponential increase in research during this decade alone has established increasing interest in the phenomenon and momentum that will help us break through the longstanding barriers to cooperation among practitioners on this issue.

For consideration: How much empirical evidence will be enough? Does one well-designed, valid, and reliable study using valid and reliable measures constitute enough evidence to justify changing clinical practice? Or will it take more and if so, how much? For this book, I examined more than 300 empirical studies in the English language. The vast majority of the evidence supports surgical intervention when tongue function is impaired. At what point does mere bulk play a role in turning the clinical tide? Or will it take that one magical, perfectly designed study to convince the unconvinced?

CHAPTER SIX TAKEAWAY

1. All babies, no matter what the feeding method, should be screened for tongue-tie, preferably within the first week of life. A universal screening process is an ideal way to prevent tongue-tie-related issues from developing as the child grows.

2. A thorough assessment process should be used when determining if tongue-tie is present. The ideal assessment process uses a valid and reliable instrument.

3. The assessment tool for infants that most closely matches these criteria is the Hazelbaker Assessment Tool for Lingual Frenulum Function. Perhaps it or another tool soon will possess all the necessary qualities that will make it the perfect tool for routine screening. The TAPP most closely matches these criteria for assessing tongue-tie in the older child, adolescent, and adult populations.

4. A determination of tongue-tie should be made first on function and second on appearance. The now-substantial body of available research shows that functional criteria supersede appearance criteria.

5. Clinicians assessing babies for feeding problems also should be thorough in their assessment of all other aspects of the feeding situation. The clinician also should suggest evidence-based or theory-driven management interventions to optimize the feeding relationship. This may include recommending and performing surgery for the tongue-tie.

6. If a clinician assesses an older child, that assessment should include speech evaluation, dental evaluation, oral toilet evaluation, orofacial development evaluation and behavior evaluation. Again, function first, and appearance second. If management strategies alone fail to correct any deficits found in these areas, surgery is indicated.

7. If a clinician recommends surgery, follow-up assessment and management of feeding and other deficits is a necessity!

CHAPTER SEVEN
TREATMENT

"I HAVE HAD MANY moms suffer for months with sore nipples and low milk supply," reports Pam, an International Board Certified Lactation Consultant, "because their pediatricians or ENTs say that the tongue is a non-issue, only to have the [frenulum] clipped and find out how much better things are." She suggests that it makes doctors look foolish when they are proven wrong, which undermines the trust that mothers put in them. She further shares that a knowledgeable pediatrician in her area of the country commented, "We have so few magic pills when it comes to breastfeeding problems, this [treating tongue-tie] is one thing we can do that makes a huge difference – and we should be doing it."

At this time, parents feel confused and remain caught in the middle. Within the ranks of professionals, there exists misunderstanding about and resistance to the various treatment procedures and the reasons that justify treatment. For example, 90 percent of pediatricians who responded to a questionnaire about tongue-tie indicated that the condition rarely, if ever, causes infant feeding problems. This same study found that disagreement exists even among lactation consultants, the group most likely to advocate tongue-tie treatment (Messner and Lalakea, 2000a).

In an effort to address these inconsistencies and take parents out of the middle, this chapter clarifies treatment procedures, illuminates the controversy surrounding the risks and benefits of treatment, addresses treatment timing, presents research-based recommendations for treating infants and older children, and closes with a discussion of post-treatment therapies.

FRENOTOMY, FRENECTOMY, STRIPPING, CLIPPING, AND DIVIDING

WHAT'S IN A NAME?

Researchers refer to and discuss three procedures for the treatment of tongue-tie: Frenotomy (also called ankylotomy, clipping, division, frenulotomy), utilizes a pair of scissors or other instrument to incise or cut through the lingual frenulum; stripping, which is a very old technique (some would say barbaric) of dividing the lingual frenulum using force; and frenectomy (frenuloplasty), a combination of techniques that removes frenular tissue and sometimes divides muscle fibers at the tongue base. One way to avoid confusion is to notice the term's suffix: otomy means incision and ectomy means excision.

The least invasive and extensive procedure – frenotomy – requires little to no anesthesia and usually can be performed in an office setting. (See Figure 7-1.) Frenectomy, which is a more difficult course of action, usually requires anesthesia and hospitalization, although it is sometimes performed on an outpatient basis.

One rarely sees the word ankylotomy, which means to cut through fused or adhesed tissue, in modern medical writings. The medical term division, meaning to separate into two or more parts, seems to have taken the place of the older word; both are used interchangeably with frenotomy, as is clipping. Clipping is perhaps the best and most accessible term; frenotomy and frenectomy are so often confused that using the word clipping aids in the distinction between these two very different procedures.

Frenotomy sometimes is referred to as frenulotomy. The extra letters in the latter come from the root word of frenulum, whereas the root word for frenotomy is frenum. Frenulum and frenum are interchangeable terms meaning restraining structure or part.

TOOLS AND PROCEDURES

Frenotomy can be further broken down into procedure types, depending upon the instrument used to cut through the tissue. Various types of scissors, lasers, and other tools currently are used. Choice of instrument depends in part on ease of use, cost, and accessibility. The vast majority of all types of practitioners seem to prefer scissors for simple frenotomy. Scalpel, electrocautery, or laser seem to be the tools of choice for oral surgeons and ear, nose, and throat physicians who perform frenectomies.

Martin (as cited in Fernando, 1998) uses a frenular clamp to cut circulation to the lingual frenulum, followed by division using fine pointed scissors. This is his preferred method even with older children. He uses frenotomy in tandem with anesthesia delivered via mask. Backes (C. Backes personal communication, 1994) also minimizes or eliminates bleeding by clamping the frenulum with hemostats prior to incision. He then uses a pair of sharp blunt-tipped scissors to incise the tissue. Rather than using an instrument to lift the tongue, Amir uses thumb and forefinger and then divides the frenulum with a small sterile scissors (Amir et al., 2005, p. 243).

Coryllos swabs the lingual frenulum with benzocaine and then performs the "simple snip" with blunt-ended scissors (Coryllos et al., 2004, p .3). Ballard (2002) uses a grooved retractor to lift the tongue before incising the lingual frenulum with sterile iris scissors. Griffiths (2004) lifts the tongue with the forefinger and holds the lower lip clear of the operative site with the thumb. Again, sterile blunt-ended scissors are used. He does not employ anesthesia because the needle punctures cause as much or more bleeding and more discomfort than the incision itself.

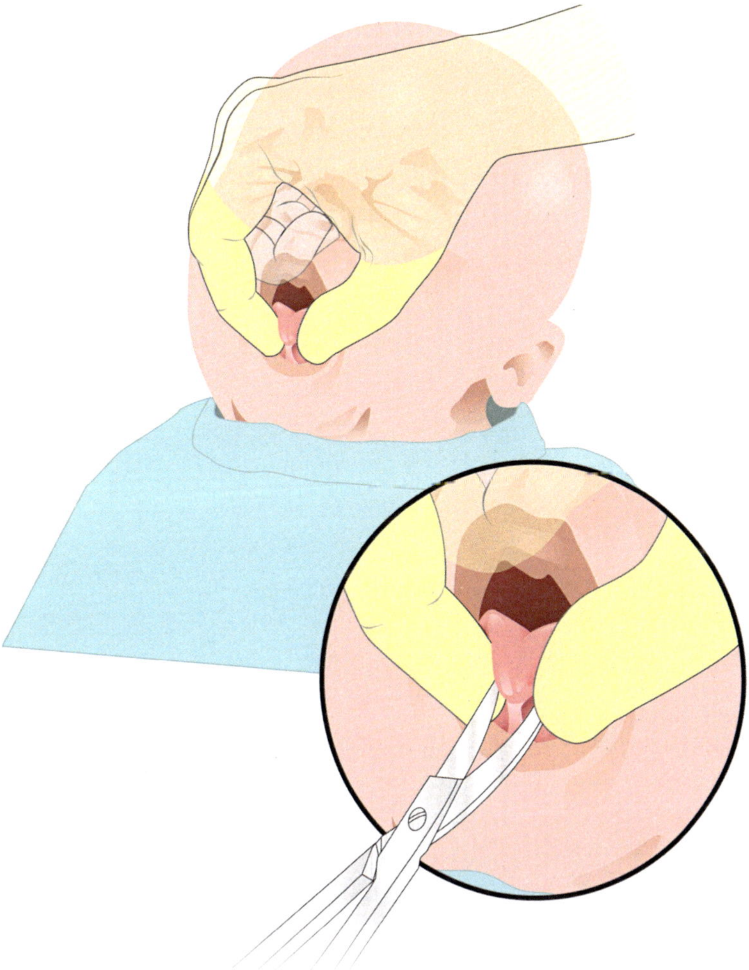

Figure 7-1 Frenotomy using sterile scissors. © 2010 Alison K. Hazelbaker. Reprinted with permission.
Artist: Paul Hughes.

Kotlow (2004) describes the frenotomy procedure performed with an Erbium: YAG laser and without anesthesia. He lifts the tongue with either his fingers or a Miltex grooved director and then "revises" (incises) the frenulum with one exposure to the laser. He indicates that dentists employ this type of laser with more and more frequency in their practices to treat a variety of soft-tissue-related dental issues because it is effective and easy, causing little to no discomfort for patients. He describes outcomes similar to those reported by practitioners using the more common scissors technique.

Two articles (Kummer, 2005; Naimer et al., 2003), discuss the use of electrocautery diathermy for frenotomy. Electrocautery uses a device that passes an electric current through an electrode.

The electrode used in oral surgery is a metal "needle" that is heated by an electrical current. This high frequency current generates enough heat to cut into tissue and cauterize the surrounding blood vessels. The zone of effect is controlled by the frequency and power of the device, in combination with the skill of the surgeon. Electrocautery does not transfer any electrical current to the patient. This procedure can be performed in an office setting and does not require general anesthetic but Naimer uses a mepivacaine local for anesthesia with great result. Kummer reports that patients can forgo anesthesia with this technique.

STRIPPING

Stripping severs the tissues underlying the tongue with a sharp instrument and usually is performed after incising the frenulum. Alternatively, the practitioner incises the frenulum, grasps the tongue, and pulls it sharply upward to rip through tissues near the tongue base. Several authors agree that stripping the tongue is dangerous at best and deadly at worst because of the damage it does to underlying structures of the tongue (Butlin and Spencer, 1900; Horton et al., 1969; Notestine, 1990). Despite the fact that this dangerous form of stripping has not been done for nearly a century (Horton), current authors write about it as if it is common practice.

Oral surgeons, however, may use a modern and less violent form of stripping when performing frenectomy. Fernando (1998, p.72) reports that Dr. Martin Glasson uses cutting diathermy to divide the lingual frenulum and then performs a transverse incision in the genioglossus muscle. This approach, she explains "achieve[s] maximum release. Just how far to go is a matter of surgical judgment and it is felt that this aspect of the operation is the single most important aspect which ensures a good result." Glasson performs this treatment on older children and adults who experience speech problems and the other complications associated with tongue-tie. Today's method of stripping, of course, utilizes modern techniques, procedures, and instruments that minimize risks.

FRENECTOMY

Frenectomy involves cutting the lingual frenulum out of the surrounding tissue. (See Figure 7-2.) Frenectomy is an extensive procedure, requiring the treated individual to receive local or general anesthetic, and undergo recovery, postoperative care, and therapy. Typically, surgeons use a procedure called frenuloplasty, ("plasty" means to shape via surgery), to excise the frenulum and possibly cut into the genioglossus muscle to free the tongue for optimal lift; they then resect, or bring together, the edges of the surgery site using sutures (Archer, 1975; Ayers and Hilton, 1977; Catlin and DeHaan, 1971). More recent techniques involve using a laser to excise the frenulum and cauterize the wound, eliminating the need for sutures (Fiorotti et al., 2004).

The typical procedure involves anesthetizing the patient and then suturing the tongue-tip, using a traction suture. The lingual frenulum is excised by making cuts at the floor of the mouth and on the underside of the tongue. This procedure leaves a diamond-shaped opening in the mucosa near the base of the tongue. The edges of the mucosa are then brought together and sutured. The

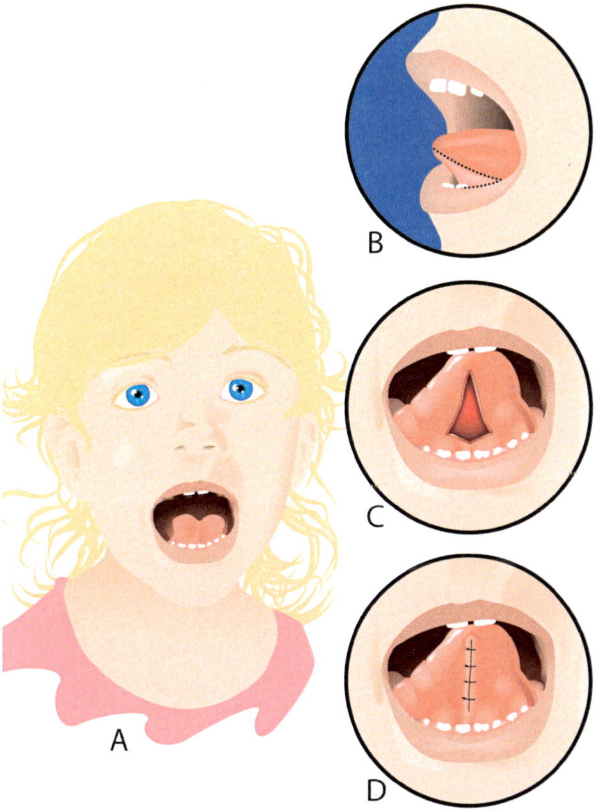

Figure 7-2. Horizontal to vertical frenuloplasty. A. Heart shaped tongue requiring surgical release. B. Excision lines. C. Diamond-shaped wound after excision. D. Vertical closure with sutures. When performed by laser, no sutures are necessary. © 2010 Alison K. Hazelbaker. Reprinted with permission. Artist: Paul Hughes.

closed wound takes on a vertical appearance (Horton et al., 1969; Jolly, 1968; Moore, 1985; Oldfield, 1955). Variations on this technique include transection of the genioglossus muscle to varying depths, creation of extra incisions on either side of the lingual frenulum to aid excision, and alternate closure techniques that involve additional incisions on either side of the primary incision to lengthen the wound, resulting in a "z" appearance of the closed wound. This latter variation is known as a z-plasty (Horton et al., 1969; Kaban, 1990; Profitt and Bell, 1980). (See Figure 7-3.)

Very little controversy seems to exist regarding the frenectomy procedure, and most descriptions of the procedure are remarkably similar (Ayers and Hilton, 1977; Fernando, 1998; Lalakea and Messner, 2003; Oldfield, 1955). The discussion about which technique to use revolves around the following issues: degree of release of the tissue; ease of surgical technique; postoperative healing time; comparative effectiveness of hemostasis (sutures vs. cautery); the type of anesthetic used (local vs. general); the prevention of scar formation; and subsequent re-ankylosis of the tissue

(Fiorotti et al., 2004; Heller et al., 2005; Lalakea and Messner, 2002, Li, Kang, Lin, Huang, and Lin, 2005; Velanovich, 1994).

The advances in the procedure come from the use of laser technology. This technology eliminates the need for sutures and general anesthesia (Fiorotti et al., 2004). The surgeon, however, must be extremely careful with the laser because it easily penetrates soft tissue. No author indicates if this technique requires special surgical skill.

As described in Fiorotti et al. (2004), using a CO_2 laser results in healing time similar to that of conventional surgery, but is superior because:

> [There is] no mechanical contact with the surgical wound and hence no risk of contamination. The absence of bleeding and a minimum amount of tissue manipulation because no suturing is needed, lead to a better postoperative result with the minimum need of symptomatic medication. (p.66)

The CO_2 laser, an infrared laser beam produced by passing electricity through carbon dioxide gas, cuts and cauterizes soft tissue. This tool performs effectively because high-water-content soft tissue, such as the oral mucosa, responds easily to this form of surgery.

Technique and technology used depends largely on the specialist performing the procedure. Different specialties lean toward different techniques, possibly determined by the nature of presenting problems and the age group with whom they are working (Messner and Lalakea, 2000a).

FRENOTOMY, FRENECTOMY. IS THERE A DIFFERENCE?

Several authors seem confused about the differences between the frenotomy and frenectomy procedures. Fleiss (1990) refers to frenectomy as a surgical incision. Wilton (1990) and Cunha (2008) describe the frenotomy procedure but call it frenectomy. Kummer (2005) describes frenulectomy as a division of the frenulum with scissors or electrocautery performed in office and requiring no anesthetic. Based on these citations, one might conclude that some physicians are reluctant to suggest treatment of tongue-tie because they are confused and think that all ties must be treated by frenectomy, the more involved and invasive of the two current treatments. Reluctance based on this assumption is understandable. Putting a patient under general anesthetic to remove tissue and place sutures is no small matter and carries specific risks.

Our discussion in the remainder of this chapter focuses on the frenotomy procedure as the preferred method of treatment for infant tongue-tie, and as a proposed treatment, using sterile scissors or laser for tongue-tied toddlers and young children. Otherwise, frenectomy remains the treatment of choice for older children, adolescents, and adults until research confirms (as in my case) that frenotomy coupled with post-surgical therapy resolves problems associated with tongue-tie in the older individual.

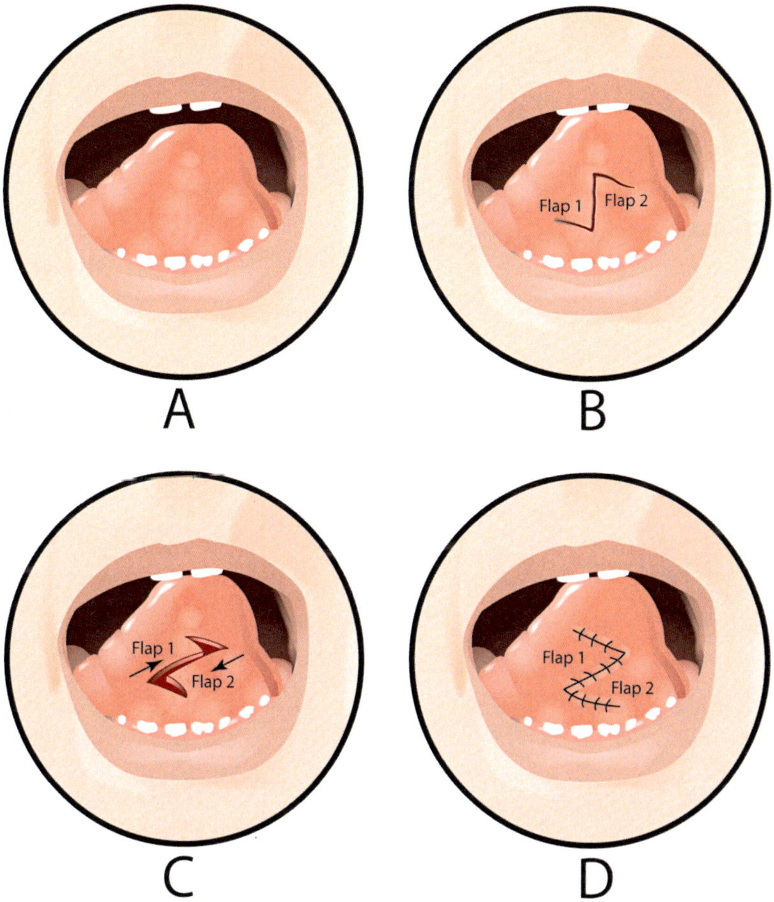

Figure 7-3. Z-plasty frenuloplasty/frenectomy. A. Tongue-tie preventing optimal tongue mobility. B. Z-shaped incision/excision. C. Rearrangement of the flaps to create tongue length and improve tongue mobility. D. Suture placement to ensure proper healing. © 2010 Alison K. Hazelbaker. Reprinted with permission. Artist: Paul Hughes.

TO CLIP OR NOT TO CLIP. IS THAT THE QUESTION?

Brinkman et al. (2004) endeavored to identify the attitudes and practices of Australian pediatric surgeons regarding tongue-tie in children. They found that 73 percent of the respondents performed surgical release of tongue-tie. Oral and maxillofacial surgeons performed surgery the most often. Pediatric general surgeons released the tongue using simple frenotomy, whereas plastic surgeons were more likely to use frenuloplasty. Across specialties, respondents believed that surgical release resulted in success more than 75 percent of the time (2004).

Messner and Lalakea (2000a) found that pediatricians are most likely to balk at treating tongue-tie, whereas lactation consultants and speech pathologists are more likely to believe that surgical treatment results in favorable outcomes. Across and within the specialties surveyed in this study, disagreement still exists regarding the significance of tongue-tie and the need for surgical treatment.

Despite the tongue-tie controversy, surprisingly only a few authors claim that treatment is never necessary. In Nelson's Textbook of Pediatrics (1987, p.361), Behrman et al. (Eds.) state, "The tongue appears relatively large; the frenulum may be short, but rarely, if ever, is this a reason for cutting it." Hoekelman (1987) says that tongue protrusion can be inhibited by a short, thick lingual frenulum, but it rarely interferes with speech and therefore requires no treatment. In Care of the Newborn, Schreiner and Bradburn (Eds., 1988, p. 24) describe tongue-tie as a "normal finding" and claim that it "never requires therapy in the neonatal period." McEnery and Gaines (1941) state that tongue-tie does not cause a problem with breastfeeding and, therefore, surgery is unnecessary.

Kummer admits that "although approximately 25 percent of newborns with ankyloglossia will have some trouble latching on to a nipple for suckling the majority have no early feeding problems." (2005, p. 2). She denies that tongue-tied individuals have speech problems despite the possible tongue mobility deficits that may produce problems with oral toilet, dental diastema, and "recreational functions like licking an ice cream cone" (p. 6). She does not advocate treatment during the newborn period.

Definitive statements such as "Ankyloglossia: an oral defect, characterized by an abnormally short lingual frenulum that limits tongue movement and impairs the speech. It may be surgically corrected by a frenotomy." (Anderson and Anderson, Eds., 1990, p. 56) are not very common in the literature. Authors most often take a circumstantial approach, i.e., treatment depends on the circumstances. For example, Berg (1990b, p.101) presented two cases of tongue-tie in which one required frenotomy and the other did not. Auerbach (1990, p. 101) says, "Each baby with a tight frenulum requires individualized evaluation, observation, care plan, and follow-up. As with most conditions, some infants need no intervention. In other situations, surgical intervention may be necessary."

Hussey (1974) based his judgments on a systematic method of assessment. If certain tongue movements could not be adequately performed, surgery would be indicated. His assessment identified tongue-tie when the tongue did not easily protrude beyond the lower gum, lateralize to the corners of the mouth, lift to the superior alveolar ridge, and notch at the tip when efforts to protrude the tongue were made. Notestine (1990) states that breast size and elasticity, baby's mouth size, and the degree of the tie are all variables to consider when deciding on a treatment plan. Butlin and Spencer (1900) say that sometimes division of the frenulum is indicated, but should be undertaken only after due deliberation. Gellis and Kagan (1964) claim that a significant number of babies are born with a short frenulum, and that most are asymptomatic; however, it is appropriate to release the tongue surgically if the tie is significant.

Preventing unnecessary frenulum division, as occurred prior to the 1950s, followed by a near ban on surgical release during infancy motivated me to author the Assessment Tool for Lingual

Frenulum Function, which distinguishes those babies who do not have tongue-tie from those who do. I found that careful and thorough assessment identified those babies who would benefit most from treatment. My scoring system (Hazelbaker, 1993) distinguishes among mild, moderate and severe tongue-tie in babies, allowing better clarity in management and treatment decisions.

Fleiss et al. (1990, p. 128) give their readers three indications for treatment that they think are widely accepted by the medical community. These are:

1. Infants with ankyloglossia who are unable to breastfeed satisfactorily as evidenced by poor latch-on, inadequate weight gain, or other problems.

2. Infants with ankyloglossia who are able to breastfeed, but who have other motor dysfunction.

3. Persons of any age with ankyloglossia who desire (or whose parents desire) a frenectomy for social reasons.

Zarem (as cited in Gellis and Kagan, 1978), thinks if a child can protrude the tongue, as in licking a lollipop, the likelihood of a speech problem is minimal. He goes on to say that significant tongue-tie may require z-plasty, but if the frenulum is extremely thin, a frenotomy may be adequate. He bases his opinion on the notion that a simple frenotomy does not release the tongue sufficiently to make a clinical and functional difference.

Marmet et al. (1990) recommend frenotomy after management and suck training efforts have failed. They describe a list of factors to take into consideration when making treatment decisions. These factors include a baby's ability to maintain tongue position over the lower gumline throughout breastfeeding, form a seal with the tongue, and perform a sufficient progressive contractile tongue action for adequate milk transfer.

Kotlow (1999) recommends that pediatric dentists assess their patients for tongue-tie starting at age 1, and to treat if he or she fails to perform certain tongue movements adequately. For Class IV, or complete tongue-tie, he recommends treatment in all cases. For Class III tongue-tie, he indicates that treatment is necessary in many cases. For moderate tongue-tie (Class I and II in his system), treatment is recommended only if tongue mobility is restricted enough to cause malocclusion, speech, swallowing or oral-toilet problems. He allows that inherent elasticity of the tongue and floor of the mouth may mitigate the development of problems.

Tongue mobility and function serve as the common denominators for these authors. Not one excludes the possibility of treatment and recommends it if tongue mobility is impaired enough to create problems, but only if problems arise. This represents a relatively conservative position based on relevant and measurable criteria. As Defabianis (2000) most eloquently asserts:

> Prophylactic treatment during the early years of life is effective in order to provide harmonious development of the dentition and of the face. When the patient is young, the elimination of negative etiological factors may enlist natural growth forces, provide different growth responses and obtain a balanced bone development before and during the eruption of most permanent teeth. (p. 32)

EFFECTIVENESS OF TREATMENT

Some practitioners would like parents to believe that tongue-tie treatment carries only risk and has relatively little or no positive impact. This belief, which is sensible if you think that tongue-tie has no negative impact on feeding, speech, orofacial development, and oral toilet, cannot be upheld in view of the multiple research studies on the subject published in the 17 years since my original study on post-frenotomy breastfeeding outcomes.

In my study, (Hazelbaker, 1993) four infants of 54 studied prospectively were tongue-tied. The three who underwent simple frenotomy experienced complete cessation of all noted breastfeeding problems. These three mothers experienced decreased nipple and breast pain and rapid healing of damaged nipple and breast tissue. Their babies showed marked improvement in tongue mobility and function, as manifested by better tongue placement and more effective milk removal. The one infant whose parents decided against treatment did not improve with careful management, was switched to bottle immediately after assessment, and was fed expressed breast milk for a short period. The mother soon stopped pumping and gave infant formula instead (Hazelbaker, 1993).

Prior to my study, Marmet et al. (1990) performed a retrospective study of all the tongue-tie cases they encountered in a given year. Of 13 infants presenting with tongue-tie that year, they recommended frenotomy for 10. Seven of those infants received treatment. Of those seven, five improved completely and immediately. The others had significant co-morbidities that required strategic support in addition to frenotomy. These clinicians also instituted suck training prior to and after treatment to ensure proper motion of the tongue at breast.

Messner and Lalakea (2002) note that immediate improvement in breastfeeding post-frenotomy commonly occurs. Mothers describe improved breastfeeding mechanics during the first post-surgery feed and thereafter. Hansen, MacKinlay, and Manson (2006) found that 80 percent of mothers noted improved ease of feeding and 64 percent noted decreased feed time. Forty partially breastfed and four bottle-fed babies comprised Hansen's study population. Hansen saw improvement in both breastfeeding and bottle-feeding skills.

Wallace and Clarke (2006, p. 1259) report on their study population of 10 mother-baby dyads. Of the 10, nine mothers experienced sore nipples, nine babies had poor latch and five of the 10 babies had extended feeding periods. Following simple frenotomy, four of the 10 mothers noticed immediate improvement, another three experienced improvement over the next two weeks and three experienced no improvement at all. The authors do not indicate if the last three had co-morbid factors that would continue to have a negative effect on the feedings.

Hogan et al. (2005) conducted a prospective study comparing the impact of management against frenotomy for the treatment of tongue-tie-related feeding problems (both breast and bottle). In their cohort of 202 tongue-tied babies, only 88 experienced feeding problems. Fifty-seven were enrolled in the study and randomized; 28 were treated with frenotomy, and 29 served as controls, receiving management alone. Of the 29 controls, only one improved with management strategies. In the treated group, all but one improved immediately post-frenotomy. At 48 hours, 28 of the babies in the control group underwent frenotomy at the parents' request. Twenty-seven experienced immediate improvement.

In another study (Masaitis and Kaempf, 1996) of 36 infants, 32 breastfed and four bottle-fed babies underwent frenotomy. Range of tongue-motion improved in all 36 infants. In one week, 27 experienced complete resolution of the feeding problem, seven had partial improvement, and two experienced no resolution. By three months post-treatment, all 36 experienced complete resolution of the feeding problems

Hall and Renfew (2006, p. 1214) complain about these various studies, citing that many contain "poorly defined outcome measures," some are guilty of "introducing a bias by raising the expectations of breastfeeding problems and of improvement from intervention," and some intervene too early, "before breastfeeding is established." These methodological considerations seem now to take on less significance under the weight of the incoming evidence in favor of early treatment. Two studies whose authors constructed them following the "gold standards of study design" achieved results that confirm those found in less-well-designed studies,

Dollberg et al. (2006, p. 1599) randomized their tongue-tie sample into two groups; one received frenotomy, and the other received a "sham" procedure. Careful blinding at each phase of the study occurred to avoid bias as described by Hall and Renfew. The investigators used nipple pain intensity as the outcome measure. Their study found there was a significant difference in pain scores between those mothers whose babies underwent the actual frenotomy and those mothers whose babies did not. Additionally, those mothers whose babies were in the sham procedure group and subsequently underwent frenotomy also showed significant decrease in nipple pain after treatment. The study concluded that frenotomy is an effective therapy for tongue-tie related nipple pain during breastfeeding.

Geddes et al. (2008) used ultrasonography and test-weighing (a proven method for assessing milk transfer) to image the tongue movements and measure the milk transfer of infants who have undergone frenotomy. Test weights and imaging were performed both prior to and after treatment. A significant increase in milk transfer occurred post-frenotomy for all the babies, as did the volume of maternal milk production in six of the eight women for whom data were collected. In all cases, maternal nipple pain decreased, infant attachment at breast improved, and rate of milk transfer increased. This study soundly confirms the many anecdotal and study reports touting the effectiveness of frenotomy for tongue-tie-related breastfeeding problems.

Frenuloplasty garners similar results in older children and adults. Z-plasty resulted in increased tongue protrusion and elevation in a study of 38 children by Li et al. (2005). Velanovich (1994, p. 715) asserts that "results with this technique [transverse-vertical frenuloplasty] are uniformly good." Wright (1995) performed a review of 287 patients presenting with tongue-tie. Of these, 156 underwent frenuloplasty. All patients receiving treatment experienced improved tongue mobility. Some required "ice-cream physiotherapy" to improve tongue motility and range of motion during the first few post-treatment days (p. 277).

Fiorotti et al. (2004) performed CO2 frenuloplasty on 15 patients. In every case, the surgery achieved the goal of increased tongue mobility. Oral motricity, however, required adjunctive speech therapy. Messner and Lalakea (2002) report immediate improvement in tongue mobility after surgical release, with improvement continuing in the first one to three months post-frenuloplasty. In their study, they also noted that speech articulation errors typical of tongue-tie also improved post-frenuloplasty. They recommend speech therapy as part of the post-surgery treatment regimen.

AND TO SUMMARIZE...

Every study on frenotomy and/or frenuloplasty demonstrates that these surgical procedures accomplish the goal of increasing tongue mobility. Not a single study concluded that surgical treatment fails enough times to warrant abandoning the practice. Only a small percentage of each group studied experienced no improvement from surgical release. No study that compares management against surgical release demonstrates that management alone can achieve the result of increased tongue mobility.

Surgical release of tongue-tie does not directly heal sore nipples. It does not directly increase maternal milk supply. It does not directly cause a person to speak plainly. These things are accomplished indirectly due to the improvements in tongue mobility. This is the reason that surgical release often will be followed by therapy to strengthen the tongue organ so it can efficiently perform its movements once its tether is removed.

RISKS OF TREATMENT

Allyson adamantly refused to have her son treated at first. "I was unwilling to even consider having [Liam's] tongue clipped," she said. "It sounded like such a scary, and, I thought, unnecessary procedure. However, a mom who had had her daughter's tongue clipped the previous week was at my [breastfeeding support] group and assured me it wasn't as big a deal as it seemed." Allyson felt reassured enough to go ahead with the procedure, which resolved her breastfeeding problems. Parents often have misconceptions about the treatment of tongue-tie, sometimes because their advising practitioner is ill-informed about treatment risks and effectiveness.

Several authors of "classic," often-cited studies have a preference for one type of procedure over another, citing risks of the less-preferred surgery and benefits of the preferred surgery. Unfortunately, these older studies still hold sway today with those who prefer to think that tongue-tie has no appreciable impact on anything, and that treating tongue-tie would be a breach of medical ethics.

Those researchers who prefer frenectomy claim it is more effective in achieving the desired result. According to these authors, frenotomy is inadequate or ineffective (Gellis and Kagan, 1964; Horton et al., 1969; Oldfield, 1955; Tuerk and Lubit, 1959), dangerous (Fleiss et al., 1990; Oldfield, 1955; and Wallace, 1964), and causes relapse (Kaban, 1990; McEnery and Gaines, 1941; and Wallace, 1964). Frenotomy may lead to infection (Hooley, 1967; McEnery and Gaines, 1941; and Summitt, 1990), hemorrhage (Mathewson, Siegel and McCanna, 1966; McEnery and Gaines, 1941; Summitt, 1990), asphyxia and tongue-swallowing (Butlin and Spencer, 1900; Mathewson et al., 1966; McEnery and Gaines, 1941), and death (Peti, as cited in Mathewson et al., 1966; and Reboul, as cited in Butlin and Spencer, 1900). Notice that many of these authors wrote during a less sophisticated time in medicine.

These risks seem to be associated with the improper performance of the frenotomy procedure, the stripping of the tongue following the incision of the lingual frenulum, and/or the use of improper instruments and procedures. Hemorrhage, for example, might occur when the blood vessels underlying the tongue are severed; infection would result from the use of a dirty instrument or fingernail; relapse would result from scar tissue formation if therapy does not follow surgery.

TRUE, FALSE, OR JUST PLAIN ABSURD?

Scar tissue formation that further impairs tongue function seems to be unsupported in the literature and appears to be an unreasonable concern. After being subjected to any surgical procedure, the tissue of the mouth rarely even forms scar tissue. Because of its vascularity, the mouth is a superb healing environment (H. Israel, personal communication, March, 1993). Mucosa is flexible enough to withstand traction, so scar tissue has much less opportunity to form. A scar would form only if the tissue remained relatively immobile (Messner and Lalakea, 2002; G. Notestine, personal communication, February 1993). Immobility is not what one associates with tongue function unless the tongue is tied. Post- surgical therapy involving purposeful movements of the tongue should ensure healing without formation of scar tissue.

Some practitioners and researchers report the appearance of a whitish bump at the base of the incision site where the division stopped (Fernando, 1998; Griffiths, 2004; and Watson Genna, 2008). Dying tissue from the edges of the incision forms this bump or patch. This dead tissue appears to be reabsorbed during the short healing process, leaving behind healthy pink tissue that may or may not look a little bumpy. I have noticed a small, pink bump at my healed incision site. It neither interferes with my tongue function nor does it bother me. I also have seen this type of bump under my sons' tongues at their healed incision sites. Others describe this phenomenon in passing, and many photographs of the underside of the tongue post-frenotomy clearly show this pinkish tissue bump. Further investigation of this phenomenon would be welcome, although its presence does not appear to be of concern.

The assertion by frenectomy proponents that frenotomy causes asphyxia and tongue-swallowing seems quite ridiculous. Frenectomy would be more likely than frenotomy to cause asphyxia due to posterior positioning of the tongue, because it removes substantially more tongue-anchoring tissue at the tongue base. However, asphyxia seems unlikely, no matter what type of procedure is performed; the tongue is anchored by more than just the lingual frenulum.

The fear of tongue swallowing, I must confess, leaves me quite amused. The tongue muscles form a complex structure, one that is quite large proportionate to the mouth. Connective tissue anchors the tongue along most of its margins: the sides of the floor of the mouth, its underside, and in the throat to the hyoid bone. It has suspensory muscular attachments to the back of the throat via the hyoid bone. Cartilaginous barriers that help form the esophagus and trachea prevent the passage of any but the most appropriate-sized object. We go to great lengths to prevent choking in babies by keeping objects smaller than a certain size away from their grasp. How in the world could a large tongue mass pass through such a small portal?

When we are mindful of the total structure of the tongue and throat, the notion that a tongue could be swallowed following the sectioning of a small tag of connective tissue seems quite absurd.

Perceived risks aside, authors and researchers have actually found frenotomy to be a relatively benign procedure (Amir et al., 2005; Ballard et al., 2002; Gartner et al., 1991; Hazelbaker, 1993; Huggins, 1990a; Marmet et al., 1990; Nezu, 1987; Segal et al., 2007). The ever-increasing contingent who have extensive experience with frenotomy claim that, when done properly, no problems but a few tears and drops of blood have resulted (Boo-Chai, 1963; Dollberg et al., 2006; Gartner et al.; Geddes and Langton et al., 2008; Griffiths, 2004; Marmet et al.; 1990; Messner and Lalakea, 2002 Nezu, 1987; Segal et al.; Wallace and Clarke, 2006). Griffiths notes that frenotomy causes less distress to the infant than immunization; 60 percent of infants cried for 15 seconds or less; 22 percent never cried, and 18 percent slept through the procedure (2004). I often have seen babies sleep through assessment and treatment.

SIMPLE FRENOTOMY

Ann shares this anecdote that underscores the notion that frenotomy is really no big deal:

> In 1950, my mom delivered my brother in Raleigh, North Carolina. She was holding him and he was crying. The doctor walked over and looked at him. He said not a word to my mother [then clipped the baby's frenulum]. My mother was shocked. 'What did you do?' she asked. The doctor said that if she was going to breastfeed him, he needed to clip that piece of skin. Otherwise [the baby] could not be breastfed. No permission slip, no anesthetic, no problem.

Current attitudes regarding informed consent would not allow such an abrupt approach, but the central message should not be lost: Frenotomy is a very simple and effective procedure.

Several descriptions of the frenotomy procedure found in the literature attest to the simplicity of the procedure, especially when performed on babies. Notestine (1990), a dentist who has performed hundreds of frenotomies on babies, says, "Since the band of tissue [frenulum] is poorly innervated or vascularized, the infant feels little pain and there is little, if any, bleeding." Ruben Marmet, M.D, (Marmet et al., 1990), also a very experienced surgeon, reports:

> There is little or no blood loss when the procedure is done properly. ... No anesthesia is necessary. It is not possible to inject the frenulum. Injecting the floor of the mouth and tongue would cause more discomfort than the frenotomy. Although the babies object to being held still, the entire procedure takes only seconds. (p. 118)

Bleeding remains a central concern for parents and some professionals. But as the literature shows, very little bleeding actually occurs, if at all. "As for the cutting procedure [frenotomy], the thin middle front section of the newborn's mouth can be cut slightly with a scissors. ... Very little bleeding will occur," states Nezu in her 1987 article (p. 61).

In a 1990 case presentation about a tongue-tied baby, Huggins commented, "He [the dentist] clipped the tongue when the mother held the baby in the dental chair. The baby tolerated the procedure well. Only slight bleeding was noted as the mother put him to her right breast" (p. 124). Berg (1990b, p. 124) states, "Clipping the frenulum is usually a simple procedure in an infant." About one of the cases described in the same article, Berg says, "The pediatrician performed the frenulotomy in his office without anesthetic. Only a 1mm-sized drop [of blood] was lost. The baby breastfed immediately after surgery" (p. 125).

Griffiths (2004, p. 411) also describes blood loss as minimal. Only nine percent of his cohort of 215 babies bled more than a few drops. Any blood loss was staved off by gentle compression to the tongue. "There were no infections, bleeding problems, feeding problems, or serious complications such as damage to the tongue or submandibular ducts."

Wallace and Clarke (2006, p. 1260) also report a zero complication rate in their study. Discomfort and bleeding were minimal. These authors are so convinced by the safety, simplicity and effectiveness of frenotomy that they advocate for the training of lactation consultants to prevent delays in treatment.

Deborah and her husband hesitated over treatment. They did extensive research and depended upon in-depth information from lactation consultants before engaging an ENT to perform a simple frenotomy. She reports:

> The procedure itself was most certainly more painful for me than for my daughter! She fussed just as much when he [the ENT] clipped the frenulum as she did when he was just exploring a bit in her mouth with his fingers. There was very little blood, and she never cried.

Parents commonly describe their experiences with frenotomy this way: The baby fusses when being examined and when his or her head is stabilized for surgery; the baby may cry a little or, very likely, not at all during the actual incision; little to no bleeding occurs; and then the baby calms. Many go to breast immediately, which stops what little bleeding may occur.

In the quarter-century that I have been working with tongue-tie, I have never heard of a story that deviates from this description. I have never heard of excessive bleeding or any other of the possible side effects that have been mentioned in the early tongue-tie literature. Lisa's story serves as emphasis for this point. Lisa chose to have a frenotomy performed on her son only after seeking the opinions of several doctors and a specialist. Her fears were for naught. Lisa shares:

> The actual procedure was a lot like ear-piercing – a little numbing spray, one quick stroke [incision] and it was over. I held Joe the whole time, and he only cried for a minute. It took 30 seconds, and there was as much blood as a tiny paper cut.

No doubt, any surgery, minor or otherwise, requires caution and skill. Proponents of frenotomy agree that frenotomies must be done properly and by an experienced practitioner to avoid damage to surrounding oral tissues (Marmet et al., 1990; Messner and Lalakea, 2002; Notestine, 1990; Segal et al., 2007). I personally refer to primary health care providers who have been taught to perform frenotomy by other skilled practitioners and who have extensive experience with the procedure.

Exactly how much knowledge and skill is required to perform a simple tongue-tie assessment and treatment? This question, now being asked in Great Britain and Australia, has led to the training of practitioners who provide care in the immediate postpartum period and who can perform frenotomy as quickly as needed to prevent development of breastfeeding problems (Breward, 2004; Wallace and Clarke, 2006).

Amir, in Australia, has been training IBCLCs to perform simple frenotomy with great success. All the IBCLCs at her hospital also are midwives, and so their scope of practice includes minor surgery. Their protocol includes thorough assessment using the Hazelbaker Assessment Tool for Lingual Frenulum Function. If they find a tongue-tie, they use Amir's frenotomy procedure to correct the tie (L. Amir, personal communication, January, 2009). If it were included in my scope of practice as an International Board Certified Lactation Consultant practicing in the United States, I would learn to do the procedure with no reservations.

In view of these descriptions of simple frenotomy, frenectomy, the more complex and interventional procedure, at least for babies, is overkill, like swatting a mosquito with a baseball bat. For anyone concerned about the Primum Non Nocere (First Do No Harm) concept, the least invasive procedure certainly would be the best choice. It seems absurd to violate this fundamental doctrine because certain historical writings, which are anecdotal reports or, worse, mere statements of personal biases, arouse fears of causing irreparable harm.

Since research confirms that frenotomy is the least complicated and very effective procedure for babies, it should be the treatment of choice whenever possible. (Amir et al., 2005; Ballard et al., 2002; Dollberg et al., 2006; Geddes and Langton et al., 2008; Griffiths, 2004; Hogan et al., 2005). As McBride (2005, p. 242) asserts in his editorial on tongue-tie, "There is no evidence that more complex procedures confer any advantage over simple division of the frenulum."

The proponents of frenectomy listed multiple made-up risks of frenotomy, perhaps to justify their use of frenectomy. Apparently using general anesthesia, creating a portal for infection, and removing pieces of tissue are not considered relevant potential risks worthy of discussion.

How does frenectomy stack up against frenotomy in the literature? The same fears regarding the risks of frenectomy appear. In spite of the possible risks of frenectomy (frenuloplasty), the research actually shows that today this procedure also carries little risk of complications. Postoperative pain seems to be the most common complication, and that is easily remedied by analgesics (Fiorotti et al., 2004; Kotlow, 1999; Li et al., 2005; Velanovich, 1994).

Professionals do little service for parents by leading them to believe that treatment carries substantial risks when there is no evidence for such an assertion. The first duty of a professional is to provide evidence-based information so that parents can make informed choices. Scare tactics about unproven risks deprive parents of good information for sound choice-making.

LET'S JUST WAIT AND SEE

On its face, a wait and see approach seems justifiable. Many authors cite multiple reasons for adopting such an approach. In situations where a condition can self-correct, or waiting will do no harm, one should wait. However, wait and see in the case of tongue-tie seems to be an unreasonable and confusing notion. The rationale for and timing of delayed treatment varies from author to author. Hooley (1967) expresses concern about treating tongue-tied infants because treatment would establish a pathway for infection. For this reason alone, he believes that tongue-tie should be left untreated until the child gets older. However, he provides no case example to back up his concern. No study has reported a single case of postoperative infection.

Several older but still often-cited articles suggest delaying treatment of the infant, sometimes for years, to allow the tongue to grow, thereby eliminating the necessity for treatment. McEnery and Gaines (1941) claim that the tongue is always short at birth, making it impossible to make an accurate diagnosis of tongue-tie. The connection between tongue length and tongue-tie is not made clear.

Tuerk and Lubit (1959) also discuss tongue shortness. They state:

> Since the tongue is always short at birth, it is not easy to determine how much the frenum interferes with its movement. In the newborn, the tip of the tongue is not completely developed, and the frenum may normally be attached well forward. As the infant grows, the tongue becomes longer and thinner toward the tip. (p.272)

Arena (1969) asserts that tongue-tie is normal and disappears with growth of the tongue. Horton et al. (1969, p.12) say that the tongue grows longer and thinner in the early weeks of life and the "frenulum stretches and its tongue attachment often recedes to a lower position." Jones (1983, p. 62), says, "Many newborn babies appear to have some degree of tongue-tie, for about twelve months, by which time both appearance and function (so far as it can be assessed) appear normal."

"The lingual frenulum extends almost to the tip of the tongue in early infancy and then gradually recedes" (Nazif and Ready, 1987, p. 184). Kaban (1990) mirrors these sentiments. He states that a prominent lingual frenulum is commonly seen in infants and becomes less prominent as the child grows. Conway (1990) reminds practitioners that a wait and see approach can be used in many cases due to the normal changes that occur as the infant grows. Breward (2004, p. 298) also claims that the tongue grows "tip forward." She goes on to misquote a significant study, claiming that the study shows that 60 percent of babies will improve with no intervention. In fact, the misquoted study actually shows that only one baby in the study's control group who was not treated immediately with frenotomy improved with management alone.

Messner and Lalakea, (2002, p. 545), researchers who have reported on several aspects of tongue-tie, deliver a mixed message in one study. They state that escalating problems as the child matures warrant early intervention, but that "a wait and see approach is also valid, as speech and social/mechanical problems may or may not develop." In a more recent article, Kummer (2005) regurgitates just about every myth perpetuated in the 20th or earlier centuries. Not once does she cite a study in support of her contentions. She reports:

> Although ankyloglossia can be significant at birth, the severity and functional effects tend to decrease with time and oral growth. During the first four to five years of life, the oral cavity changes significantly in shape and size. The alveolar ridge grows in height, the teeth begin to erupt, and the tongue grows and narrows at the tip. At the same time, the lingual frenulum recedes, stretches, and may even rupture. Therefore as the child grows, the severity of the tongue-tie lessens and the initial restrictions of lingual movement are diminished. (p. 6)

THE PERSONAL PERSPECTIVE

The official stance taken by researchers is one side of the coin; on the other side are personal perspectives of those who experience tongue-tie. It was this perspective that intrigued Messner and Lalakea (2002) enough to do a study looking at adolescent and adult attitudes related to tongue-tie. Two important findings emerged from this study:

1. No person choosing to undergo treatment regretted the decision and would definitely recommend treatment to others.

2. Participants did not know how badly affected they were until they experienced freedom from their problems.

The bottom-line reality is that no one who is not tongue-tied can possibly understand what it is like to be tongue-tied, and that some people who are tongue-tied do not realize how badly the tongue-tie is affecting them until they live without the condition for a time.

I certainly fall into the latter category. As a youth, I had no idea why I wasn't like normal people in regard to speaking and eating. As a better-informed adult pre-frenotomy, I could easily identify certain deficits in my tongue mobility and function. As an adult post-frenotomy, I realized just how pervasive and challenging those deficits were and came to regret not having the tie treated earlier in life. I wish my parents had chosen treatment for me as an infant. Early treatment would have saved three molars from abscess, enabled me to breathe effectively during eating, and altered my speech articulation patterns. The significant issues that developed over time warranted early intervention as prevention.

TIMING OF TREATMENT

Several writers believe that tongue-tie should not be treated until the child is at least 4 years old. Gardner (as cited in Block, 1968) suggests that a short frenum cannot be diagnosed definitively until the age of 4, therefore making this age the earliest at which treatment would be indicated. Warden (1991) seems to agree with Gardner. McEnery and Gaines (1941) hint at this same timing. Their rationale, however, seems to be related to the fact that their clients were never younger than 4 years of age. Wright (1995) disagrees with the age rule, saying:

> There are also categorical statements in the literature that frenulotomy should not be performed before 4-5 years of age, but there is little basis for this dogma. The appropriate age for any operation is when the surgeon is convinced that it needs to be done in the interests of the patient. (p. 278)

Tuerk and Lubit (1959, pp. 274-275) state that treatment should occur "prior to the institution or completion of corrective orthodontic care." Ketty and Sciullo (1974) claim that a diagnosis can be made after the development of the primary dentition, but surgery should not be performed until the preschool years so that the child can undergo tongue exercises and speech therapy.

Fernando (1998, p. 3) adamantly opposes this wait-and-see notion: "The propensity to put off surgical intervention in the hope that the patient will adjust to the disability is equally disastrous, because the best effects are achieved by surgery before poor speech habits can be formed"

Fernando (1998, p. 35) indicates that the best and fastest outcomes with small children occur when intervention is applied before the child is three. "Children who have surgery under the age of 3 years are able to acquire normal speech, improve feeding habits, and gradually adopt normal oro-muscular movements without the need for regular speech therapy" (p. 35). The bottom line for Fernando is to treat the tongue-tie in infancy, providing a good developmental foundation for sucking, swallowing, and chewing, and thereby preventing the development of problems in these areas.

Some writers believe in the "spontaneous cure." Shafer et al. (1974) state that some cases of tongue tie are self-corrective. Wallace (1964) personally witnessed the rupturing of a frenulum in a crying child. He asserts, based on this one personal experience, that tongue-tie is extremely rare in adults because it spontaneously cures itself. MacCarthy (1964) suggests that the strenuous movements of the tongue will stretch the frenulum over time. Smithells (1959) wrote a case study of a spontaneously ruptured lingual frenulum. The case history describes a slow-gaining, tongue-tied baby who, on the 15th day of life, gave a sudden cry at breast. Examination of the infant's mouth revealed a ruptured lingual frenulum.

How convenient it would be if we could count on spontaneous frenotomy. But we can't. The reported incidence range of tongue-tie in the general child and adult population is the same as it is for infants. So exactly how many tongue-ties are self-corrective? We have no research that identifies an exact statistic. It is possible that some will rupture, but most will not. Unfortunately, mine did not. I was as tongue-tied at the age of 42 as I was as an infant, only with more severe problems. Continual citation of these older and inaccurate articles as justification for the wait-and-see approach undermines the treatment decisions of today.

PROBLEMS WITH THE WAIT-AND-SEE APPROACH

The wait-and-see idea seems appropriately cautious at first glance; however, several issues arise upon closer examination of this concept:

1. The tongue grows proportionately (J. Pensyl, personal communication, January, 1993). There is no solid evidence that supports the idea that the tongue-tip grows longer or beyond the frenular insertion into the tongue despite the repetition of this concept in multiple texts. A frenulum attached at the tongue-tip will always be attached at the tongue-tip (Fernando, 1998; D. Garliner, personal communication, April 1, 1993). My heart-shaped tongue in childhood became my heart-shaped tongue in adulthood.

2. The frenulum appears to grow in proportion to the tongue. If this is so, the frenulum will always be tight relative to what it would have been had it not been short.

3. Garliner, the formulator of myofunctional therapy, and Notestine, a dentist who is an expert on tongue-tie agree: There is no concrete evidence that the frenulum increases in elasticity as a child grows (D. Garliner, personal communication, April 1, 1993; G. Notestine, personal communication, March, 1993). The frenulum is

fibrous connective tissue, which is relatively inelastic (Avery and Chiego, 2006). There might be some merit to the idea that the force that tongue use exerts on the tissue causes it to stretch beyond its inherent ability, but careful observations would be required to confirm this hypothesis. On the other hand, if it is true that lingual frenula can rupture under traction, one must consider that as partial evidence that lingual frenula do not stretch under traction. Further, the oral mucosa that forms the lingual frenulum is consistent with all the oral mucosa that anchors the tongue (Nanci, 2008). If all this tissue were elastic and able to stretch over time and with use, what would happen to the tongue's mobility? Would it become hypermobile? Unstable?

4. If lingual frenula always stretch or rupture, then no older children or adults would be tongue-tied.

5. The wait-and-see approach does not resolve a breastfeeding problem or prevent orofacial development issues, speech articulation errors, oral toilet problems, airway collapse and other breathing issues, and/or embarrassment issues.

6. There is absolutely no evidence that tongue function improves if treatment is put off until a later date. In fact, the experience of several clinicians would indicate the opposite: Tongue-function without intervention leans toward ever-increasing levels of compensation. What is a relatively minor tongue mobility problem in early infancy becomes a much larger problem as the infant grows into childhood – and beyond – and the structures in the throat become less apposed. This separation of structures as an infant sits up and starts to walk and talk creates more vulnerability of the airway, demanding more compensation from the airway protective mechanisms: the gag reflex, the cough reflex, and movements and positioning of the tongue to control the swallow. As speech develops, aspects of it depend upon an optimally mobile tongue. If there is any possibility that a child will develop any of these other issues, why would any parent take a wait-and-see approach, trading off a simple procedure for a more complex and invasive one?

7. Premature weaning remains a significant risk factor of delaying treatment, as does dooming the mother to continuing pain and damage, which itself will most likely lead to premature weaning. Breastfeeding remains the ideal feeding method, confers lifelong health benefits to both mothers and their infants, and should be protected.

SURGICAL ALTERNATIVES

Marmet et al. (1990, p.120), developers of suck training, concluded from their study, "In our experience, if the tongue is physically restricted in movement, no amount of suck training or physical therapy will solve the problem. The frenulum needs to be surgically clipped."

I agree. My research (Hazelbaker, 1993) demonstrated that even the best of management strategies fails to resolve the tongue function issues when a baby is truly tongue-tied. My definition of tongue-tie, unlike some others, is one of impaired function, rather than one of appearance deviation. A tongue can appear and act restricted because of other factors: a torticollis, a fascial restriction in the throat that pulls the tongue back, or a congenitally short tongue. These problems respond to therapy and management. Thorough and appropriate assessment distinguishes one type of problem from another and aids in identification of a targeted treatment and therapy plan.

Two recent studies confirm the notion that management alone fails to properly address infant feeding problems related to tongue-tie. Griffiths (2004) conducted a prospective study of 215 infants younger than 3 months. All mother-baby pairs received professional management assistance with no resolution of the reported problems. Within 24 hours of surgical correction by frenotomy without anesthesia, 80 percent of babies were feeding better. Geddes and Langton et al. (2008) also performed a prospective study on mother-infant pairs who had received professional management support. The management failed to resolve the breastfeeding problems. Surgery, however, resolved the feeding problems for all enrollees.

Multiple issues arise when we examine the management vs. surgery argument. Typically, any mother-infant dyad experiencing uncomplicated feeding will not ask for or receive professional support and management. Only those mother-infant dyads experiencing feeding problems will present themselves for help. We will never know how many babies are tongue-tied in the no-problem group until we perform a screening procedure on all babies to separate one group from the other.

It very well may be that mild to moderately tongue-tied babies will improve with management alone. However, we have no idea how many of these tongue-tied babies and/or those whose feeding goes well will develop problems with speech, oral toilet, and tongue motility later on until we study this cohort separately.

Additionally, an ethics issue emerges. If surgical correction carries little to no risk and is effective, it would be unethical to withhold such treatment from a mother-baby dyad for the sake of a prospective randomized trial comparing management to surgery. It is therefore premature to conclude that management alone constitutes a reasonable option to surgical correction in those babies who have feeding difficulties.

In my estimation, the current climate of ignorance and unwarranted fear plays a role in the parents' decision-making processes, although there is no study to confirm my hypothesis. If parents and professionals alike were more properly informed, they might freely choose early surgical correction.

Some adults choose to forgo treatment because they have learned to cope with their problems (Lalakea and Messner, 2003a). For them, the perceived benefits of surgical correction do not outweigh the discomforts of the tongue mobility deficits. More studies looking at the impact of management vs. surgical treatment in this population would give us important information about the adult perspective and help guide our clinical decision making with infants.

Lalakea and Messner (2003a) contend that the few cases of adult tongue-tie who consented to surgical treatment in their sample wished they had been diagnosed and treated sooner and would recommend treatment to anyone who also was found to be affected. Part of the problem for adults is the lack of knowledge. We have such a poor popular understanding of this congenital anomaly that adults today may not know they have a tie.

During the writing of this book, my friend Evi discovered she was tongue-tied when a lactation consultant colleague noticed it during casual conversation. She recommended that Evi have her frenulum clipped, even though Evi is 64 years old. Evi mentioned the conversation to me, and I encouraged her to find a dentist who would consider performing a simple frenotomy. There was just such a dentist in her area, who subsequently clipped her frenulum using a local anesthetic and scissors. She reports her mouth was sore for a few days, but that she noticed immediate difference in her tongue mobility. She wishes she had known she was tongue-tied sooner so she could have undergone treatment as a younger woman. (E. Adams, personal communication, January 19, 2009).

My hesitation in treating my own tie was the concern over the frenuloplasty procedure. I strongly felt that frenuloplasty was too much intervention, with no functional advantage and far too much postoperative pain. I wanted my dentist to perform simple frenotomy without anesthetic. He had no qualms about my preferred method; he just wanted to be sure he wasn't going to hurt me in the process. He didn't. That raises a question. If we performed frenotomy on adults instead of frenuloplasty, would they be more willing to undergo surgical correction?

For whatever reason, some parents of tongue-tied babies will choose not to treat their children surgically. Watson Genna (2008) provides an extensive and useful set of management tools and instructions to attempt mitigation of tongue-tie-related feeding problems when parents must delay or decline treatment altogether. When considering such an option, however, I suggest practitioners and parents consider the following:

1. Only the most dedicated mothers will adhere to such a management regimen. Unfortunately, it is easier for some to switch to bottle-feeding than to perform some of these exercises consistently and correctly. If the management fails to adequately address nipple and breast pain or milk-transfer issues, premature weaning becomes a very real risk.

2. Most babies will respond to management strategies quickly if they are going to be effective in that baby's situation. If management fails to provide relief to the mother within a few days, practitioners should again discuss the surgery option with the mother. Weeks and weeks of management with no significant result constitutes a failed clinical strategy. Delay of treatment for months or years in a case of true tongue-tie is now unjustifiable.

3. According to the extensive research now available on the subject, frenotomy is the current treatment of choice for infants and should be presented as such. In most communities, there are many skilled practitioners in various disciplines who will perform the procedure should a parent encounter resistance from his or her pediatrician.

4. Parents who decline surgery should be educated regarding the possible problems their children will face as they mature. They should be properly informed of the risks of forgoing treatment. Enough literature on this subject has been published to warrant such a discussion and to pursue it confidently. Parents also should be informed that delayed surgical treatment usually results in use of the more extensive and invasive frenuloplasty.

5. Professionals should know who in their community or nearby communities are trained and available to perform frenotomies so mothers can be given multiple options. Dentists, midwives, advanced practice nurses, naturopathic doctors, non-resistant pediatricians and, in some countries, lactation consultants are most likely to use simple frenotomy with little to no anesthetic.

Of course, parents should be informed of the risks of any treatment, but now they also must be informed about the risks of not treating.

POST-TREATMENT THERAPY

In the last century, a few authors suggested that some cases of tongue-tie will need post-treatment tongue retraining. Douglas and Kresberg (1954) cite a case in which a woman who underwent surgery to release her tongue-tie had to undergo tongue retraining. McEnery and Gaines (1941) recommend tongue retraining in addition to speech therapy. Archer (1975) suggests that speech therapy that includes tongue retraining might be required after surgery because of bad habits that developed as a result of restricted tongue motion.

Marmet et al. (1990) state:

> Due to the impaired tongue movement, the babies tried a variety of compensatory movements of their tongues or other oral anatomy. ... Occasionally this [clipping] is sufficient; but usually suck training and other management techniques are also needed to resolve breastfeeding problems. (p. 120)

Earlier in this same article they state that if the frenotomy is performed within days after birth, tongue retraining may not be necessary. This statement on the subject from Whitman and Rankow (1961) predates Marmet et al. (1990). They say:

> If it [abnormal tongue function] is the result of an anatomic abnormality [such as tongue-tie], correction calls for surgical intervention followed by tongue training. The muscles of the tongue are as readily trainable as muscles of any other part of the body. (p. 424)

For Fernando (1998), tongue training is a given except in the youngest patients. The older the patients (the study sample included young adults over 18), the more extensive the therapy, and the longer it takes for them to achieve optimal results – in some cases more than a year. Variations in problem presentation related to the severity of the tie also influenced the postoperative course. Increased severity of impact lengthens the therapeutic timeline.

The stories of many of the mothers who wrote to me reinforce the notion that some tongue-retraining is needed postoperatively, especially if the procedure has been delayed. It would be irresponsible, however, not to acknowledge that some older babies will have no difficulty using their tongue after the surgery. Conversely, some babies who are only hours old may need to be suck-trained. The responsibility of health professionals is to hold a realistic view about the matter and not lead the parents down the path of an "easy fix."

Practitioners should provide anticipatory guidance regarding the possibility of tongue therapy after treatment. Such therapy may consist merely of frequent breastfeeds, because breastfeeding alone may be the most effective muscle retraining exercise. Or the baby may need intervention, such as finger-feeding, or special suck retraining administered by a trained IBCLC, and/or speech or occupational therapist. Newer therapies, such as craniosacral therapy, also may be of benefit.

Several authors have concluded that a percentage of tongue-tied babies, whether due to delay of treatment, to co-morbid factors, or just to the normal presentation of signs and symptoms characteristic of tongue-tie, do not improve after surgical release. Marmet et al. (1990) first noted the use of suck training pre-and post-frenotomy. This strategy ensured the development of appropriate tongue positioning and strengthening to completely resolve any weakness or compensatory tongue motions. More recently, Amir et al. (2005) reported that 17 percent of their cohort did not improve with frenotomy alone. They do not elaborate on the type of support provided for this segment of their study population.

Sometimes, co-morbidities adversely influence a feeding situation. The frenotomy resolves the tongue movement deficits, and the other form of therapy or intervention resolves the co-morbidity. In my own experience, my oldest son, whose frenulum was clipped within the first day after birth, needed no further intervention. My second son, who also had a sensory-based sucking problem due to intracranial soft-tissue nerve impingement during childbirth, required craniosacral therapy in addition to frenotomy to restore his feeding to a normal, effective pattern. In his case, post-surgical therapy for the nerve impingement required three treatments in a two-week period.

Fernando (1998), Kotlow (1999), and Holtzman (S. Holtzman, personal communication, 1998) describe therapy regimens for their older patients that include exercises to improve oral kinesthesia, bolus manipulation, oral hygiene, swallowing, and speech production. My frenotomy was followed by a twice-daily regimen of myofunctional speech therapy (See Appendix B for resource information). Forty-two years of tongue-tie resulted in complex compensatory tongue-movements and tongue strength imbalances. The prescribed exercises strengthened underperforming muscles and rebalanced tone so that more functional tongue movements could replace the less functional compensations. The prescribed exercises were so easy to perform that even a 4-year-old could have done them.

A simple, 20-minute regimen put my tongue through its "circuit." It didn't take long before my tongue learned more productive habits, improving my chewing, swallowing, oral toilet, breathing, and speech articulation.

SUCK RETRAINING

Allyson's breastfeeding problem did not resolve with frenotomy. Her nipples, so badly damaged from the improper sucking Liam did while tongue-tied, took weeks to heal. The situation required that she pump and use a nipple shield to protect her nipple tissue. Her husband also fed Liam, often with finger-feeding, to help him learn to bring his tongue down and forward. Finger-feeding often serves as a suck training method that works quickly and with little mess or fuss. (See Instructions for Finger-Feeding in Appendix E.) Finger-feeding provides consistent sensory input to the tongue, enabling it to better feel itself as a mobile organ in the oral cavity, resulting in better placement and motion. If a few days of finger-feeding exclusively or on every second or third feed does not correct any tongue strength deficiencies, more complex suck training may be indicated (Hazelbaker, 1993, 2003).

Older babies who refuse to suck on a finger (this is a developmental issue, not one of defiance) who need suck retraining will need to be seen by a specially trained therapist – an International Board Certified Lactation Consultant, a speech-language pathologist, an occupational therapist, or an orofacial myologist – who can accurately assess deficits and prescribe a targeted and effective training regimen. Exercises may include such techniques as gentle pressure on the blade of the tongue to encourage the edges to curl and the dorsum to groove for a better tongue seal at breast; tongue walking, to bring the tongue forward in the mouth; or tip teasing, which encourages the baby to lengthen the tongue, sticking it out to touch the teasing finger. No regimen should be applied without first knowing what deficits require correction. More harm than good can be done by applying the wrong techniques.

Marmet and Shell have devised a suck-training regimen that many IBCLCs have been trained to use. The technique combines finger-feeding with various intra-oral finger movements during the feed itself to promote proper tongue placement, tongue seal, and progressive contractions. Watson Genna (2008, pp. 197-201) describes a regimen that may include one or more of the following exercises: Press-down, which encourages the infant's tongue to come down and forward in the mouth for proper placement; tongue massage for improving tongue extension; tongue lateralization, to improve lateral movements of the tongue necessary for seal, bolus formation, and progressive contractions; and palate desensitization for the infant presenting with a high palate and a sensitive gag reflex.

Simply putting the baby to breast with proper attachment technique can encourage proper tongue function during breastfeeds. Proper positioning and attachment always should be the first step in any postoperative regimen. Watson Genna (2008) describes a latch technique that encourages an asymmetrical latch, making more of the areola directly available to the infant's tongue. She indicates that this placement also can help prior to frenotomy and should be instituted while waiting for surgical release. In my experience, focused effort to properly tickle the baby's lip-midline, eliciting a wide gape and good tongue extension, followed by quick and deep attachment, works the vast majority of times. Adjustment to this technique, as Watson Genna suggests, can be useful when simple technique does not garner a satisfactory result.

Mothers always must receive follow-up assessment and support after frenotomy. Every mother also must employ excellent attachment technique to ensure her baby has good tongue placement, seal, and efficient milk transfer. One mother with whom I worked had difficulty mastering proper positioning and deep attachment technique. The baby already had had a frenotomy when she came to me. Her nipples were not healing, but the baby's suck was excellent. She had yet to master positioning and attachment. No other professional had taken the time to teach her this fundamental skill. Once she had learned, her breastfeeding problem was remedied quickly.

The above suggestions also apply to the bottle-fed baby. The care provider may need to suggest an alternate bottle teat, one that encourages better tongue placement and use. The bottle-fed baby may benefit from a post-surgery course of finger-feeding and/or suck-retraining. An appropriate therapy regimen will correct skill and strength deficits identified during the post-frenotomy evaluation.

CRANIOSACRAL THERAPY

Craniosacral therapy, a light-touch form of bodywork designed to make both structural and physiological changes in the body through gentle communication with the various soft tissues, especially the fascia, plays a key role in resolving suck problems associated with structural restrictions. Structural restrictions may occur as a result of intrauterine lie issues; intrapartum interventions such as epidurals, forceps, or vacuum delivery; or from anomalies such as tongue-tie. Several lactation consultants around the United States, and perhaps elsewhere, have undergone training as craniosacral therapists and achieve excellent results with their sucking-compromised breastfeeding-baby clients (Hazelbaker, 2003). A subset of these practitioners works specifically with babies who are tongue-tied.

Variations in approach exist, but those practitioners with whom I spoke perform several treatments of craniosacral therapy on their infant clients to optimize the structural alignment of the mouth, throat and thorax – supporting or restoring as much functional stability as the tongue-tie allows. This approach clears away any functional issues not directly associated with the tie and places the infant in the best possible position for post-surgical recovery. Following frenotomy or frenectomy, several more treatments speed healing, help strengthen weak musculature, and reinforce optimal communication and function between the nerves and muscles involved in the suck-swallow-breathe mechanism.

Craniosacral therapy also serves as an excellent companion to other therapeutic techniques. For example, basic suck training and craniosacral therapy work well together, one reinforcing proper tongue placement and function, the other priming and encouraging the nerves and muscles to send and receive the right signals.

This gentle bodywork technique, in its current form, took root in the 1970s. Based on osteopathic principles developed in the late 1800s by Dr. Andrew Taylor Still, the father of osteopathy, and reformulated in the mid-20th century by Dr. William Sutherland and Dr. Rollin Becker, the technique parted company in mode of application from osteopathic manipulative technique under the brilliant reconceptualizations of Dr. John Upledger and Dr. Franklyn Sills. Several "schools" of form exist at this point, the two most known being Upledger CranioSacral Therapy and Biodynamic Craniosacral Therapy.

Regardless of the school attended, certified craniosacral therapists receive extensive training, and those who specialize in working with pediatric problems undergo more training in pediatric application of the technique. Despite unfounded concerns to the contrary, the technique has always been safe and effective. (See Appendix B for resource information.)

As discussed in a previous chapter, baby Elijah underwent craniosacral therapy for several weeks before having a second frenotomy performed. Although effective in releasing the most visible portion of his tight lingual frenulum, his first frenotomy did not address the tight posterior tie. The lactation consultant wanted to be sure that a true posterior tie was present and so used craniosacral therapy to clear away the various throat tissue and other restrictions caused by his traumatic birth. Elijah experienced dramatic improvement overall, but still was unable to bring his tongue over his lower gumline. A second frenotomy corrected his posterior tie and then several more craniosacral treatments helped with his recovery and set the stage for optimal function.

TREATMENT RECOMMENDATIONS

One must wonder what would have happened had Liam's frenulum been clipped in the hospital. Would he have learned to use his tongue correctly and faster? Would Allyson's nipples been spared pain and damage? What is our professional obligation in preventing problems by using early-intervention strategies? It seems we need to re-examine our priorities and hearken back to an earlier day when assessment for tongue-tie was done in the early postpartum period, and steps were taken to correct any problems before they snowballed, mandating a more complex treatment regimen.

After a thorough assessment has been done to verify that an individual is, in fact, tongue-tied, the evidence proves that the following sound recommendations can be made regarding treatment:

1. Tongue-tie, by definition, limits tongue mobility thereby negatively impacting feeding, chewing, swallowing, breathing, speech articulation, orofacial development and oral toilet. Treatment should commence if simple management provided by a knowledgeable professional fails to produce improvement in an appropriate time window. For breastfed and bottle-fed babies, management should produce some result within 24 to 48 hours.

2. Practitioners ought to perform frenotomy as an early intervention strategy, when problems first manifest, or if tongue-mobility restrictions are noticed during a thorough screening evaluation directly after birth. Problem prevention should once again become a high priority. Too many breastfeeding mothers prematurely wean, often within the first two weeks, warranting universal assessment of and treatment for tongue-tie in the early days postpartum. Bottle-feeders often go months without anyone's noticing an issue because of a failure to screen for the anomaly and a lack of ability to determine if bottle-feeders are handling their feeds well.

3. Given that most tongue-tied individuals are not currently treated shortly after birth, treatment method depends upon the age of the affected individual, the severity of the problems and the amount of tissue involved in the restriction. Consideration of all these issues after careful and thorough assessment guides the decision-making process.

4. Whenever possible, and that will be in the highest percentage of infant cases, simple frenotomy (possibly followed by tongue strengthening exercises), should be utilized. In some cases of older children and adults, simple frenotomy followed by speech therapy and tongue strengthening exercises may suffice. More research needs to be done comparing treatment outcomes of simple frenotomy, especially that using laser, with frenectomy in older populations.

5. Frenectomy (frenuloplasty) or laser frenotomy currently remain the treatments of choice in older children, adolescents, and adults. Researchers should continue discussions about the type of procedure used for frenuloplasty. Everyone benefits when procedures evolve to an optimal state, thus improving outcomes, reducing recovery time, and minimizing risks.

CHAPTER SEVEN TAKEAWAY

1. Frenotomy is the indicated procedure in infancy. Severely affected babies and older children may require a more interventional approach such as frenuloplasty, followed by speech, myofunctional, or craniosacral therapy.

2. Frenotomy is safe in the vast majority of cases. No significant side effects of treatment are reported in the research studies where frenotomy was used as the intervention of choice. Reported side effects are limited to a drop or two of blood when scissors are employed and minor discomfort for a day or two.

3. Frenotomy is effective in the vast majority of cases. Sometimes babies need a few days to two weeks to completely master breast or bottle-feeding. Most studies that followed breastfeeding women indicate that it may take a few days to several weeks for nipple and breast damage to heal satisfactorily.

4. In a small percentage of infant cases, further therapy is needed to achieve optimal results, especially where a co-morbidity exists. Treatment for tongue-tie in older children, adolescents, and adults definitely will require further therapy to rectify problems that developed because the tongue-tie was not treated earlier.

5. Treatment during infancy may prevent the development of other associated problems, such as speech articulation errors, oral toilet, and orofacial development problems. If treatment is not undertaken during infancy, more intervention may be required to correct future problems.

AFTERWORD

A SOON-TO-BE-PUBLISHED ARTICLE TELLS THE dramatic tale of a baby, who after having seen myriad health care providers, finally was ordered to the hospital for medical evaluation by the Department of Child and Family Services. The exclusively breastfed infant was Failure to Thrive at the age of 6 months. What was wrong?

The baby was tongue-tied, and the tongue-tie was the sole cause of the problem. Post-frenotomy, the infant began gaining appropriately, eventually resolving the medical issues. Had the infant been properly diagnosed at the beginning, this situation could have been prevented (Forlenza, Paradise Black, McNamara, and Sullivan, in press).

Dramatic? Absolutely. Common? Unfortunately common enough that many similar stories were shared with me during the writing of this book. Clearly, we need a universal attitude change coupled with a change in the way we provide care for these babies.

I have had the honor of interfacing with experts around the world through the uniting format of the Internet. In my various e-mail discussions, not only was the consensus about the definition of tongue-tie underscored, but also the desire for universal acceptance of its impact and treatment. The experts want everyone to have access to accurate research-based information. These experts are passionate people. They dedicate themselves daily to helping babies, children, and adults receive the education and the assistance they need to flourish without the impediment of tongue-tie. Many feel frustrated by the resistance they encounter from well-meaning but less informed colleagues.

OBJECTIONS

The sole, but huge, remaining barrier to the routine treatment of tongue-tie is ignorance: The notion that tongue-tie never causes any problems and therefore never needs treatment persists simply because health care providers are not taught otherwise in their professional training programs. The view from the late 1950s haunts us. Some – perhaps many – doctors still insist that clipping a lingual frenulum is bad medicine because it is unnecessary and potentially could cause harm. At the time this view held sway, very little research had been done to demonstrate that tongue-tie caused multiple problems with infant feeding and subsequent orofacial development and easily could be remedied with little to no complication.

Year after year, practitioners receive little to no accurate information about tongue-tie. Times have changed and so must our attitudes, educational programs and clinical approaches.

Not treating a baby who needs it is wrong. But treating a baby who has been improperly diagnosed with tongue-tie also is wrong. In the past, far too many babies who had no functional problems received frenotomies based on simple visualization. We now know that evaluation of function must take precedence over appearance criteria so overtreatment can be avoided. What we now should strive for in our clinical approach is to prevent problem development by clipping the frenula of babies who actually are tongue-tied.

Today we have an excellent body of literature on which to rely. There is no doubt that more research needs to be performed. However, consensus has emerged on two main points: (1) Tongue-tie causes a multitude of problems, especially with infant feeding, and (2) Treatment is effective in mobilizing the tongue so it can perform its various functions optimally. Any health care professional unwilling to acknowledge these two research-based understandings operates out of a lack of information. That lack must be addressed as quickly as possible.

POOR SYSTEMS

As noted in many of the personal stories generously shared by parents for publication in this book, parents often know that something is wrong, but have no place to turn for appropriate information to explain their child's problems. Backed against a wall of misinformation and resistance, some parents just give up. More persistent parents search until they find even a shred of information that can lead them to a knowledgeable practitioner willing to help. We need a system, both in the United States and abroad, that can help parents fill in the gaps and ensure timely access to treatment.

In the United Kingdom, the National Health Service educates any qualified health practitioner to perform frenotomy, yet recently a British woman needing such a practitioner was not referred for treatment by her general physician. He knew where to refer her, but he didn't make the referral until an American dentist with whom the mother corresponded told her about the referral service. When the mother asked the doctor to make a referral, he finally did so. She received the help she needed very quickly once she was directed to the correct practitioner. Despite this attitudinal glitch, Great Britain's National Health Service leads the way by making it fairly easy for parents to obtain treatment.

In the United States, many primary care doctors no longer think of tongue-tie as a cause of breast or bottle-feeding difficulties or other problems, and therefore they don't pursue this line of diagnostic thinking. Some doctors provide categorically incorrect information, misleading parents into thinking that tongue-tie poses no problem, or if it does, it should be treated later and only with the most invasive surgery. Parents often find their answers elsewhere – not by choice, but by necessity – from La Leche League, their lactation consultant, a neighbor, or on the World Wide Web.

Parents tell story after story about the inefficiencies of the U.S. system. Fortunately, a few very passionate and knowledgeable physicians are helping to change their colleagues' attitudes, but even they find enormous resistance in some quarters (B. Coryllos, personal communication, February, 2009; J. Murphy, personal communication, February 2009, B. Palmer, personal communication, May 2009).

The roadblock to efficient treatment seems to be education of health care providers. Old attitudes and understandings/beliefs cannot be changed without proper re-education, which should begin with initial medical, dental, nursing and allied health training programs and be updated in continuing education programs. Textbooks should be revised based on current research findings.

Although lactation consultants may be in the best position to inform the uninformed, even their training does not ensure that every practitioner possesses adequate knowledge on the subject. Lay persons positioned to support parents need education as well. They may often be the first line of help for a tongue-tied baby whose primary care practitioner missed the tie during the newborn exam.

INFORMATION ACCESSIBILITY

Real change relies on both top-down and bottom-up strategies. Educating parents so they can make informed choices seems to be a strategy that works well when professional resistance to change is high. A grassroots effort to change attitudes puts pressure on practitioners to re-educate themselves simply because of the demand generated by parent "consumers." Providing easily accessible information to parents via popular channels makes such a task more doable.

The Web serves as an excellent and accessible format for parents to gather information. Despite criticism from health professionals that health information on the Web often may be inaccurate or inadequate, where else are parents supposed to look for help if their primary care physician knows nothing about the problem with which they are faced? Criticizing parents for trying to solve their child's problem does nothing to remedy their situation. Cultivating an excellent source of information for parents on the Internet remains the responsibility of those who know the most and thus are the true experts.

I often have found information on these "unreliable" sites to be more accurate than that found on medical sites. The Web, rather than being a bane, provides a rich and easy opportunity to support parents with up-to-date information and resources. A well-designed tongue-tie site, such as that under construction at the time of this writing (www.tongue-tie.net), also provides a list of practitioners around the world who are both knowledgeable on the subject and have the ability to surgically treat and/or perform therapy. (See Appendix B for a brief list of organizations that provide practitioner referrals.) Through continued re-education efforts, the rest of the healthcare world will catch up, making routine examination and treatment readily accessible and such a Web site obsolete.

LOOKING FOR MORE ANSWERS

The opportunities for tongue-tie research are virtually endless. The more we find out, the more we want to know. At one time, we speculated that tongue-tie was a heritable condition. Now, through the work of researchers in genetics, the gene responsible for ankyloglossia and tongue-tie has been located. Speculation has been turned into fact.

Clinicians speculate anew. A rise in tongue-tie incidence has some questioning the role that environment plays in the phenotypic expression of tongue-tie in individuals carrying the genetic mutation. Is this rise their imagination or do epigenetic influences account for a real increase in incidence? Have environmental influences created the emergence of a non-genetic form of tongue-tie that will in turn be expressed hereditarily through non-gene mediated epigenetic programming? Further research in this area would be welcome.

The excellent clinical work of the Coryllos team has identified the existence of a hidden tongue-tie they have termed the "posterior tie." Due to the educational efforts of the team, many practitioners around the world now perform an extensive frenotomy for these ties. Recently, concerns about overdiagnosis of the posterior tie have been raised. Even clinicians once extremely enthusiastic about treating these ties have become more hesitant, wondering if other influences, such as childbirth interventions, may be responsible for tongue movement deficits that only appear to be posterior ties.

Several of these clinicians arrived at their new understanding by examining the results of bodywork in these cases. Bodywork, such as craniosacral therapy, is designed to resolve soft tissue restrictions that may feel and act like a restricted tongue base. Several lactation consultants who also are trained to perform such bodywork claim that what has been diagnosed as a posterior tie may disappear after several treatments. That is not to say that posterior ties do not exist; it is certain that they do, but better assessment and a differential diagnostic approach need to be discussed and adopted before this issue is finally clarified and settled.

If a surgical intervention is chosen, the degree to which pre- and post-treatment therapy should be employed appears to be a brand new discussion among researchers. In speech therapy circles, postoperative therapy has been a given. In breastfeeding circles, the prevalent assumption that the frenotomy alone would correct the problem has persisted until recently. Several clinicians experimenting with pre- and post-surgical treatment have new insights. What approach works best should emerge as inquiry continues. What role therapy plays as a substitute for surgical treatment also is an area for investigation.

Recent excellent research builds on the foundational work from the mid-20th century. Consensus regarding articulation errors emerges slowly. Research in the field of speech suffers from the same problem as does breastfeeding research – the lack of a standardized assessment. Although each study reveals tidbits of information about various aspects of speech articulation, we, as yet, do not see the complete picture. The story presented at the beginning of Chapter Five shows clearly that speech delay can result from tongue-tie, yet clinicians may cling to the notion that tongue-tie cannot and does not delay speech, ever. Clearly, research needs to be done in this area.

The role of technology as a means to make diagnoses remains uncertain. Recent studies employing ultrasound dramatically demonstrate the sucking deficits that result from tongue-tie in breastfed babies. Should such technology be employed in lieu of clinical assessment using standardized assessment processes? The technology remains expensive, so if the clinical assessment accurately reflects that which is seen by these imaging techniques, then clinical assessment probably will remain the diagnostic approach of choice.

EARLY INTERVENTION VS. WAIT AND SEE

Because of the high incidence of tongue-tie, routine assessment at birth for the condition constitutes good medical practice. A return to the good old days, in this case, makes good old sense. Should all tongue-ties then be clipped as a matter of routine shortly after birth? Is the need for early intervention so significant that all babies who appear to have tongue-tie should receive a frenotomy?

As breastfeeding rates continue to increase, many question the role of a wait-and-see attitude. However, their concern for lack of a standardized assessment process keeps them from once again performing routine frenotomy right after birth. At the same time, the need to optimally support breastfeeding makes holding off on treatment an unacceptable approach.

Some experts suggest that waiting until the baby's suck has matured warrants putting off treatment for a few days to weeks. If a problem develops, then treatment may be warranted. Even I see this side of the argument, despite my being a proponent of clipping at birth or soon thereafter. However, studies in the last decade have shown that in full-term babies, suck maturation occurs within the first 24 to 48 hours of life, and what occurs in the following month is the refinement of feeding style. Therefore, waiting to clip a lingual frenulum for only a few days may end up being the responsible yet conservative approach.

To add complexity to the argument, sucking problems have multiple causes; intrauterine lie issues, intra-partum and postpartum interventions and routines; and congenital problems all may interfere with the integrity of the suck-swallow-breathe mechanism. Waiting a few days prior to treating may help to sort out what actual influences are playing a role in the sucking deficits.

A knowledgeable therapist can also tease out the various influences on suck and provide an assessment of any deficits. Parents shouldn't hesitate to see a therapist if the baby's suck has not improved and stabilized by day 7. Advice to wait and see what happens, especially if the mother has sore nipples, constitutes inappropriate management. If a baby is not sucking well within the first week, action must be taken to avoid further deterioration of the breastfeeding relationship. Erring on the side of caution for fear of the "side effects" of treatment simply does not make sense.

If, despite appearances and without significant intervention, a baby transfers milk well (whether breast or bottle-fed); has a stable suck mechanism; continues to grow well; and seems happy and content, waiting to treat the "tongue-tie" when and if a problem develops may be the most responsible choice. Tongue-tie, however, does not improve on its own. If it causes problems at any point, it must be addressed – and the sooner, the better.

CONCLUSION

I find this time period an exciting one. Never before has there been such ability for clinicians and researchers to discuss tongue-tie with this much clarity. We still have much to learn, but what we now know provides us with enough information to assist individuals afflicted with this condition, which is, at best, inconvenient, and at worst, severely limiting. The momentum established by researchers in the past decade ignites the imagination: Study after study will follow as researchers become fascinated by what they could know about tongue-tie in the near future.

I am gratified to have been a small part of that process.

GLOSSARY

ANKYLOGLOSSIA (Complete): A condition in which the tongue is fused to the floor of the mouth.

ANKYLOGLOSSIA (Partial): Tongue-tie; impaired tongue function resulting from a tight and/or short lingual frenulum; the condition also may involve the genioglossus muscle.

ANTERIOR: Situated in front of or in the forward part of an organ (*Dorland's Illustrated Medical Dictionary, 25th Edition,* 1974).

BOTTLE-SUCK: Deviation from the normal sucking pattern for extracting milk from the breast to extract milk from a bottle.

DEGLUTITION: The action of swallowing.

DENTITION: The teeth in their dental arch; ordinarily used to designate the natural teeth in position in their alveoli (*Dorland's Medical Dictionary, 25th Edition,* 1974).

DIASTEMA: A space between two adjacent teeth.

EXCISION: Removal by cutting.

FRENECTOMY: Excision of a frenum.

FRENOTOMY: Incision of a frenum; frenulotomy; "clipping."

GENIOGLOSSUS MUSCLE: The muscle that protrudes and depresses the tongue.

INCISION: A cut or a wound produced by cutting with a sharp instrument (*Dorland's Medical Dictionary, 25th Edition,* 1974).

IBCLC: International Board Certified Lactation Consultant; the official title granted a person who has successfully completed the board examination of the International Board of Lactation Consultant Examiners. IBCLCs provide lactation counseling to breastfeeding families and may teach the science and art of lactation management and breastfeeding counseling to others. They may practice in hospitals, doctors' offices, home health care agencies, government program offices, and/or may have a private practice.

INFERIOR: Situated below or lower; the lower surface of an organ or structure, or the lower of two similar structures (*Dorland's Medical Dictionary, 25th Edition,* 1974).

INTER-RATER RELIABILITY: The rate of agreement between two observers or the same observer measuring twice with the same measuring tool during the course of scientific research that requires human beings to be measurers.

LATERALIZATION: The movement of the tongue from one side of the mouth to the other side when gentle pressure is placed on the lateral surface of the tongue.

LINGUAL FRENULUM: The piece of tissue in the mouth that attaches the tongue to the floor of the mouth. Typically, it will be connected to the underside of the tongue at least 1cm behind the tongue-tip and to the floor of the mouth well below the ridge of the inferior alveolus.

MALOCCLUSION: Improper relationship of the upper dentition to the lower dentition caused by one or more influences and causing one or more effects.

MASTICATION: Chewing.

ORBICULARIS ORIS: The orbicular muscle of the mouth that closes and protrudes the lips and is innervated by the facial nerve. (*Dorland's Medical Dictionary, 25th Edition,* 1974). This muscle contains some fibers that are restricted to the lip and some fibers that blend with adjacent muscles

PERISTALSIS: Wave-like progressive contractions of muscles, usually referring to the esophagus and lower digestive tract.

POSTERIOR: Behind, in back of, at the back part of.

PREDICTIVE VALUE: The probability of a characteristic's being present, in the case of a positive result, or absent, in the case of a negative result.

PROGNATHISM: Protrusion of the jaw.

RAPHE: A seam where two halves of a part unite.

REFLEX: A reflected action or movement; the sum total of any particular involuntary activity (*Dorland's Medical Dictionary, 25th Edition,* 1974).

RUGAE: Ridges, wrinkles, or folds. Rugae palatina—the transverse ridges that extend outward on both sides of the raphe of the hard palate just behind the upper gum.

SENSITIVITY (in testing): The extent to which a true characteristic is classified correctly. A highly sensitive test will identify the majority of individuals with a given characteristic (*Handbook of Research Methodology,* 1988).

SPECIFICITY (in testing): The extent to which the absence of a characteristic is correctly classified. A highly specific test will correctly identify those individuals who are free of a given characteristic (*Handbook of Research Methodology,* 1988).

SUCKING: The combination of tongue and other orofacial muscle movements that removes milk from the breast or bottle. Proper sucking is characterized by a front to back progressive contraction of the tongue. The tongue remains over the lower gumline during its contractile action while simultaneously cupping the breast.

SUPERIOR: Upper, above, closest to the top, uppermost part of an organ or body part.

TEST-RETEST RELIABILITY: Degree of correlation between two successive measurements with the same test (*Handbook in Research and Evaluation, 2nd Edition,* 1981).

TONGUE-TIE: Impaired tongue function resulting from a tight and/or short lingual frenulum; the condition may or may not involve fibers of the genioglossus muscle.

TONGUE-THRUST: The abnormal forward movement of the tongue that replaces the normal front-to-back progressive contraction of the tongue that precedes swallowing.

TRANSVERSE TONGUE REFLEX: The side-to-side movement of the body and tip of the tongue that is elicited by touching the sides of the tongue (lateralization). This reflex forms the foundation for masticatory tongue movements.

VALIDITY: The degree to which a test measures what it was designed to measure.

BIBLIOGRAPHY

Aarts, C., Hornell, A., Kylberg, E., Hofvander, Y., & Gebre-Medhin, M. (1999). Breastfeeding patterns in relation to thumb sucking and pacifier use [Electronic version]. *Pediatrics,* 104, e50.

Agarwal, P., & Raina, V. K. (2003). Tongue-tie: An update. *Indian Pediatrics*, 40, 404-405.

American Academy of Pediatrics. (2005). Breastfeeding and the use of human milk. *Pediatrics,* 115, 496-506.

American Psychological Association. (2001). *Publication manual of the American Psychological Association* (5th ed.). Washington, DC: Amir, L. H. (2005, July 28). Tongue-tie: A view from Down Under. *Pediatric Alert,* 81.

Amir, L. H., James, J. P., & Beatty, J. (2005). Review of tongue-tie at a tertiary maternity hospital. *Journal of Pediatric and Child Health*, 41, 243-245.

Amir, L. H., James, J. P., & Donath, S. M. (2006). Reliability of the Hazelbaker assessment tool for lingual frenulum function [Electronic version]. *International Breastfeeding Journal*, 1, 3.

Anderson, K. N., & Anderson, L. E. (Eds.). (1990). *Mosby's pocket dictionary of medicine, nursing, and allied health* (3rd ed.). St. Louis, MO: C. V. Mosby.

Apgar, V. (1953). A proposal for a new method of evaluation of the newborn infant. *Current Researches in Anesthesia and Analgesia,* 32, 260-267.

Apgar, V. (1966). The newborn (Apgar) scoring system: Reflections and advice. *Pediatric Clinics of North America,* 13, 645-650.

Apgar, V., Holaday, D., James, L., Weisbrot, I., & Berrin, C. (1958). Evaluation of the newborn infant—Second report. *Journal of the American Medical Association,* 168, 1985-1988.

Apgar, V., & James, L. (1962). Further observations on newborn scoring system. *American Journal of Diseases of Children,* 104, 419–428.

Archer, W. H. (1975). *Oral and maxillofacial surgery* (5th ed.). Philadelphia: W. B. Saunders.

Ardran, G. M., Kemp, F. H., & Linda, J. (1958). A cineradiographic study of breastfeeding. *British Journal of Radiology,* 31, 156–162.

Arena, J. M. (Ed.). (1969). *Davison's compleat pediatrician* (9th ed.). Philadelphia: Lea & Febiger.

Arvedson, J. C., & Brodsky, L. (2002). *Pediatric swallowing and feeding: Assessment and management* (2nd ed.). Albany, NY: Singular Publishing Group/Thomson Learning.

Auerbach, K. H. (1990). Our first thematic issue: Ankyloglossia in infancy. *Journal of Human Lactation,* 6 (Suppl. 1), 101.

Avery, J. K., & Chiego, D. J. (2006). *Essentials of oral histology and embryology* (3rd ed.). St. Louis, MO: Mosby Elsevier.

Avery, M. E., & First, L. (Eds.). (1989). *Pediatric medicine.* Baltimore: Williams and Wilkins.

Ayers, F. J., & Hilton, L. M. (1977). Treatment of ankyloglossia: Report of a case. *Journal of Dentistry for Children,* 44, 237–239.

Ballard, J. L., Auer, C. E., & Khoury, J. C. (2002). Ankyloglossia: Assessment, incidence, and effect of frenuloplasty on the breastfeeding dyad [Electronic version]. *Pediatrics,* 110, e63.

Bauchner, H. (2008, July 10). Does frenulotomy improve breast-feeding? [Electronic version]. *Journal Watch General Medicine.* Retrieved April 8, 2010, from http://general-medicine.jwatch.org/cgi/content/full/2008/710/1

Becker, L. E., Zhang, W., & Pereyra, P. M. (1993). Delayed maturation of the vagus nerve in sudden infant death syndrome. *Acta Neuropathologica,* 86, 617–622.

Behrman, R. E., Vaughan, V. C., & Nelson, W. E. (Eds.). (1987). *Nelson's textbook of pediatrics.* Philadelphia: W. B. Saunders.

Bell, W. H. (1989). *Surgical correction of dentofacial deformities.* Philadelphia: W. B. Saunders.

Bellinger, D. C., Stiles, K. M., & Needleman, H. L. (1992). Low-level lead exposure, intelligence and academic achievement: A long-term follow-up study. *Pediatrics,* 90, 855–861.

Berg, K. (1990a). Tongue-tie (ankyloglossia) and breastfeeding: A review. *Journal of Human Lactation,* 6(Suppl. 1), 109–112.

Berg, K. (1990b). Two cases of tongue-tie and breastfeeding. *Journal of Human Lactation,* 6 (Suppl. 1), 124–126.

Bhaskar, S. N. (Ed.). (1991). *Orban's oral histology and embryology* (11th ed.). St. Louis, MO: C. V. Mosby.

Bjornsson, A., Arnason, A., & Tippet, P. (1989). X-linked cleft palate and ankyloglossia in an Icelandic family. *Cleft Palate Journal,* 26, 3-8.

Block, J. R. (1968). The role of the speech clinician in determining indications for frenulotomy in cases of ankyloglossia. *New York State Dental Journal,* 34, 479–481.

Boiron, M., Da Nobrega, L., Roux, S., Henrot, A., & Saliba, E. (2007). Effects of oral stimulation and oral support on non-nutritive sucking and feeding performance in infants. *Developmental Medicine & Child Neurology,* 49, 439–444.

Boo-Chai, K. (1963). The tongue-tie. *Singapore Medical Journal,* 4, 84–85.

Booth, I., & Wozniak, E. R. (1984). *Pocket picture guide for nurses: Pediatrics.* Baltimore: Williams and Wilkins.

Bosma, J. F. (1985). Postnatal ontogeny of performance of the pharynx, larynx, and mouth. *American Review of Respiratory Disease,* 131, S10–S15.

Bosma, J. F., Hepburn, L. G., Josell, S. D., & Baker, K. (1990). Ultrasound demonstrations of tongue motions during suckle feeding. *Developmental Medicine and Child Neurology,* 32, 223–229.

Bowen, C. (2000). Tongue-tie, ankyloglossia or short lingual fraenum. *Speech-language-therapy dot com.* Retrieved April 8, 2010, from http://www.speech-language-therapy.com/tonguetie.html

Braybrook, C., Doudney, K., Marcano, A. C. B., Arnason, A., Bjornsson, A., Patton, M. A., et al. (2001). The T-box transcription factor gene TBX22 is mutated in X-linked cleft palate and ankyloglossia. *Nature Genetics*, 29, 179–183.

Braybrook, C., Lisgo, S., Doudney, K., Henderson, D., Marcano, A. C. B., Strachan, T., et al. (2002). Craniofacial expression of human and murine TBX22 correlates with the cleft palate and ankyloglossia phenotype observed in CPX patients. *Human Molecular Genetics,* 11, 2793-2804.

Breastfeeding and birthing: Do birthing practices affect breastfeeding? (2007, Winter). *INFACT Newsletter,* 1-2.

Breward, S. (2004). Tongue tie and breastfeeding: Assessing and overcoming the difficulties. *Community Practitioner,* 79, 298-299.

Brinkman, S., Reilly, S., & Meara, J. G. (2004). Management of tongue-tie in children: A survey of paediatric surgeons in Australia. *Journal of Paediatric and Child Health,* 40, 600–605.

Broad, F. E. (1972a). The effects of infant feeding on speech quality. *New Zealand Journal of Medicine*, 76, 28–31.

Broad, F. E. (1972b). In the beginning was the word: Suckling and speech. *Bulletin of the Federation of New Zealand Parents Centers*, 53, 4–6.

Brookes, M., & Zeitman, A. (1998). *Clinical embryology: A color atlas and text.* Boca Raton, FL: CRC Press.

Broussard, D. L., & Altschuler, S. M. (2000). Central integration of swallow and airway-protective reflexes. *American Journal of Medicine,* 108, 62S–67S.

Browne, D. (1959). Tongue-tie. *British Medical Journal,* 2, 952.

Butlin, H., & Spencer, W. (1900). *Diseases of the tongue* (pp. 1-21, 30-35, 50-51). London: Cassell and Company.

Cancer risks of oral contraception [Editorial]. (1989). *Lancet,* 1, 21-22.

Catlin F. I., & De Haan, V. (1971). Tongue-tie. *Archives of Otolaryngology,* 94, 548-557.

Cesar, J. A., Victora, C. G., Barros, F. C., Santos, I. S., & Flores, J. A. (1999). Impact of breastfeeding on admission for pneumonia during postneonatal period in Brazil: Nested case-control study. *British Medical Journal,* 318, 1316-1320.

Chamberlain, G., & Banks, J. (1974). Assessment of the Apgar score. *Lancet,* 2, 1225-1288.

Cinar, F., & Onat, N. (2005). Prevalence and consequences of a forgotten entity: Ankyloglossia. *Plastic and Reconstructive Surgery,* 115, 355-356.

Colley, J. R. T., & Creamer, B. (1958). Sucking and swallowing in infants. *British Medical Journal,* 2, 422-423.

Conway, A. (1990). Ankyloglossia-To snip or not to snip: Is that the question? *Journal of Human Lactation,* 6(Suppl. 1), 101-102.

Corbin-Lewis, K., Liss, J. M., & Sciortino, K. L. (2005). *Clinical anatomy & physiology of the swallow mechanism.* Clifton Park, NY: Thomson Delmar Learning.

Coryllos, E., Watson Genna, C., & Salloum, A. C. (2004, Summer). Congenital tongue-tie and its impact on breastfeeding. *Breastfeeding: Best for Mother and Baby Newsletter,* 1-6.

Crook, C. K., & Lipsitt, L. P. (1976). Neonatal nutritive sucking effects of taste stimulation upon sucking rhythm and heart rate. *Child Development,* 47, 518-522.

Cullum, I. M. (1959). Nova et vetera: An old wives' tale. *British Medical Journal, European Society of Haematology,* 2, 497-498.

Cunha, R. F., Silva, J. Z., & Faria, M. D. (2008). Clinical approach of ankyloglossia in babies: Report of two cases. *The Journal of Clinical Pediatric Dentistry,* 32, 277-281.

Cunningham, A. S. (1979). Morbidity in breast-fed and artificially fed babies. *Journal of Pediatrics,* 95, 685-689.

Cunningham, A. S., Jelliffe, D. B., & Jelliffe, E. F. (1991). Breastfeeding and health in the 1980s: A global epidemiological review. *Journal of Pediatrics,* 118, 659-666.

Daly, S. E. J., Kent, J. C., Owens, R. A., & Hartmann, P. E. (1996). Frequency and degree of milk removal and the short-term control of human milk synthesis. *Experimental Physiology,* 81, 861-875.

Davis, M. K., Savitz, D. E., & Graubard, B. I. (1988). Infant feeding and childhood cancer. *Lancet,* 2, 365-368.

Defabianis, P. (2000). Ankyloglossia and its influence on maxillary and mandibular development. *The Functional Orthodontist,* 17, 25-33.

DePorte, J. V., & Parkhurst, E. (1945). Congenital malformations and birth injuries among the children born in New York State, outside of New York City, in 1940-1942. *New York State Journal of Medicine,* 45, 1097-1100.

Dollberg, S., Botzer, E., Grunis, E., & Mimouni, F. B. (2006). Immediate nipple pain relief after frenotomy in breast-fed infants with ankyloglossia: A randomized, prospective study. *Journal of Pediatric Surgery,* 41, 1598-1600.

Dorland's illustrated medical dictionary. (1988). Philadelphia: W. B. Saunders.

Dorland's illustrated medical dictionary. (25th ed.). (1989). Philadelphia: W. B. Saunders.

Dorland's pocket medical dictionary. (24th ed.). (1989). Philadelphia: W. B. Saunders.

Dorland's pocket medical dictionary. (2001). Philadelphia: W. B. Saunders.

Douglas, B. L. (1961, May). "Elephant gun" anesthesia [Editorial]. *The Journal of the American Dental Society of Anesthesiology,* 156-158.

Douglas, B. L., & Kresberg, H. (1954). Surgical correction of ankyloglossia. *New York State Dental Journal,* 20, 477-479.

Downs, F. S. (Ed.). (1988). *Handbook of research methodology—Considerations in efficient research design and data analysis.* New York: American Journal of Nursing.

Ekenze, S. O., Ikechukwu, R. N., & Oparaocha, D. C. (2005). Surgically correctable congenital anomalies: Prospective analysis of management problems and outcome in a developing country. *Journal of Tropical Pediatrics,* 52, 126-131.

Evans, C. (1978). Muscles involved in oral-motor function. In J. M. Wilson (Ed.), *Oral-motor function and dysfunction in children* (pp. 79-95). Chapel Hill: University of North Carolina.

Fanibunda, K., & Adams, A. (1998). Are the features of ankyloglossia limited to the lingual fraenum? *Dental Update, September,* 296-297.

Fernando, C. (1998). *Tongue Tie: From confusion to clarity.* Concord, New South Wales, Australia: Tandem.

Fessler, D. M. T., & Abrams, E. T. (2004). Infant mouthing behavior: The immunocalibration hypothesis. *Medical Hypotheses,* 63, 925-932.

Finn, S. B. (1973). *Clinical periodontics.* Philadelphia: W. B. Saunders.

Fiorotti, R. C., Bertolini, M. M., Nicola, J. H., & Nicola, E. M. D. (2004, November). Early lingual frenectomy assisted by CO2 laser helps prevention and treatment of functional alterations caused by ankyloglossia. *International Journal of Orofacial Myology,* 30, 64-71.

Fitz-Desorgher, R. (2003). All tied up: Tongue-tie and its implications for breastfeeding. *The Practising Midwife,* 6, 20-22.

Fleiss, P. M., Burger, M., Ramkumar, H., & Carrington, P. (1990). Ankyloglossia: A cause of breastfeeding problems? *Journal of Human Lactation,* 6(Suppl. 1), 128-129.

Fletcher, S. G., & Daly, D. A. (1974). Sublingual dimensions. *Archives of Otolaryngology,* 99, 292-296.

Fletcher, S. G., & Meldrum, J. R. (1968). Lingual function and relative length of the lingual frenulum. *Journal of Speech and Hearing Research,* 11, 382-390.

Forlenza, G. P., Paradise Black, N. M., McNamara, E. G., & Sullivan, S. E. (In press). Ankyloglossia, exclusive breastfeeding, and failure to thrive lead to child abuse investigation.

Forbes, S. A., Brennan, L., Richardson, M., Coffey, A., Cole, C. G., Gregory, S. G., et al. (1996). Refined mapping and YAC contig construction of the X-linked cleft palate and ankyloglossia locus (CPX) including the proximal X-Y homology breakpoint within Xq21.3. *Genomics,* 31, 36-43.

Forbes, S. A., Richardson, M., Brennan, L., Arnason, A., Bjornsson, A., Campbell, L., et al. (1995). Refinement of the X-linked cleft palate and ankyloglossia (CPX) localization by genetic mapping in an Icelandic kindred. *Human Genetics,* 95, 342-346.

Friend, G. W., Harris, E. F., Mincer, H. H., Fong, T. L., & Carruth, K. R. (1990). Oral anomalies in the neonate, by race and gender, in an urban setting. *Pediatric Dentistry,* 12, 157-161.

Furer, R. (2008). *Subfunctional tongue and upper lip release in nursing babies.* Retrieved April 10, 2010, from http://roeefurer.blogspot.com

Garcia Pola, J., Gonzalez Garcia, M., Garcia Martin, J. M., Gallas, M., & Leston, J. S. (2002). A study of pathology associated with short lingual frenum. *Journal of Dentistry for Children,* 69, 59-63.

Gardner, A. F. (1949). Dental, oral, and general causes of speech pathology. *Oral Surgery, Oral Medicine, and Oral Pathology,* 2, 742-751.

Garliner, D. (1968). Effects of unrecognized abnormal swallowing. *Journal of the Canadian Dental Association,* 34, 301-304.

Garliner, D. (1974). *Myofunctional therapy in dental practice.* Coral Gables, FL: Institute for Myofunctional Therapy.

Garliner, D. (1975). Myofunctional therapy. *I.C.D., Sc. Ed. Journal,* 8, 39–46.

Garliner, D. (1976). Stress and the dentition. *Basal Facts,* 1, 98–109.

Garliner, D. (1981). *Myofunctional therapy.* Philadelphia: W. B. Saunders.

Garrison, C. P. (2002). Nipple vasospasms, Raynaud's syndrome, and nifedipine. *Journal of Human Lactation,* 18, 382–385.

Gartner, L., Tanis, A., & Lawrence, R. A. (1991, Spring). Wrap-up session: Physician's Seminar, 1991 [Transcript]. *Medical Associates Newsletter,* 7(1).

Geddes, D. T., Kent, J. C., Mitoulas, L. R., & Hartmann, P. E. (2008). Tongue movement and intra-oral vacuum in breastfeeding infants. *Early Human Development,* 84, 471–477.

Geddes, D. T., Langton, D. B., Gollow, I., Jacobs, L. A., Hartman, P. E., & Simmer, K. (2008). Frenulotomy for breastfeeding infants with ankyloglossia: Effect on milk removal and sucking mechanism as imaged by ultrasound [Electronic version]. *Pediatrics,* 122, e188–e194.

Gellis, S. S., & Kagan, B. M. (1964). *Current pediatric therapy.* Philadelphia: W. B. Saunders.

Gellis, S. S., & Kagan, B. M. (1978). *Current pediatric therapy.* Philadelphia: W. B. Saunders.

Gellis, S. S., & Kagan, B. M. (1990). *Current pediatric therapy.* Philadelphia: W. B. Saunders.

Gewolb, I. H., Bosma, J. F., Taciak, V. L., & Vice, F. L. (2001). Abnormal developmental patterns of suck and swallow rhythms during feeding in preterm infants with bronchopulmonary dysplasia. *Developmental Medicine and Child Neurology,* 43, 454–459.

Glass, R. P., & Wolf, L. S. (1994). Incoordination of sucking, swallowing, and breathing as an etiology for breastfeeding difficulty. *Journal of Human Lactation,* 10, 185–189.

Goldberger, J. M. (1973). Tongue thrust: Report of cases. *Journal of the American Dental Association,* 86, 667-671.

Good, M. E. (1987). Breastfeeding and the short frenulum. *Journal of Human Lactation,* 3, 154–156.

Gorski, S. M., Adams, K. J. Birch, P. H., Friedman, J. M., & Goodfellow, P. J. (1992). The gene responsible for X-linked cleft palate (CPX) in a British Columbia native kindred is localized between PGK1 and DXYS1. *American Journal of Medical Genetics,* 50, 1129–1136.

Green, M., & Richmond, J. B. (1962). *Pediatric diagnosis.* Philadelphia: W. B. Saunders.

Greene, J. S. (1937). Speech defects and related oral anomalies. *The Journal of the American Dental Association and the Dental Cosmos,* 24, 1969–1974.

Greene, J. S. (1945). Anomalies of the speech mechanism and associated voice and speech disorders. *New York State Journal of Medicine*, 45, 605–608.

Griffiths, D. M. (2004). Do tongue ties affect breastfeeding? *Journal of Human Lactation,* 20, 409–414.

Griffiths, M., Hall, D., Renfrew, M. (2006, June 1). Tongue ties and breastfeeding [Author's reply]. *Archives of Diseases in Childhood,* 91(6), 542.

Gryboski, J. D. (1969). Suck and swallow in the premature infant. *Pediatrics,* 43, 96–102.

Gunther, M. (1970). *Infant feeding.* Chicago: Henry Regnery.

Gutman, G. (1990, July). Blocked atlantal nerve syndrome in infants and small children. *International Review of Chiropractic*, 37–42.

Gwinn, M. L., Lee, N. C., Rhodes, P. H., Layde, P. M., & Rubin, G. L. (1990). Pregnancy, breastfeeding, and oral contraceptives and the risk of epithelial ovarian cancer. *Journal of Clinical Epidemiology*, 43, 559–568.

Hall, D. M., & Renfew, M. J. (2005). Tongue tie. *Archives of Disease in Childhood,* 90(12), 1211–1215.

Hall, D. M., & Renfew, M. J. (2006). Tongue tie: More research needed [Letter to the editor]. *Archives of Diseases in Childhood,* 91, 542.

Hammond-McKibbon, D., Karges, W., Gaedigk, R., & Dosch, H-M. (1997). Immunological mechanisms that link cow milk protein and insulin dependent diabetes: A synopsis. *Canadian Journal of Allergy and Clinical Immunology,* 2, 136–146.

Hansen, R., MacKinlay, G. A., & Manson, W. G. (2006). Ankyloglossia intervention in outpatients is safe: Our experience [Letter to the editor]. *Archives of Diseases in Childhood,* 91, 541–542.

Harper, R. M., & Hoffman, H. D. (Eds.). (1988). *Sudden infant death syndrome: Risk factors and basic mechanisms.* New York: PMA.

Hasan, N. (1973). Tongue tie as a cause of deformity of lower central incisor. *Journal of Pediatric Surgery,* 8, 985.

Hayashi, Y, Hoashi, E., & Nara, T. (1997, July 24). Ultrasonographic analysis of sucking behavior of newborn infants: The driving force of sucking pressure. *Early Human Development,* 49(1), pp. 33–38.

Hazelbaker, A. K. (1993). *The assessment tool for lingual frenulum function: Use in a lactation consultant private practice.* Unpublished master's thesis, Pacific Oaks College, Pasadena, CA. (Available from A. K. Hazelbaker, 5095 Olentangy River Road, Columbus, OH 43235)

Hazelbaker, A. K. (1994, February, June, and October). *Tongue-tie.* Columbus, OH: A.B.R.E.A.S.T. [Associates for Breastfeeding Research, Education, Advocacy, Support and Treatment center for breastfeeding] seminars [Unpublished],

Hazelbaker, A. K. (2003). *The impact of craniosacral therapy on infant sucking dysfunction: A pilot study.* (Available from A. K. Hazelbaker, 5095 Olentangy River Road, Columbus, OH 43235)

Hazelbaker, A. K. (2005). Newborn tongue-tie and breast-feeding [Letter to the editor]. *Journal of the American Board of Family Practice,* 18, 326.

Hedberg Nyqvist, K., Farnstrand, C., Eeg-Olofsson, K., & Ewald, U. (2001). Early oral behaviour in pre-term infants during breastfeeding: An electromyographic study. *Acta Pediatrica,* 90, 658–663.

Heller, J., Gabbay, J., O'Hara, C., Heller, M., & Bradley, J. P. (2005). Improved ankyloglossia correction with four-flap Z-frenuloplasty. *Annals of Plastic Surgery,* 54, 623–628.

Herbst, J. J. (1983). Development of suck and swallow. *Journal of Pediatric Gastroenterology and Nutrition,* 2(Suppl. 1), S131–S135.

Hillan, R. (2008). Division of tongue-tie: Wicked and barbaric? *The Practising Midwife,* 11, 22–25.

Hingley, G. (1990). Ankyloglossia [Letter to the editor]. *Journal of Human Lactation,* 6(Suppl. 1), 103.

Hoekelman, R. A. (1987). *Primary pediatric care.* St. Louis, MO: C. V. Mosby.

Hogan, M., Westcott, C., & Griffiths, M. (2005). Randomized, controlled trial of division of tongue-tie in infants with feeding problems. *Journal of Paediatric and Child Health,* 41, 246–250.

Hong, P., Lago, D., Seargeant, J., Pellman, L., Magit, A.E., & Pransky, S.M. (2010). Defining ankyloglossia: A case series of anterior and posterior tongue ties. *Int. J. Pediatr. Otorhinolaryngol.* Doi:10.1016/j.ijporl.2010.05.025.

Hooley, J. R. (1967). The infant's mouth. *Journal of the American Dental Association,* 75, 95–103.

Horton, C. E., Crawford, H. H., Adamson, J. E., & Ashbell, T. S. (1969). Tongue-tie. *Cleft Palate Journal,* 6, 8–23.

Howie, P. W., Forsyth, J. S., Ogston, S. A., Clark, A., & Florey, C. (1990). Protective effect of breast-feeding against infection. *British Medical Journal,* 300, 11–16.

Huggins, K. (1986). *Nursing mother's companion.* Boston: Harvard Common Press.

Huggins, K. (1990a). Ankyloglossia–One lactation consultant's personal experience. *Journal of Human Lactation,* 6(Suppl. 1), 123–124.

Huggins, K. (1990b). *Nursing mother's companion.* Boston: Harvard Common Press.

Hussey, H. H. (1974). Tongue-tie. *Journal of the American Medical Association,* 228, 735.

Hyashi, Y., Hoashi, E., & Nara, T. (1997). Ultrasonograhic analysis of sucking behavior of newborn infants: The driving force of sucking pressure. *Early Human Development,* 49, 33–38.

Illingworth, R. S. (1969). Sucking and swallowing difficulties in infancy: Diagnostic problem of dysphagia. *Archives of Diseases in Childhood,* 44, 655-665.

Inoue, N., Sakashita, R., & Kamegai, T. (1995). Reduction of masseter muscle activity in bottle-fed babies. *Early Human Development,* 42, 185-193.

Is the Apgar score outmoded? [Editorial]. *Lancet,* 1, 591-592.

Isaac, S., & Michael, W. B. (1981). *Handbook in research and evaluation* (2nd ed.). San Diego, CA: EdITS/Educational and Industrial Testing Service.

Ivens, A., Moore, G. E., Chambers, J., Arnason, A., Jensson, O., Bjornsson, A., & Williamson, R. (1988). X-linked cleft palate: The gene is localized between polymorphic DNA markers DXYS12 and DXS17. *Human Genetics,* 78, 356-358.

Jacobs, L. A., Dickenson, J. E., Hart, P. D., Doherty, D. A., & Faulkner, S. J. (2007). Normal nipple position in term infants measured on breastfeeding ultrasound. *Journal of Human Lactation,* 23, 52-59.

Jain, E. (1995). Tongue-tie: Its impact on breastfeeding. *AARN Newsletter,* 51, 18.

Jean, A. (1984). Brainstem organization of the swallowing network. *Brain, Behavior and Evolution,* 25, 109-116.

Jepson, H. A., Talashek, M. L., & Tichy, A. M. (1991). The Apgar score: Evolution, limitations, and scoring guidelines. *Birth,* 18, 83-92.

Jolly, M. (1968). Soft tissue surgery in general dental practice. *Australian Dental Journal,* 13, 10.

Jones, F. Z. (1989). Tongue-tied. *New Beginnings,* 5, 122.

Jones, P. J. (Ed.). (1983). A grooved table-spoon for tongue-tie release and hernial neck transfixion [Editorial comment]. *Australia and New Zealand Journal of Surgery,* 53, 62.

Kaban, L. (1990). *Pediatric oral maxillofacial surgery.* Philadelphia: W. B. Saunders.

Karabulut, R., Sonmez, K., Turkyilmaz, Z., Demirogullari, B., Ozen, I. O., Bagbanci, B., et al. (2008). Ankyloglossia and effects on breast-feeding, speech problems and mechanical/social issues in children. *B-ENT,* 4, 81-85.

Kent, J. C., Mitoulas, L. R., Cregan, M. D., Ramsay, D. T., Doherty, D. A., & Hartmann, P. E. (2006). Volume and frequency of breastfeedings and fat content of breast milk throughout the day [Electronic version]. *Pediatrics,* 117, e387-e395.

Ketty, N., & Sciullo, P. A. (1974). Ankyloglossia with psychological implications. *Journal of Dentistry for Children,* 41, 43-46.

Kidd, H. R. (1976). Examination of the mouth. *Canadian Family Physician,* 22, 59-62.

Klockars, T. (2007). Familial ankyloglossia. *International Journal of Pediatric Otorhinolaryngology,* 71, 1321-1324.

Klockars, T., & Pitkäranta, A. (2009). Pediatric tongue-tie division: Indications technique and patient satisfaction. *International Journal of Pediatric Otorhinolaryngology, August* 4. [Abstract obtained from Epub ahead of print.] Retrieved May 22, 2010, from *www.ncbi.nlm.nih.gov/pubmed/*19660817

Koletzko, S., Sherman, P., Corey, M., Griffiths, A., & Smith, C. (1989). Role of infant feeding practices in development of Crohn's disease in childhood. *British Medical Journal,* 298, 1617-1618.

Kotlow, L. A. (1999). Ankyloglossia (tongue-tie): A diagnostic and treatment quandary. *Pediatric Dentistry,* 30, 259-262.

Kotlow, L. A. (2004). Using the Erbium: YAG laser to correct an abnormal lingual frenum attachment in newborns. *The Journal of the Academy of Laser Dentistry,* 12, 22-23.

Kotlow, L. A. (2009). Using photobiostimulating lasers in the practice of pediatric dentistry. *Laser,* 3(User Report).

Kummer, A. (2005). Ankyloglossia: To clip or not to clip? That's the question. *The ASHA Leader,* 10, 6-7, 30.

Kupietzky, A., & Botzer, E. (2005). Ankyloglossia in the infant and young child: Clinical suggestions for diagnosis and management. *Pediatric Dentistry,* 27, 40-46.

Labbok, M. H., & Hendershot, G .E. (1987). Does breast-feeding protect against malocclusion? An analysis of the 1981 child health supplement to the national health interview survey. *American Journal of Preventive Medicine,* 3, 227-232.

Lalakea, M. L., & Messner, A. H. (2002). Frenotomy and frenuloplasty: If, when, and how. *Otolaryngology-Head and Neck Surgery,* 13, 93-97.

Lalakea, M. L., & Messner, A. H. (2003a). Ankyloglossia: The adolescent and adult perspective. *Otolaryngology-Head and Neck Surgery,* 128, 746-752.

Lalakea, M. L., & Messner, A. H. (2003b). Ankyloglossia: Does it matter? *Pediatric Clinics of North America,* 50, 381-397.

Lau, C., & Kusnierczyk, I. (2001). Quantitative evaluation of infant's nonnutritive and nutritive sucking. *Dysphagia,* 16, 58-67.

Lau, J. T. K., & Ong, G. B. (1983). A grooved table-spoon for tongue-tie release and hernial neck transfixion. *Australia and New Zealand Journal of Surgery,* 53, 61-62.

Lauwers, J., & Woessner, C. (1983). *Counseling the nursing mother.* Wayne, NJ: Avery.

Lawrence, R. A. (1989). *Breastfeeding: A guide for the medical profession* (3rd ed.). St. Louis, MO: C. V. Mosby.

Leith, D. E. (1985). The development of cough. *The American Review of Respiratory Disease,* 131, S39-S42.

Li, H. M., Kang, B., Lin, J. B., Huang, J. Y., & Lin, L. E. (2005). Use of Z-plasty for ankyloglossia: Report of 38 cases. *Shanghai Kou Qiang Yi Xue,* 14, 203-204.

Logemann, J. A. (1998). *Evaluation of treatment and swallowing disorders.* (2nd ed.). Austin, TX: Pro-Ed.

Lomcali, G. (1987). Ankyloglossia (A case report). *Dentistry,* 2, 124-127.

Lowe, A. A. (1984). Tongue movements–Brainstem mechanisms and clinical postulates. *Brain, Behavior and Evolution,* 25, 128-137.

Lucas, A., & Cole, T. J. (1990). Breastmilk and neonatal necrotizing enterocolitis. *Lancet,* 336, 1519-1523.

Lucas A., Morley, R., Cole, T. J., Lister, G., & Lesson-Payne, C. (1992). Breastmilk and subsequent intelligence quotient in children born preterm. *Lancet,* 339, 261-264.

Luz, C. L. F., Garib, D. G., & Arouca, R. (2006). Association between breastfeeding duration and mandibular retrusion: A cross-sectional study of children in the mixed dentition. *American Journal of Orthodontics and Dentofacial Orthopedics,* 130, 531-534.

MacCarthy, D. (1964). Minor disorders in infancy. *British Medical Journal,* 2, 1512.

Makuen, G. H. (1897). Faculty of speech, with some cases illustrating anomalies of the organs of speech and the operative measures for their correction. *International Clinics,* 1, 319-326.

Malec, M. (1977). *Essential statistics for social research.* Philadelphia: J. B. Lippincott.

Mangelsdorf, M. (1986). Effective suckling and how to encourage it. *Breastfeeding Review,* 8, 28-33.

Marcano, A. C. B., Doudney, K., Braybrook, C., Squires, R., Patton, M. A., Lees, M. M., et al. (2004). TBX22 mutations are a frequent cause of cleft palate. *Journal of Medical Genetics,* 41, 68-74.

Marchesan, I. Q. (2004). Lingual frenulum: Classification and speech interference. *International Journal of Orofacial Myology,* 30, 31-38.

Marmet, C., & Shell, E. (1984). Training neonates to suck correctly. *American Journal of Maternal Child Nursing,* 9, 401-407.

Marmet, C., Shell, E., & Aldana, S. (2000). Assessing infant suck dysfunction: Case management. *The Journal of Human Lactation,* 16, 332-336.

Marmet, C., Shell, E., & Marmet, R. (1990). Neonatal frenotomy may be necessary to correct breast-feeding problems. *Journal of Human Lactation,* 6(Suppl. 1), 117-121.

Masaitis, N. S., & Kaempf, J. W. (1996). *Journal of Human Lactation,* 12, 229-232.

Mathewson, R. J., Siegel, M. J., & McCanna, D. L. (1966). Ankyloglossia: A review of the literature and a case report. *Journal of Dentistry for Children,* 33, 238-243.

Mayer, E. J., Hamman, R. F., Gay, E. C., Lezotte, D. C., Savitz, D. A., & Klingensmith, G. J. (1988). Reduced risk of insulin-dependent diabetes mellitus (IDDM) among breastfed children. *Diabetes,* 37, 1625-1632.

MacTavish, W. K., & Matthews, R. L. (1960). *Airways: The key to early facial growth and malocclusions.* (Available from 17200 Red Oak Drive, Suite 200, Houston, TX 77090)

McBride, C. (2005). Tongue-tie. *Journal of Pediatric and Child Health,* 41, 242.

McEnery, E. T., & Gaines, F. P. (1941). Tongue-tie in infants and children. *Journal of Pediatrics,* 18, 252-255.

McNeilly, A. S. (1994). Suckling and the control of gonadotropin secretion. In E. Knobil & J. D. Neill (Eds.), *The physiology of reproduction* (2nd ed). New York: Raven Press.

Medoff-Cooper, B., McGrath, J. M., & Shults, J. (2002). Feeding patterns of full-term and preterm infants at forty weeks postconceptional age. *Journal of Developmental & Behavioral Pediatrics,* 23, 231-236.

Medoff-Cooper, B., Weininger, S., & Zukowsky, K. (1969). A clinical assessment tool: Preliminary findings. *Nursing Research,* 36, 162-165.

Meier, P. (1988). Bottle and breast-feeding: Effects on transcutaneous oxygen pressure in preterm infants. *Nursing Research,* 37, 36-41.

Meintz-Maher, S. (1988). *An overview of solutions to breastfeeding and sucking problems.* Franklin Park, IL: La Leche League International.

Messner, A. H., & Lalakea, M. L. (2000a). Ankyloglossia: Controversies in management. *International Journal of Pediatric Otorhinolaryngology,* 54, 123-131.

Messner, A. H., & Lalakea, M. L. (2000b). Ankyloglossia: Incidence and associated feeding difficulties. *Archives of Otolaryngology Head and Neck Surgery,* 126, 36-39.

Messner, A. H., & Lalakea, M. L. (2002). The effect of ankyloglossia on speech in children. *Otolaryngology-Head and Neck Surgery,* 127, 539-545.

Meyer Palmer, M. (1995). NOMAS certification course. [Taught by Marjorie Meyer Palmer.]

Meyer Palmer, M. (2002). Recognizing and resolving infant suck difficulties. *Journal of Human Lactation,* 18, 166.

Meyer Palmer, M., & VandenBerg, K. A. (1998). A closer look at neonatal sucking. *Neonatal Network,* 17, 77-79.

Miller, A. J. (1986). Neurophysiological basis of swallowing. *Dysphagia,* 1, 91-100.

Miller, B. F., & Keane, C. B. (1983). *Encyclopedia and dictionary of medicine, nursing and allied health.* Philadelphia: W. B. Saunders.

Miller, M. J., Martin, R. J., Carlo, W. A., Fouke, J. M., Strohl, K. P., & Fanaroff, A. A. (1985). Oral breathing in newborn infants. *Journal of Pediatrics,* 107, 465-469.

Min, M. O., Singer, L. T., Kirchner, H. L., Minnes, S., Short, E., Hussain, Z., et al. (2009). Cognitive development and low-level lead exposure in poly-drug exposed children. *Neurotoxicology and Teratology,* 31, 225-231.

Minchin, M. (1985). *Breastfeeding matters.* Armadale, Victoria, Australia: Alma.

Mitchell, E. A., Scragg, R., Stewart, A. W., Becroft, D. M., Taylor, B. J., Ford, R. P., et al. (1991). Results from the first year of the New Zealand cot death study. *New Zealand Medical Journal,* 104, 71-76.

Mizuno, K., & Ueda, A. (2006). Changes in sucking performance from nonnutritive sucking to nutritive sucking during breast- and bottle-feeding. *Pediatric Research,* 59, 728-731.

Mohrbacher, N., & Stock, J. (1991). *The breastfeeding answer book.* Franklin Park, IL: La Leche League International.

Moore, J. R. (1985). *Surgery of the mouth and jaws.* Boston: Blackwell Scientific.

Moore, K. L., & Persaud, T. V. N. (1998). *The developing human: Clinically oriented embryology* (6th ed.). Philadelphia: W. B. Saunders.

Morino, C., & Winn, S .M. (2007). Raynaud's phenomenon of the nipples: An elusive diagnosis. *Journal of Human Lactation,* 23, 191-193.

Morris, S. E. (1978). A glossary of terms describing the feeding process. In J. M. Wilson (Ed.), *Oral-motor function and dysfunction in children* (pp. 156-162). Chapel Hill: University of North Carolina.

Morselli, P., Vecchiet, F., & Marini, I. (1999). Frenuloplasty by means of a triangular flap. *Oral Surgery, Oral Medicine, Oral Pathology,* 87, 142-144.

Mueller, D. T., & Callanan, V. P. (2007). Congenital malformations of the oral cavity. *Otolaryngologic Clinics of North America,* 40, 141-160.

Mukai, S., Mukai, C., & Asaoka, K. (1991). Ankyloglossia with deviation of the epiglottis and larynx. *Annals of Otolaryngology, Rhinology and Laryngology,* 100, 3-20.

Naimer, S. A., Biton, A., Vardy, D., & Zvulunov, A. (2003). Office treatment of congenital ankyloglossia. *Medical Science Monitor,* 9, 432–435.

Nanci, A. (2008). *Ten Cate's oral histology: Development, structure, and function* (7th ed.). St. Louis, MO: Mosby Elsevier.

Nazif, M. M., & Ready, M. A. (1987). Oral disorders. In H. W. Davis & B. J. Zitelli (Eds.), *Atlas of pediatric physical diagnosis* (pp. 18.1-18.13). St. Louis, MO: C. V. Mosby.

Needleman, H. L., Gunnoe, C., Leviton, A., Reed, R., Peresie, H., Maher, C., et al. (1979). Deficits in psychologic and classroom performance of children with elevated dentine lead levels. *New England Journal of Medicine,* 300, 689–695.

Newman, L. A., Cleveland, R. H., Blickman, J. G., Hillman, R. E., & Jaramillo, D. (1991). Videofluoroscopic analysis of the infant swallow. *Investigative Radiology,* 26, 870–873.

Nezu, H. (1987). Breastfeeding question and answer (K. J. Shenk, Trans.). *Josanpu Zasshi,* 41, 61.

Nicholson, W. L. (1991). Tongue-tie (ankyloglossia) associated with breastfeeding problems. *Journal of Human Lactation,* 7, 82–84.

Notestine, G. E. (1990). The importance of the identification of ankyloglossia (short lingual frenulum) as a cause of breastfeeding problems. *Journal of Human Lactation,* 6(Suppl. 1), 113–115.

Nowak, A. J., Smith, W. L., & Erenberg, A. (1995). Imaging evaluation of breast-feeding and bottle-feeding systems. *Journal of Pediatrics,* 126, S130–S134.

Oddy, W. H., Holt, P. G., Sly, P. D., Read, A. W., Landau, L. I., Stanley, F. J., et al. (1999). Association between breastfeeding and asthma in 6 year old children: Findings of a prospective birth cohort study. *British Medical Journal*, 319, 815–819.

Oldfield, M. C. (1955). Congenitally short frenula of the upper lip and tongue. *Lancet,* 1, 528–530.

Oldfield, M. C. (1959). Tongue-tie. *British Medical Journal,* 2, 1181-1182.

O'Shea, M. (2002). Licking the problem of tongue-tie. *British Journal of Midwifery,* 10, 90–92.

Ostapiuk, B. (2006). Tongue mobility in ankyloglossia with regard to articulation. *Annales Academiae Medicae Stetinensis,* 52(Suppl. 3), 37–47.

Page, D. C. (2001). Breastfeeding is early functional jaw orthopedics. *The Functional Orthodontist,* 18, 24–27.

Paine, R., & Cable, R. D. (1982). Breast-feeding and infant health in a rural US community. *American Journal of Diseases in Children,* 136, 36–38.

Palmer, B. (2001). Frenums. *Brian Palmer, DDS, For Better Health.* Retrieved April 8, 2010, from http://www.brianpalmerdds.com

Palmer, B. (2005, August). Snoring and sleep apnea: How it can be prevented in childhood. Retrieved April 8, 2010, from http://www.brianpalmerdds.com/pdf/Master_2_27_06.pdf

Paradise, J. L. (1990). Evaluation and treatment for ankyloglossia. *Journal of the American Medical Association, 263,* 2371.

Parida, P. K. (2008). Ankyloglossia (tongue tie) [Electronic version]. *Internet Journal of Otorhinolaryngology,* 8.

Patterson, G. T., Ramasastry, S. S., & Davis J. U. (1988). Macroglossia and ankyloglossia in Beckwith-Wiedemann syndrome. *Oral surgery, Oral Medicine, Oral Pathology,* 65, 29-31.

Phillips, V. T. (1992). Correcting faulty suck: Tongue protrusion and the breastfed infant. *The Medical Journal of Australia,* 156, 508.

Ploude, F. (1991). Kudos for issue on ankyloglossia [Letter to the editor]. *Journal of Human Lactation, 7,* 3.

Porter, N. (Ed.). (1913). Tongue-tied [Definition]. *Webster's Revised Unabridged Dictionary.* Springfield, MA: G. & C. Merriam. Retrieved April 8, 2010, from http://everything2.com/title/Tongue-tied Pottenger, F. M., & Krohn, B. (1950). Influence of breastfeeding on facial development. *Archives of Pediatrics,* 67, 454-461.

Prieto, C. R., Cardenas, H., Salvatierra, A. M., Boza, C., Montes, C. G., & Croxatto, H. B. (1996). Sucking pressure and its relationship to milk transfer during breastfeeding in humans. *Journal of Reproduction and Fertility,* 108, 69-74.

Qureshi, M. A., Vice, F. L., Taciak, V. L., Bosma, J. F., & Gewolb, I. H. (2002). Changes in rhythmic suckle feeding patterns in term infants in the first month of life. *Developmental Medicine & Child Neurology,* 44, 34-39.

Ramsay, D. T., & Hartmann, P. E. (2005). Milk removal from the breast. *Breastfeeding Review,* 13, 5-7.

Ramsay, D. T., Kent, J. C., Hartmann, R. A., & Hartmann, P. E. (2005). *Journal of Anatomy,* 206, 525-534.

Ramsay, M., Gisel, E. G., McCusker, J., Bellavance, F., & Platt, R. (2002). Infant sucking ability, non-organic failure to thrive, maternal characteristics, and feeding practices: A prospective cohort study. *Developmental Medicine and Child Neurology,* 44, 405-414.

Rendon-Macias, M. E., Cruz-Perez, L. A., Mosco-Peralta, M. R., Saraiba-Russell, M. M., Levi-Tajfeld, S., & Morales-Lopez, M. G. (1999). Assessment of sensorial oral stimulation in infants with suck feeding disabilities. *Indian Journal of Pediatrics,* 66, 319-329.

Ricke, L. A., Baker, N. J., Madlon-Kay, D. J., & DeFor, T. A. (2005a, July-August). Newborn tongue-tie and breast-feeding [Authors' reply as letter to the editor]. *Journal of the American Board of Family Practice,* 18, 326-327.

Ricke, L. A., Baker, N. J., Madlon-Kay, D. J., & DeFor, T. A. (2005b, January). Newborn tongue-tie: Prevalence and effect on breast-feeding. *Journal of the American Board of Family Practice,* 18, 1-7.

Righard, L., & Alade, M. (1992). Sucking technique and its effect on success of breastfeeding. *Birth,* 19, 185-189.

Riordan, J. (1983). *A practical guide to breastfeeding.* St. Louis, MO: C. V. Mosby.

Rogers, J. G., & Douglas, B. L. (1952). Surgical correction of ankyloglossia. *United States Armed Forces Medical Journal,* 3, 695-697.

Ruffoli, R., Giambelluca, M. A., Scavuzzo, M. C., Bonfigli, D., Cristofani, R., Gabriele, M., et al. (2005). Ankyloglossia: A morphofunctional investigation in children. *Oral Diseases,* 2, 170-174.

Saarinen, U. M. (1982). Prolonged breastfeeding as prophylaxis for recurrent otitis media. *Acta Pediatrica Scandinavica,* 71, 567-571.

Salinas, C. F. (1982). Orodental findings and genetic disorders. *Birth Defects: Original Article Series,* 18, 97-99.

Sato, T., Iida, M., & Yamaguchi, Y. (1983). A family with hereditary ankyloglossia complicated by heterochromia irides and a congenital clasped thumb. *International Journal of Oral Surgery,* 12, 359-362.

Sawyer, D. R., Taiwo, E. O., & Mosadomi, A. (1984). Oral anomalies in Nigerian children. *Community Dentistry and Oral Epidemiology,* 12, 269-273.

Schmidt, B., Kirpalani, H., Rosenbaum, P., & Cadman, D. (1988). Strengths and limitations of the Apgar score: A critical appraisal. *Journal of Clinical Epidemiology,* 41, 843-850.

Schreiner, R. L., & Bradburn, N. C. (Eds.). (1988). *Care of the newborn.* New York: Raven Press.

Sedano, H. O. (1975). Congenital oral anomalies in Argentinean children. *Community Dentistry and Oral Epidemiology,* 3, 61-63.

Segal, L., Stephenson, R., Dawes, M., & Feldman, P. (2007). Prevalence, diagnosis, and treatment of ankyloglossia: Methodologic review. *Canadian Family Physician,* 53, 1027-1033.

Shafer, W. G., Hine, M. K., & Levy, B. M. (1974). *A textbook of oral pathology.* Philadelphia: W. B. Saunders.

Shepard, J. W., Geffler, W. B., Guilleminault, C., Hoffman, E. A., Hoffstein, V., Hudgel, D. W., et al. (1991). Evaluation of the upper airway in patients with OSA. *Sleep,* 14(4), 361-371.

Silverman, F. (1985). The Apgar score: Is it enough? *Obstetrics and Gynecology,* 66, 331-336.

Smith, H., & Smith, L. (1992). *The fact pack.* Dayton, OH: www.bflrc.com Smith, T. L., & Smith, J. M. (2001). Electrosurgery in otolaryngology: Head and neck surgery: Principles, advances, and complications. *Laryngoscope,* 111, 769-780.

Smith, W. L., Erenberg, A., & Nowak, A. (1988). Imaging evaluation of the human nipple during breastfeeding. *American Journal of Diseases in Children,* 142, 76-78.

Smith, W. L., Erenberg, A., Nowak, A., & Franken, E. A. (1985). Physiology of sucking in the normal term infant using real-time ultrasound. *Radiology,* 156, 379-381.

Smithells, R. W. (1959). Spontaneous rupture of tongue-tie. *British Medical Journal,* 1, 236.

Sperber, G. H. (2001). *Craniofacial development.* Hamilton, Ontario, Canada: B. C. Decker.

Srinivasan, A., Dobrich, C., Mitnick, H., & Feldman, P. (2006). Ankyloglossia in breastfeeding infants: The effect of frenotomy on maternal nipple pain and latch. *Breastfeeding Medicine,* 1, 216-224.

Stal, P. S., Marklund, S., Thornell, L. E., De Paul, R., & Eriksson, P. O. (2003). Fibre composition of human intrinsic tongue muscles. *Cells Tissues Organs,* 173, 147-161.

Stevenson, R. D., & Allaire, J. H. (1991). The development of normal feeding and swallowing. *Development and Behavior: The Very Young Child,* 38, 1439-1453.

Stice, E., Agras, W. S., & Hammer, L. D. (1999). Risk factors for the emergence of childhood eating disturbances: A five-year prospective study. *International Journal of Eating Disorders,* 25, 375-387.

Summitt, R. (1990). *Comprehensive pediatrics.* St. Louis, MO: C. V. Mosby.

Tait, P. (2000). Nipple pain in breastfeeding women: Causes, treatment, and prevention strategies. *Journal of Midwifery & Women's Health,* 45, 212-215.

Takemoto, H. (2001). Morphological analyses of the human tongue musculature for three-dimensional modeling. *Journal of Speech, Language, and Hearing Research,* 44, 95-107.

Teele, D. W., Klein, J. O., & Rosner, B. (1980). Epidemiology of otitis media in children. *Ann Otol Rhinol Laryngol Suppl.* 89(3 Pt 2), :5-6.

Thomas, C. L. (Ed.). (1985). *Taber's cyclopedic medical dictionary* (16th ed.). Philadelphia: F. A. Davis.

Tuerk, M., & Lubit, E. (1959). Ankyloglossia. *Plastic and Reconstructive Surgery,* 24, 271-276.

Velanovich, V. (1994). The transverse-vertical frenuloplasty for ankyloglossia. *Military Medicine,* 159, 714-715.

Voloschin, L. M., Althabe, O., Olive, H., Diena, V., & Repezza, B. (1998). A new tool for measuring the suckling stimulus during breastfeeding in humans: The orokinetogram and the Fourier series. *Journal of Reproduction and Fertility,* 114, 219-224.

Walker, M. (1989). Management of selected early breastfeeding problems seen in clinical practice. *Birth,* 16, 150–151.

Walker, M. (1993). A fresh look at the risks of artificial feeding. *Journal of Human Lactation,* 9, 97–107.

Wall, V., & Glass, R. (2006). Mandibular asymmetry and breastfeeding problems: Experience from 11 cases. *Journal of Human Lactation,* 22, 328–334.

Wallace, A. F. (1964). The tongue-tie controversy. *Nursing Times,* 60, 527–528.

Wallace, A. F., & Lond, M. B. (1963). Tongue-tie. *Lancet,* 2, 377.

Wallace, H., & Clarke, S. (2006). Tongue tie division in infants with breast feeding difficulties. *International Journal of Pediatric Otorhinolaryngology,* 70, 1257–1261.

Wang, Y. S., & Wu, S. Y. (1996). The effect of exclusive breastfeeding on development and incidence of infection in infants. *Journal of Human Lactation,* 12, 27–30.

Ward, N. (1990). Ankyloglossia: A case study in which clipping was not necessary. *Journal of Human Lactation,* 6(Suppl. 1), 126–127.

Warden, P. J. (1991, August). Ankyloglossia: A review of the literature. *General Dentistry,* 252–253.

Watson Genna, C. (2002). Tongue-tie and breastfeeding. *Leaven,* 38, 27–29.

Watson Genna, C. (2008). *Supporting sucking skills in infants.* Sudbury, Suffolk, England: Jones and Bartlett.

Weber, F., Woolridge, M. W., & Baum, J. D. (1986). An ultrasonographic study of the organization of suck and swallow. *Developmental Medicine and Child Neurology,* 28, 19–24.

West, D., & Marasco, L. (2008). *The Breastfeeding Mother's Guide to Making More Milk.* New York: McGraw-Hill.

Whaley, L. F., & Wong, D. L. (1985). *Essentials of pediatric nursing* (2nd ed.). St. Louis, MO: C. V. Mosby.

Whitman, C. L., & Rankow, R. M. (1961). Diagnosis and management of ankyloglossia. *American Journal of Orthodontics,* 47, 423–428.

Whorwell, P. J., Holdstock, G., Whorwell, G. M., & Wright, R. (1979). Bottle-feeding, early gastroenteritis, and inflammatory bowel disease. *British Medical Journal,* 1, 382.

Williams, W. N., & Waldron, C. M. (1985). Assessment of lingual function when ankyloglossia (tongue-tie) is suspected. *Journal of the American Dental Association,* 110, 353–356.

Wilson, A. C., Forsyth, J. S., Greene, S. A., Irvine, L., Hau, C., & Howie, P. W. (1998). Relation of infant diet to childhood health: Seven year follow up of cohort children in Dundee infant feeding study. *British Medical Journal,* 316, 21–25.

Wilson, S. L., Thach, B. T., Brouillette, R. T., & Abu-Osba, Y. K. (1980). Upper airway patency in the human infant: Influence of airway pressure and posture. *Journal of Applied Physiology: Respiration, Environmental, and Exercise Physiology,* 48, 500-504.

Wilton, J. M. (1990). Sore nipples and slow weight gain related to a short frenulum. *Journal of Human Lactation,* 6(Suppl. 1), 122-123.

Winberg, J. (2005). Mother and newborn baby: Mutual regulation of physiology and behavior–A selective review. *Developmental Psychobiology,* 47, 217-229.

Wolf, R. P., & Glass, L. S. (1992). *Feeding and swallowing disorders in infancy: Assessment and management.* Tucson, AZ: Therapy Skill Builders.

Woods, R. H. (1973). Structural normalization in infants and children with particular reference to disturbances of the CNS. *Journal of the American Osteopathic Association,* 72, 903-908.

Woolridge, M. W. (1986a). Aetiology of sore nipples. *Midwifery,* 2, 172-176.

Woolridge, M. W. (1986b). The anatomy of infant sucking. *Midwifery,* 2, 164-171.

Wright, A. L., Holberg, C. J., Martinez, F. R., Morgan, W. J., & Taussig, L. M. (1989). Breastfeeding and lower respiratory tract illness in the first year of life. *British Medical Journal,* 299, 946-949.

Wright, J. E. (1995). Tongue-tie. *Journal of Pediatric and Child Health,* 31, 276-278.

Young, E. C., & Sacks, G. K. (1979). Examining for tongue-tie. *Clinical Pediatrics,* 18, 298.

Zarem, H. A. (1978). Diseases and injuries of the oral region. In S. S. Gellis & G. M. Kagan (Eds.), *Current pediatric therapy.* Philadelphia: W. B. Saunders.

APPENDIX A

FREQUENTLY ASKED QUESTIONS

Q: What is tongue-tie?

A: Tongue-tie, or partial ankyloglossia, is an inherited condition in which the connective tissue on the underside of the tongue is too tight or too short. It keeps the tongue from performing its full range of motion and can thereby affect infant feeding, eating, chewing, speech, and even breathing if left untreated for too long.

Q: How common is tongue-tie?

A: Worldwide, about 3 to 4 percent of people have a tied tongue.

Q: What causes tongue-tie?

A: Tongue-tie is inherited. It is a minor genetic mutation attached to the X chromosome. Environmental influences may play a role, but to what degree is unknown.

Q: How would I know if my baby, my child, or I have a tongue-tie?

A: Tongue-tie may not be obvious. If your baby has sucking or feeding problems, or if you or your child has difficulties with speech articulation, speech delay, chewing and/or swallowing issues, and/or tooth misalignment or other dental problems, you should see a knowledgeable practitioner to receive an evaluation. Be sure the practitioner has experience evaluating tongue-tie; many do not. See Appendix B for a list of organizations that can help you locate a practitioner.

Q: What kinds of problems are caused by tongue-tie?

A: In infants, tongue-tie can impair their sucking, both at breast and on a bottle. Babies can have minor to severe difficulty coordinating their sucking, swallowing, and breathing. Some may have such severe problems that they aspirate milk into their lungs, fail to thrive, or damage their mothers' breasts and nipples.

Children who are tongue-tied may have speech delay or speech articulation problems, malocclusion of the teeth, tongue-thrusting or other swallowing problems, excessive salivation, a recessive or protruding lower jaw and/or an increased incidence of dental caries. As the child grows older, these problems can worsen.

Adults will most likely exhibit a worsening of any problems they experienced during childhood. Gum recession, tooth loosening, decay at the gumline, and tooth abcesses all can result from untreated tongue-tie. Tongue-tied adults also may experience sleep apnea and airway collapse, which can lead to significant problems, including stroke and, possibly, death.

Q: Is tongue-tie so bad that it should always be treated?

A: The negative impact of tongue-tie varies from person to person. For some, the impact is very slight; for others the impact can be substantial and affect the daily quality of life. The problem is that it is impossible to predict which babies will experience the worst problems as they grow up. Most knowledgeable health practitioners recommend treating tongue-tie during early infancy to prevent problems from developing.

Q: How is tongue-tie treated?

A: There are two treatments for tongue-tie. One, called a frenotomy, consists of a simple incision into the connective tissue to free the tongue from the floor of the mouth. Many practitioners perform this procedure with little to no anesthetic in an office setting. A little post-surgery soreness may occur but an analgesic usually takes care of this minor issue.

Another procedure, called a frenectomy, involves removing the connective tissue from the underside of the tongue. This procedure requires either extensive numbing or general anesthesia. If done with a scalpel, the practitioner places sutures in the incision to help the wound heal. If done with laser, no sutures are required. Post-surgical healing takes from one to two weeks. About a week of soreness usually follows this procedure. Again, an analgesic usually takes care of the issue.

The research so far demonstrates that both procedures carry little to no risk and are effective. The benefit of one over the other remains unproven.

Individuals may need post-surgery therapy to correct tongue function problems and to strengthen the tongue muscles. Suck training, speech-language therapy, and myofunctional therapy are three common post-surgical therapy methods for infants and older individuals, respectively.

Q: How do I find a doctor or other practitioner who will treat my or my baby's tongue tie?

A: First, ask your pediatrician or general practitioner about tongue-tie treatment or a referral to an ear, nose, and throat specialist. If neither can be of help, ask your dentist. If your dentist cannot help, contact the International Lactation Consultant Association for a local referral to a lactation consultant who may know of a practitioner. You may also want to contact La Leche League International for a referral to a local La Leche League Leader. League Leaders often know of practitioners willing to treat tongue-tie. Speech-language pathologists may know of an ear, nose, and throat specialist or oral surgeon who performs frenotomies and frenectomies. Contact information for many of the organizations who have practitioner listings can be found in Appendix B.

Q: How difficult is it to find a practitioner to treat my or my child's tongue-tie?

A: One of the great frustrations for many people has been finding a physician willing to treat tongue-tie. Hopefully, in the near future, a listing of practitioners will become available. Currently in the United States, finding a practitioner to treat a tongue-tie may be somewhat difficult. Generally speaking, few pediatricians are willing to treat tongue-tie, and it may be more difficult to find a knowledgeable practitioner in smaller communities. The larger the city, the more likely you'll be able to find a practitioner knowledgeable on the subject.

Do not hesitate to seek help from dentists, oral surgeons, midwives, lactation consultants and La Leche League Leaders. They often know of the practitioners willing to assist.

In countries, such as Great Britain, that have national health services, finding a practitioner may be as easy as asking the general practitioner for a referral.

Q: Can the condition worsen after treatment?

A: Research shows that the only risk of treatment that can cause the tongue to become less mobile is scar tissue formation after a frenectomy or a deep frenotomy. This relatively rare risk can be eliminated if the individual moves his or her tongue frequently after the surgery. Often, a myofunctional therapist or speech-language pathologist will suggest exercises that both prevent scar tissue formation and strengthen the tongue. If the affected individual undergoing treatment is a breastfed baby, putting the baby to breast directly after treatment and often thereafter usually prevents problems.

APPENDIX B
RESOURCES

GENERAL AND RESEARCH-BASED INFORMATION AND PRACTITIONER REFERRAL

INTERNATIONAL AFFILIATION OF TONGUE-TIE PROFESSIONALS (IATP)

A large group of dedicated researchers and clinicians comprise this organization. The IATP's mission is to educate other health professionals and parents about tongue-tie and to reinstate sane and research-based clinical practices.

An international referral list for assessment and treatment can be found on this site:
www.tongue-tie.net

INFANT FEEDING

Academy of Breastfeeding Medicine
140 Huguenot Street, 3rd Floor
New Rochelle, New York 10801 USA
1-800-990-4ABM (Toll Free)
914-740-2115
Fax 914-740-2101
e-mail: abm@bfmed.org
www.bfmed.org

International Board of Lactation Consultant Examiners
6402 Arlington Boulevard, Suite 350
Falls Church, Virginia 22042 USA
703-560-7330
Fax 703-560-7332
www.iblce.org

International Lactation Consultant Association
2501 Aerial Center Parkway, Suite 103
Morrisville, North Carolina 27560 USA
919-861-5577
Fax 919-459-2075
e-mail: info@ilca.org
www.ilca.org

La Leche League International
P.O. Box 4079
Schaumberg, Illinois 60168-4079 USA
847-519-7730
1-800-525-3243 (Toll Free)
Fax 847-969-0460
www.llli.org

TREATMENT

American Academy of Family Physicians
www.familydoctor.org

American Academy of Pediatrics
141 Northwest Point Boulevard
Elk Grove Village, Illinois 60007-1098 USA
847-434-4000
Fax 434-8000
www.aap.org

American Academy of Otolaryngology-Head and Neck Surgery
1650 Diagonal Road
Alexandria, Virginia 22314-2857 USA
703-836-4444
www.entnet.org

American Association of Oral and Maxillofacial Surgeons
9700 West Bryn Mawr Avenue
Rosemont, Illinois 60018-5701 USA
847-678-6200
www.aaoms.org

American Osteopathic Association
142 East Ontario Street
Chicago, Illinois 60611 USA
1-800-621-1773 (Toll Free)

312-202-8000
Fax 312-202-8200
www.osteopathic.org

THERAPY

American Occupational Therapy Association, Inc.
4720 Montgomery Lane
P.O. Box 31220
Bethesda, Maryland 20824-1220 USA
301-652-2682
Fax 301-652-7711
www1.aota.org

American Speech-Language-Hearing Association
2200 Research Boulevard
Rockville, Maryland 20850-3289 USA
301-296-5700
www.asha.org

International Association of Orofacial Myology
www.iaom.com

The Biodynamic Craniosacral Therapy Association of North America
e-mail: info@craniosacraltherapy.org
www.craniosacraltherapy.org

The Craniosacral Therapy Association of the United Kingdom
www.craniosacral.co.uk

The Craniosacral Therapy Association of Australia
www.craniosacraltherapy.org.au

The Upledger Institute, Inc.
11211 Prosperity Farms Rd., Suite D-325
Palm Beach Gardens, Florida 33410 USA
561-622-4334
1-800-233-5880 (Toll Free)
Fax 561-622-4771
e-mail: upledger@upledger.com
www.upledger.com

APPENDIX C

THE ASSESSMENT TOOL FOR LINGUAL FRENULUM FUNCTION

BECAUSE OF MY PERSONAL EXPERIENCES with ankyloglossia and my frustration with the lack of a formal way to assess its presence in breastfed babies, I wanted to develop an assessment approach that could make it easier to determine the extent of the impact that tongue-tie had on tongue mobility in the breastfed baby.

Prior to 1989, I used as my assessment tools a combination of tongue appearance criteria and function criteria assessed during oral-digital exam. Prominence of the frenulum, notching at the tip of the tongue, and the heart-shaped tongue were the appearance criteria; proper tongue peristalsis, side-to-side tongue movement, and proper maintenance of suction were the function criteria.

This method seemed sufficient at first, but each time I worked with a tongue-tied baby and had to advocate for treatment, I had nothing but my word and experience with which I could "convince" an unconvinced doctor of what I had assessed. More times than I care to say, my recommendations went unheeded and the problem went unresolved, with the all-too-often result of premature weaning.

With the publication of the September 1990 Ankyloglossia Theme Issue of the *Journal of Human Lactation*, much discussion was generated among lactation consultants. Although that special theme issue validated the observations of many clinicians, it raised many more questions than it answered. After reading more articles, I came to realize that no screening tool yet existed. It seemed that most assessors were content to rely on their personal beliefs and experiences, regardless of how limited those beliefs or experiences.

To remedy this situation, I spent three years researching the subject of tongue-tie, observing babies and experimenting with an screening process that eventually became the Assessment Tool for Lingual Frenulum Function (Hazelbaker, 1993).

The 2009 version of the ATLFF appears below. Although I recommend that new users take a course to learn how to use the ATLFF optimally, I feel confident that screening 30-40 babies (any baby under 6 months, not just those suspected of being tongue-tied) using the tool as a screening-assessment will lessen the learning curve considerably.

I designed the ATLFF to be used on infants younger than 6 months of age, and most ideally on babies under 3 months of age. An assessor will have to find another way (other than oral-digital examination) to assess certain items, e.g., progressive contraction of the tongue, in a baby over 3 months because babies of this age or older usually will not suck on an assessor's finger.

The assessor must have a working knowledge of normal tongue function and normal infant oral anatomy and sucking physiology. It is also beneficial for inexperienced assessors to be taught how to use the tool before they employ it in their own practices. An incomplete understanding of oral function and of proper assessment can lead to inappropriate scoring and treatment recommendations.

Scoring: If the baby receives 2s under each Function heading, he or she has a perfect score, regardless of the Appearance Score. If he or she receives 11 out of 14 on the Function Items, then his or her score is acceptable only if the Appearance Score is 10. A score less than 11 on the Function Items indicates impaired function. The clinician should consider frenotomy if management alone fails, i.e., if correct positioning and latch-on technique do not fix the problem. If the baby scores less than 11 on Function Items and less than 8 on Appearance Items, then a frenotomy is considered necessary.

ASSESSMENT PROCESS

When performing the assessment, the number one rule is to RESPECT the baby. Do not attempt to enter the baby's oral space if the baby is giving aversion signs. Wait for a time when the baby is calmer and willing to be assessed. Proceed gently, calmly, and as quickly as possible. *Do not perform this assessment before the baby has been at the breast the first time unless the baby's exposure to the breast is delayed for medical reasons.*

All items need to be assessed. Any missed items will skew scoring, preventing the assessor from making an accurate assessment and appropriate, timely treatment recommendations.

Starting with the **LATERALIZATION** heading (see below), assess the baby's side-to-side tongue movement. The tongue will follow your finger as you trace the lower gum ridge back to the jaw. Your finger must brush the lateral edge of the tongue. With this action, you will elicit the **transverse tongue reflex** (see glossary). Score the baby as a 2 if the body and tip of the tongue follow your finger. Score the baby as a 1 if only the body of the tongue follows, and as a 0 if the tongue does not follow your finger at all.

Next, pull your finger out of the baby's mouth and gently brush the midline of the tongue tip and lower lip down toward the chin. This action will usually elicit the **tongue extrusion reflex**. Under the **EXTENSION OF TONGUE** heading, score the baby as a 2 if the tip of the tongue extends over the lower lip. Score the baby as a 1 if the tongue-tip extends only over the lower gum ridge and as a 0 if the tongue-tip does neither, or if the anterior or mid-tongue humps and/or dimples as the baby attempts to extend his tongue-tip outward.

Now elicit a **rooting reflex** by tickling the midline of the baby's lower lip in an up-and-down motion. When the baby opens his mouth wide enough for you to insert your finger, place the pad of your finger on the **palatal rugae** (see glossary), just behind the superior alveolar ridge. Take note of the prominence of the rugae and the shape and height of the palate (prominent rugae and bubble-like or high palates can be the result of a tied tongue); then move your finger back a little. Allow the baby to cup his tongue around your finger. Be aware of the spreading of the anterior tongue as the baby starts the cupping action. Under the heading **SPREAD OF ANTERIOR TONGUE**, score the baby as a 2 if he spreads his tongue completely. With a complete spread you should feel the anterior tongue thin out evenly. Score the baby as a 1 if the spread is moderate or partial. Usually in tongue-tied babies, the part of the tongue involved in the tie will not thin and expand, and will feel thick and/or "bunchy." Score the baby as a 0 if there is little or no spread.

Under **CUPPING OF TONGUE**, score the baby as a 2 if you feel the entire edge form a firm cup around your finger. The tongue edges should come up and "hug" your finger securely, thereby creating a furrow, or trough along the midline of the tongue. Score the baby as a 1 if you feel only the side edges form a moderate cup around your finger and as a 0 if the baby's tongue forms no cup or a poor cup. Once you have felt the cupping motion, allow the baby to draw your finger back into his or her mouth. Your goal is to nearly reach the tip of your finger to the junction of the hard and soft palates. If the tongue does not cup well, or humps inhibiting the drawing-back of your finger, gently trace the hard palate with your finger pad until you reach the junction of the hard and soft palates. Note if the baby gags during this movement.

As the baby sucks, you will be able to score the **PERISTALSIS** (progressive contraction) item. Score the baby as a 2 if you feel the progressive contraction originating at the tongue-tip and proceeding anterior to posterior, as in normal, proper sucking. Score the baby as a 1 if you feel progressive contraction originating posterior to the tongue-tip. (If the tip is restricted by an anterior tie, it cannot effectively originate the progressive contraction.) Score the baby as a 0 if the tongue does not move in a wavelike fashion or if it thrusts anteriorly. During this assessment of tongue motion, you will be able to determine if the tongue is "snapping-back."

"Snap-back" is the involuntary pulling-back of the tongue, sometimes accompanied by a release of suction that occurs in some tongue-tied babies. When a tie is so tight preventing the tongue from extending well when the baby attempts to maintain traction on the breast, the tie pulls the tongue backward—like the release of a taut rubber band—thereby causing the baby to lose its grasp of the breast. This "snap-back" accompanied by release of suction can make a "clucking" or "chucking" sound. Under the **SNAP-BACK** heading, score the baby as a 2 if there is no snap-back, as a 1 if snap-back is periodic (occasionally or every few sucks), and as a 0 if the snap-back is more frequent than every few sucks or is with every suck.

Mothers name: ____________________ Baby's age: ____________________

Baby's name: ____________________ Date of assessment: ____________________

FUNCTION ITEMS	
LATERALIZATION	CUPPING OF TONGUE
2 Complete **1** Body of tongue but not tongue-tip **0** None	**2** Entire edge, firm cup **1** Side edges only, moderate cup **0** Poor OR no cup
LIFT OF TONGUE	PERISTALSIS (PROGRESSIVE CONTRACTION)
2 Tip to mid-mouth **1** Only edges to mid mouth **0** Tip stays at alveolar ridge OR tip rises only to mid-mouth with jaw closure AND/OR mid-tongue dimples	**2** Complete anterior to posterior (originates at tip) **1** Partial: originating posterior to tip **0** None OR Anterior thrusting
EXTENSION OF TONGUE	SNAP BACK
2 Tip over lower lip **1** Tip over lower gum only **0** Neither of the above OR anterior or mid-tongue humps AND/OR dimples	**2** None **1** Periodic **0** Frequent OR with each suck
SPREAD OF ANTERIOR TONGUE	
2 Complete **1** Moderate OR partial **0** Little OR none	

APPEARANCE ITEMS	
APPEARANCE OF TONGUE WHEN LIFTED	ELASTICITY OF LINGUAL FRENULUM
2 Round OR square **1** Slight cleft in tip apparent **0** Heart shaped	**2** Very elastic (excellent) **1** Moderately elastic **0** Little OR no elasticity
LENGTH OF LINGUAL FRENULUM WHEN TONGUE LIFTED	ATTACHMENT OF LINGUAL FRENULUM TO TONGUE
2 More than 1 cm OR absent frenulum **1** 1 cm **0** Less than 1 cm	**2** Posterior to tip **1** At tip **0** Notched OR under the mucosa at the tongue base
ATTACHMENT OF LINGUAL FRENULUM TO INFERIOR ALVEOLAR RIDGE	
2 Attached to floor of mouth OR well below ridge **1** Attached just below ridge **0** Attached to ridge	

SCORING	
Function Item score: ____________ Appearance Item score: ____________	Combined Score: ____ / ____

TREATMENT RECOMMENDATIONS BASED ON SCORING

14 Perfect Function score regardless of Appearance Item score. Surgical treatment not recommended.

11 Acceptable Function score only if Appearance Item score is **10**.

< 11 Function Score indicates function impaired. Frenotomy should be considered if management fails. Frenotomy necessary if Appearance Item score is **< 8**.

If the baby gags during your assessment of progressive contraction and snap-back, you may have dropped your finger onto the tongue. Your finger-pad should stay in contact with the baby's palate at all times. If the baby gags even if your finger stays up at the palate, you may have gone beyond the hard/soft palate junction, OR the baby's suck may be so disorganized from tongue bunching, humping, or other causes that the gag occurs when it should not. In any case, take note of when the gag occurs in the assessment process. It is useful information that could aid you in formulating a treatment plan.

Gently remove your finger from the baby's mouth and watch for **LIFT OF TONGUE**. Sometimes the baby has to be crying for you to assess this item. Normally, a baby cannot lift his or her tongue-tip all the way to the roof of his or her mouth without some jaw closure, so we score the baby as a 2 if he is able to lift his tongue-tip to the mid-point in his mouth without jaw closure. Score the baby as a 1 if only his tongue edges are able to lift to mid-mouth. Score the baby as a 0 if the tongue-tip stays at the inferior alveolar ridge or if the tongue-tip rises to mid-mouth with jaw closure and/or if the mid-tongue dimples during the lift. The dimpling may signify that a posterior tie is present.

At first, assessing the Appearance items is more time-consuming than assessing the Function items because there is no guarantee that you will witness every item on the first try. With experience, the assessor can assess every item while observing the **LIFT OF TONGUE**. The typical appearance of the baby's lifted anterior tongue-edge is round OR square. Score the baby as a 2 under the **APPEARANCE OF TONGUE WHEN LIFTED** heading if you see a round or square anterior tongue-edge. Score the baby as a 1 if you see a slight cleft in the anterior tongue-edge when the tongue is lifted, and as a 0 if the anterior tongue appears heart-shaped.

Take notice of the lingual frenulum at this point. You will be looking at its inherent elasticity, length, and point of attachment to the tongue and to the floor of the mouth. Under **ELASTICITY OF FRENULUM**, score the baby as a 2 if the lingual frenulum appears to be very elastic or to have excellent elasticity. Score the baby as a 1 if the frenulum appears to be moderately elastic and as a 0 if the frenulum appears to have little or no elasticity. You may need to put your fingers underneath the tongue and gently pull the tongue upward to make an accurate assessment.

While you are assessing elasticity, also take note of **THE LENGTH OF THE LINGUAL FRENULUM WHEN TONGUE LIFTED**. The length of the infant's lingual frenulum when the tongue is lifted is typically longer than 1cm. You may have to measure at first, but with experience, will be able to "eyeball" and be accurate. In some infants, the frenulum is entirely absent. Score the baby as a 2 if the lingual frenulum is longer than 1cm or is entirely absent, as a 1 if it is 1cm, and as a 0 if it is less than 1cm or hidden under the mucosa.

The superior attachment point is typically underneath the tongue and about 1cm behind the tongue-tip. Score the baby as a 2 under the **ATTACHMENT OF LINGUAL FRENULUM TO TONGUE** heading if the baby's lingual frenulum is attached posterior to the tongue-tip, as a 1 if the attachment is at the tip and as a 0 if the attachment causes a notch at the tongue-tip or is under the mucosa at the tongue base.

Just after you assess the superior attachment, assess the inferior attachment. The inferior attachment of the lingual frenulum is typically on the floor of the mouth, but in tongue-tied babies, it can be as high as the crest of the inferior alveolar ridge. Under the **ATTACHMENT OF LINGUAL FRENULUM TO INFERIOR ALVEOLAR RIDGE** heading, score the baby as a 2 if the lingual frenulum is attached to the floor of the mouth or well below the alveolar ridge. Score the baby as a 1 if the lingual frenulum is attached just below the alveolar ridge, and as a 0 if it is attached at the ridge.

I additionally recommend that the assessor visualize and feel at the base of the tongue for a hidden or posterior tie. When you use the fingers to lift the tongue, take a good look at the base to see if there is a tight strip or band that may restrict tongue motion. You may have to also swipe your finger across the base to feel for this tightness because some frenula are located under the superficial mucosal layer.

Dr. Jim Murphy describes this motion as sweeping. He places his finger under the tongue on one side of the mouth and sweeps it across. If he hits a "speedbump" (his finger bounces a little but can make it across without withdrawing), the baby may or may not need treatment (he treats if breastfeeding is going poorly). If he hits a fence (needs to withdraw his finger partially or completely to come around the frenulum) he definitely treats. This process has come to be known as the "Murphy Maneuver."

APPENDIX D

FINGER-FEEDING

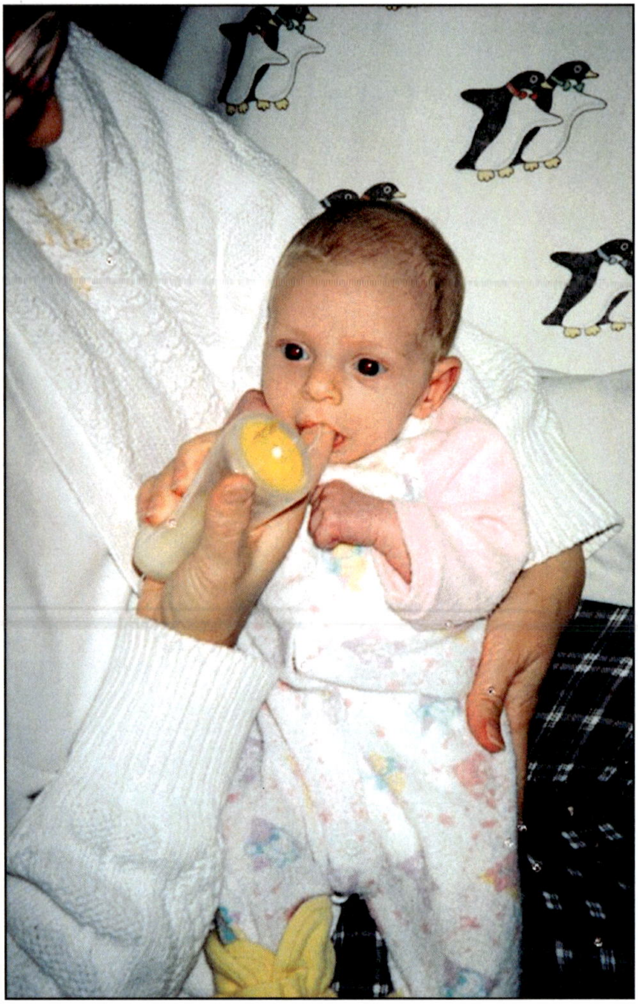

Either before or after surgery, finger-feeding can be an important adjunct approach to keep baby fed or to help strengthen his or her suck. The Hazelbaker™ FingerFeeder can assist the feeding and/or therapy process.

Instructions for Finger-Feeding (© 2009 Aidan & Éva, LLC. Adapted with Permission).

1. Position yourself and baby in a proper feeding position such as that shown in the photo. Placing a pillow under baby will make feeding more comfortable for both of you by raising the baby to chest height.

2. Young babies tend to orient to the right so holding the baby with your left hand and finger-feeding with your right can capitalize on this tendency. However, you may use whichever side you and your baby feel most comfortable using.

3. Keep your shoulders and elbows down and relaxed to reduce muscle strain. Support yourself with extra pillows if needed to achieve this goal.

4. Gently tickle your baby's lower lip in the middle, in an up-and-down direction to elicit both the rooting and tongue extrusion reflexes. Keep tickling, just as you would with the breast or bottle, until the baby opens as wide as he or she can.

5. When you see the "gape," gently insert your finger, pad up, against the hard palate near the upper gumline. The baby will bring up his or her tongue to create a seal around your finger. If your baby is still tongue-tied or is weak, he or she may not do this well. Eventually, this ability will improve.

6. As the baby starts the sucking sequence, move your finger back to near the hard and soft palate juncture where the breast nipple would go if the baby were at breast. While moving your finger back, keep your finger pad in gentle contact with the hard palate. If your finger drops down on the tongue, your baby may gag.

7. Once you have reached the appropriate "landmark," keep your finger in the same position and stationary unless your therapist directs you to perform certain movements.

8. There is usually no need to squeeze the bulb unless your baby needs a therapeutic reminder or is so weak that he or she needs a little extra help. Allow the baby to set the pace. He or she will do best synchronizing suck, swallow and breathe if allowed to determine the right pace for that feed.

The Hazelbaker™ FingerFeeder can be ordered from:

Aidan & Éva, LLC
5115 Olentangy River Rd.
Columbus, Ohio 43235 USA
(614) 451-1154
www.fingerfeeder.com

INDEX

Page numbers followed by an *f* or *t* indicate figures or tables.

A

B

D

H

I

M

P

R

S